DATE DUE
Fecha Para Retornar

			PRINTED IN U.S.A.

Critic ... *and*

D1567906

ROWMAN & LITTLEFIELD
Lanham • Boulder • New York • London

ECC, Osgood Library
Iowa Falls, IA 50126

306.874
M8799
2013

Published by Rowman & Littlefield
A wholly owned subsidiary of The Rowman & Littlefield Publishing Group, Inc.
4501 Forbes Boulevard, Suite 200, Lanham, Maryland 20706
www.rowman.com

Unit A, Whitacre Mews, 26-34 Stannary Street, London SE11 4AB

Copyright © 2013 by Scarecrow Press, Inc.
First Rowman & Littlefield paperback edition 2015

All rights reserved. No part of this book may be reproduced in any form or by any
electronic or mechanical means, including information storage and retrieval systems,
without written permission from the publisher, except by a reviewer who may quote
passages in a review.

British Library Cataloguing in Publication Information Available

Library of Congress Cataloging-in-Publication Data
The hardback edition of this book was previously catalogued by the Library of Congress as follows:

MTV and teen pregnancy : critical essays on 16 and pregnant and Teen mom / edited by Letizia
Guglielmo.
p. cm.
Includes bibliographical references and index.
1. Teenage mothers. 2. Teenage pregnancy 3. 16 and pregnant (Television program) 4. Teen mom
(Television program) 5. Reality television programs—Social aspects. 6. Mass media and teenage
girls. I. Guglielmo, Letizia, 1977–
HQ759.4.M78 2013
306.874'3—dc23
2013004949

ISBN 978-0-8108-9169-2 (cloth : alk. paper)
ISBN 978-1-4422-5618-7 (pbk.   )
ISBN 978-0-8108-9170-8 (ebook)

Printed in the United States of America

OCT 1 3 2016

Contents

iii

ECC, Osgood Library
Iowa Falls, IA 50126

Acknowledgments

I would like to thank the collection's contributors for their dedication to the project, their many insights and thoughtful reflections throughout the writing and revision process, and their willingness to add their voices to this conversation. I offer my sincere thanks to Kimberly Wallace Stewart, whose interest in and commitment to research in gender and women's studies helped to generate the seeds for this project as well as a truly rewarding collaboration. And finally, enormous thanks to John for watching countless episodes of *16 and Pregnant*, *Teen Mom*, and *Teen Mom 2*, for listening to ongoing analysis throughout the project, and for offering unending support.

Introduction: Teen Moms and Baby Daddies

Interrupting the Conversation on Teen Pregnancy

Letizia Guglielmo

The September 2008 announcement of Bristol Palin's pregnancy, teen daughter of then vice presidential candidate Sarah Palin, propelled the topic of teen pregnancy to the forefront of mainstream news media reports, prompting discussion on abstinence-only programs, conservative "family values," and the fiercely pro-life politics of the Republican vice presidential candidate. Although by 2008 teen pregnancy rates within the United States had been on the decline since the early 1990s,[1] this "problem" generated renewed interest and media attention. With the premiers of the film *Juno* in 2007, the television series *The Secret Life of the American Teenager* in 2008, and the very public pregnancies of Bristol Palin and teen idol Jamie Lynn Spears before her, one might argue that "[teen] pregnancy is no longer in the shadows"[2] and that, unlike young women facing unplanned pregnancies forty or fifty years earlier, Palin and Spears were fortunate to have the choice to raise their children and speak publicly about their pregnancies.[3] Framed as "teachable moments," however, these public discussions of teen pregnancy came with a clear message for young women: don't let this happen to you. In the months following the birth of her son, Bristol Palin became a spokesperson for abstinence just as Jamie Lynn Spears had announced, "It's better to wait,"[4] and this unveiling of teen pregnancy did little to disrupt assumptions about young women, teen sexuality, or reproductive choice.

As government funding for comprehensive sex education has continued to decrease since the 1980s, entertainment media has played an increasing role "in educating the public about significant health issues," including teen pregnancy.[5] In 2000, a Centers for Disease Control and Prevention survey revealed that a "majority of viewers (52%) report picking up health information that they trust to be accurate from prime time TV shows, and 1 in 4 (26%) say that these shows are among their top three sources for health information."[6] By 2004, a partnership between the Kaiser Family Foundation and MTV, for example, resulted in nineteen programs of varying formats "designed to entertain and educate audiences . . . of over 95 million viewers."[7] In 2009, MTV again partnered with the Kaiser Family Foundation as well as the National Campaign to Prevent Teen and Unplanned Pregnancy to create a documentary-style series on teen pregnancy: *16 and Pregnant.*

Since its premiere, *16 and Pregnant* has received ongoing media attention for the extent to which it contributes to the conversation on teen pregnancy in the United States as a potential factor in reducing the number of teen pregnancies at one extreme and as culpable for exploiting young women and glamorizing teen pregnancy at another. Although the program and its spin-offs, *Teen Mom* and *Teen Mom 2,* have been cited for their high ratings among teen viewers, resulting in a kind of celebrity status for the teen moms and suggesting that *16 and Pregnant* does potentially fill a niche, the program content—specifically, the messages shared with the audience—remains largely unexplored. Although feminists such as Jessica Valenti have questioned the absence of the whole story of teen pregnancy in these programs— namely, the omission of any sustained discussion of abortion as a viable choice for teens facing an unplanned pregnancy—of significant concern are questions of authentic voice and meaningful intervention in the national discussion surrounding teen pregnancy, representations of teen sexuality and motherhood, and the place of the programs (and teen moms) within popular culture. Furthermore, what are viewers—particularly, teenagers—learning about contraception, reproductive rights, poverty, social systems of support, gender roles, relationships, domestic violence, and education? Given the programs' focus on teen pregnancy and, by default, young women, scholars in gender and women's studies, media studies, motherhood studies, sexuality education, and adolescent development, among other fields, have both an opportunity and an obligation to approach the programs critically and help young people interrogate the social and cultural norms in which these messages are grounded. To that end, the chapters in this collection offer critical interdisciplinary thought on the programs and, where applicable, their companion spaces online.

Multivocal in nature, this collection provides scholarly work grounded in theory and, in some cases, personal narrative to expand the national discussion on teen pregnancy and teen sexuality with critical lenses that have the potential to foster social change. Divided into four parts, the volume is informed by the varied backgrounds and disciplinary expertise of its authors, yet each chapter calls for an approach to *16 and Pregnant, Teen Mom, Teen*

Mom 2, and programs like them with questions that prompt ongoing analysis. In part I, "Feminist Interventions or Tired Narratives?" Caryn Murphy, in "Teen Momism on MTV: Postfeminist Subjectivities in *16 and Pregnant*," argues that these series construct a postfeminist, neoliberal subject position through discourses of individual choice and personal responsibility, the incorporation of a maternal role into adolescent identity, and the internalization of gendered social expectations of "successful" female adolescence and parenting. Continuing this analysis of gendered social norms in "*16 and Pregnant* and the 'Unvarnished' Truth about Teen Pregnancy," Kimberly Wallace Stewart and I explore the extent to which *16 and Pregnant* offers a meaningful intervention in discourses on teen sexuality and sex education, particularly given distribution of the program's first season as an educational resource. Drawing from individual episodes, online resources associated with the program, and educational materials prepared and distributed by the Kaiser Family Foundation, Wallace Stewart and I question through our analysis the dominant narratives being retold and the limited opportunities that the program offers teens to consider their sexuality and sexual choices within the context of reproductive justice.

In "Teen Moms Negotiate Desire: The (Re)Production of Patriarchal Motherhood in MTV's *Teen Mom*," Anastasia Todd employs discourse analysis as a method to deconstruct representations of teenage mothers and motherhood in *Teen Mom*. Todd argues that these hypervisible representations of teen moms on the program aid in the (re)production of the hegemonic discourse of patriarchal motherhood. Characterized by a mother's willingness to forgo all "selfish desire," this ideal teenage motherhood, Todd argues, includes forgoing teenage sexual desire, already constructed as inappropriate and "dangerous" by the larger discourse on teenage girls' sexuality. Jennifer A. Fallas further develops this analysis, arguing that although *Teen Mom* bears great potential to inform and thereby empower young women about sexual autonomy and bodily sovereignty, especially in regard to maintaining healthy active sexual lives, the program inevitably returns to a fixed notion of appropriate femaleness through its focus on and responses to prescriptive gender norms. Despite its potential to serve as a site of feminist intervention, Fallas argues, *Teen Mom* works almost entirely through a postfeminist framework.

Part II, "'The Personal Is Political': Teen Pregnancy and Hegemony," prompts readers to consider the intersections of race, class, gender, and the social and cultural power structures often glossed in the these MTV programs. In "'100% Preventable': Teen Motherhood, Morality, and the Myth of Choice," May Friedman illustrates the extent to which the young women of *16 and Pregnant* and *Teen Mom* are presented as unfolding disasters: stripped of autonomy, with limited opportunities and all future promise taken away by their own poor choices. She considers the ways that dominant themes of poverty and violence are presented as logical conclusions to the perceived moral failings of the shows' protagonists, and she calls on readers and viewers to resist this heavy-handed moralizing. Using visual and discursive analysis in "Teen Sex: An Equal Opportunity Menace—Multicultural Politics in *16 and Pregnant*," Clare Daniel examines the racial, sexual, gender, and class politics of the first two seasons of *16 and Pregnant*. The episodes, she argues, naturalize authoritative claims about who should have sex and who should reproduce, obscuring the complexity of social forces by which people's reproductive behaviors are produced, enabled, regulated, and prevented. Intersecting feminist, queer, and cultural theory in "Sensationalizing the Sentimental: National Culture and Futurity," Melanie Anne Stewart argues that the intended aim of *16 and Pregnant* and *Teen Mom* to prevent teen pregnancy is thwarted by its situation in two conflicting national cultures. The sentimental culture, she argues, focuses on the regulation of sexuality and citizenship in the name of protecting the child, family life, and, thus, the national image and futurity, while the sensational culture is concerned with mug shots, celebrity, and scandal. Drawing examples from the programs as well as their online spaces, Stewart argues that a sentimental national culture built around normative ideas of family life and reproduction is perpetuating the prevalence of teen pregnancy. In the final chapter of this section, Martina Thomas explores the extent to which the teen mothers' narratives are presented as abnormal while the mothers are stereotyped as problematic, infantile, and deviant. Through her analysis of the first three seasons of *Teen Mom*, she explains how counseling experts, difficult relationships between the teen mothers and their parents, and the mothers' struggle for "normal" family structures create both reassurance and anxiety for these young women in ways that overshadow the true complexity of their situations.

Conspicuously absent from most teen pregnancy prevention campaigns, teen fathers—often referred to as "baby daddies" to further characterize this role as "other"—receive sustained attention in part III: "Making Room for Daddy: Images of Teen Fatherhood." First, in "*16 and Pregnant*, Masculinity, and Teen Fatherhood: Reconciling or Reinforcing Stereotypes?" Jennifer Beggs Weber and Enid Schatz explain that while the norms of femininity and expectations of motherhood are well defined and often complimentary for teen mothers, for young fathers the rules for what it means to be a "man" and a "good father" often come into conflict. The authors explore the ways in which particular tropes of masculinity are represented and reinforced on *16 and Pregnant*, with a focus on tensions between masculinity and representations of "good fathers" and "bad fathers." This conflict or, at the very least, liminality, they argue, influences the ways in which these young men navigate fatherhood and masculinity and the ways in which "good fathers" and "bad fathers" are defined for the viewing audience.

Further developing this analysis, Andrea McClanahan interrogates the representations of fathers in *16 and Pregnant* and *Teen Mom* to uncover the key themes constructed about fathers and how these narratives disrupt the heterosexual imaginary as a deterrent to teenage pregnancy. Through a textual analysis of individual episodes, McClanahan analyzes the positioning of teen fathers on these programs in one of three dominant roles—dad as dunce, donor dad, and fantasy father—and considers their impact on teenage viewers. Finally, in "What's a Baby Daddy to Do? Fathers on the Fringe in MTV's *16 and Pregnant*," Laura Tropp extends this conversation with a focus on the gatekeeping role of teen moms who choose to limit and guide how much involvement the fathers have in the lives of their babies. Drawing from motherhood research, feminist theory, and fatherhood literature, Tropp explores how the program represents ambivalent views of fatherhood and frames the teen fathers' primary role as serving, first and most important, an economic function.

In the final section, "Is This Real Life? Mediating the Whole Story of Teen Pregnancy and Motherhood," the authors draw from "real life" and from the programs' representations of the reality of teenage pregnancy and parenting. Addressing the topic of abortion—one for which *16 and Pregnant* has received a great deal of criticism—JoAnne Gordon helps readers to question how abortion is discussed on the programs and the impact that these discussions may have on the larger viewing audience. In "'Having an Abortion Is Not Uncommon, but Talking about It Publicly Is': Exploring the Potential for Positive, Feminist, Pro-Choice Portrayals of Young Women's Experiences with Abortion in Mass Media through MTV's 'No Easy Decision,'" Gordon uses the special episode as a case study to explore the potential of mass media to disseminate positive, feminist, and pro-choice portrayals of abortion. Given the current political climate of hostility and regressive federal and state policies against women's reproductive rights and access in the United States, Gordon explores how mass media can be utilized as a tool to fill in the gaps in representations and information pertaining to sexual and reproductive health available to youth. Moreover, she examines how we can look at "No Easy Decision" as a counterhegemonic site and a potential feminist success for representations of not only abortion but teen pregnancy and pregnancy options. Exploring the ways in which legal issues are framed within *16 and Pregnant*, *Teen Mom*, and *Teen Mom 2*, Alison N. Novak and India J. McGhee critically examine the teen mothers' interactions with the legal system, with implications for understanding the way that legal empowerment of young mothers is discussed and showcased in popular mass media more broadly. Legal frames, the authors argue, present viewers with a complicated view of the teen mom's relationship to the law and her ability to traverse a legal and social system intended to support her. In the chapter that follows, Margaret Tally explores the larger question of how these programs fit into the genre of reality television known as *edutainment*, one that seeks to educate an audience, usually women, with the explicit purpose of teaching them to lead their lives in a different manner and one that accords with more acceptable forms of behavior. Ultimately, she argues, the moralizing discourses of these shows end up remaining silent as to how to really address this social problem, other than to watch with pleasure and fascination as these young lives become even more precarious. In the section's final chapter, through her own narrative intervention, Allison Bass describes growing up in the religious South as a young girl and being faced with "True Love Waits" pledges in place of comprehensive sexuality education. Bass explains that she did not learn about condoms or birth control until after she became pregnant at the age of sixteen and that after marrying and then divorcing the abusive twenty-year-old father of the baby, she found herself confused and alone at eighteen with a one-year-old and no education. Sharing her journey as a teenage mom, Bass argues that programs such as *16 and Pregnant* and *Teen Mom* do not show the reality of life as a single teen mom and fail to promote self-advocacy.

Throughout this project, it was never my goal nor the goal of the other authors in this collection to suggest that the programs *16 and Pregnant*, *Teen Mom*, and *Teen Mom 2* be taken off the air or replaced with something "better." Instead, we hope that these chapters prompt critical analysis and reviewing of the programs' episodes with the larger goals of promoting advocacy, media literacy, and intervention in discourses of power. Whether you read the text from cover to cover or plot your own unique journey through the volume, we hope that you engage in conversation with the authors, with the sources cited, and with the many examples we share from the programs. We also hope that you take these conversations into your classrooms, your community centers, and your homes and that you add your own voices to the broader social and culture discourses that speak for and about you and for those whose voices have been silenced.

NOTES

1. National Campaign to Prevent Teen and Unplanned Pregnancy, *Fast Facts*.
2. Oliver, "Motherhood, Sexuality, and Pregnant Embodiment."
3. Fessler, *The Girls Who Went Away*.
4. Bute and Russell, "Public Discourses about Teenage Pregnancy."
5. Henry J. Kaiser Family Foundation, *Issue Brief*.
6. Cited in Henry J. Kaiser Family Foundation, *Issue Brief*.
7. Henry J. Kaiser Family Foundation, *Issue Brief*.

Part I

Feminist Interventions or Tired Narratives?

Chapter One

Teen Momism on MTV

Postfeminist Subjectivities in 16 and Pregnant

Caryn Murphy

A previous version of this chapter appeared in Networking Knowledge: Journal of the MeCCSA-PGN, *Volume 5, Issue 1, 2012.*

Farrah Abraham and Maci Bookout appeared on the August 2010 cover of *Us Weekly*, a celebrity gossip magazine. Unlike conventional tabloid subjects, these young women were not pursuing careers in film, television, or music; instead, they drew national attention when they appeared in the first season of MTV's hit reality series *16 and Pregnant* and its spinoff *Teen Mom*. The magazine's headline, "Inside Their Struggles," is belied by the flawless physical appearance of the teenage mothers, who are posed with their smiling children. This issue kicked off a flurry of press coverage in which the "average" young women from MTV's series joined the ranks of high-profile teen parents, including Bristol Palin and Jamie Lynn Spears, on the covers of *People*, *In Touch*, and *OK!* in feature stories about the trials of teen pregnancy that are ultimately presented as triumphs over adversity.

16 and Pregnant and *Teen Mom* have been documenting the lives of pregnant teenagers since 2009, in what MTV promotes as an educational effort. These series target a youth audience with depictions of how teen pregnancy causes family stress, derails romantic relationships, and radically alters career plans. They also have been criticized for glamorizing teen motherhood, a charge that seems borne out in the *Us Weekly* cover story: Farrah, who has an eighteen-month-old, announces her plans to open her own restaurant in a major city; Amber Portwood, whose baby is twenty-one months, is lauded as a weight-loss success story. [1] I argue that these television series rely on discourses of choice and agency to present teenage mothers as postfeminist neoliberal subjects. Accusations of glamorization result from the manner in which these shows individualize the experience of teen pregnancy and position each subject as a success or failure based on her ability to reconstitute her identity around motherhood. Within these series, the responsibilities related to bearing and raising children become part of a larger fabric of educational and social achievements associated with feminine adolescence.

POSTFEMINISM, NEOLIBERALISM, AND YOUNG MOTHERHOOD

Research on postfeminism within media studies has taken two major directions since the early 1990s. One school of thought argues that the term *postfeminism* signifies a change of direction within feminist studies from a focus on inequality to a focus on difference.[2] The other direction examines widespread social and cultural retractions of feminist gains as a symptom of struggle over the continuing necessity of feminism.[3] In a recent intervention, Rosalind Gill argues that postfeminism is best conceptualized as a "sensibility" that is manifested in discursive themes of choice and empowerment, individualism and self-discipline, and a reassertion of sexual difference.[4] Postfeminist media culture negates the realities of continuing gender inequities by representing women as autonomous individuals who can overcome institutionalized barriers through self-regulation and discipline. I rely on Rosalind Gill's perspective that postfeminism is a pervasive sensibility because it positions postfeminist media culture as the object of analysis and because her work is specifically invested in the correlation between postfeminist and neoliberal constructions of subjectivity. MTV's educational entertainment on sex and relationships becomes part of a postfeminist media culture, and as such the programming demonstrates the salient aspects of postfeminist discourse, including themes of individual choice, empowerment, and self-discipline.

The theory of neoliberalism is based in economist Adam Smith's conception of the "invisible hand of the market," arguing that without state interventions or controls, the market will regulate itself to optimal levels of efficiency. Neoliberal economic policies have resulted in transformed conceptions of the public and private spheres as subject to the logic of the free market. Rosemary Hennessy claims that since the 1970s, this deregulatory philosophy has worked to extend "the rationality of the market—its schemes of analysis and decision-making criteria—to areas of social life that have not been primarily economic."[5] In *Young Femininity*, social science researchers Sinikka Aapola et al. document "the neo-liberal process of individualization" in an examination of the changing global conditions in which contemporary constructions of girlhood are taking place. The authors argue, "The neoliberal incitement of individualism, rational choice and self-realization bumps up against discourses of femininity, creating contradictory and complex positions for girls."[6] The recent expansion of girls' media hails young women with multiple messages proclaiming their freedom from constraints and their ability to create themselves and their own lives, unhampered by markers of gender, race, class, or sexuality.

Rosalind Gill's position is that neoliberal and postfeminist discourses are interrelated. Both ideological positions separate the individual from social and institutional forces to form an idealized, self-monitoring subject. For Gill, postfeminism and neoliberalism "both appear to be structured by a current of individualism that has almost entirely replaced notions of the social or political, or any idea of the individual as subject to pressures, constraints, or influence from outside themselves."[7] She calls for critical work on the construction of postfeminist neoliberal subjectivity, and because my analysis focuses on adolescence, it necessarily complicates already troubled ideals of individualism, autonomy, and choice. In her examination of contemporary constructions of girlhood, Anita Harris identifies two major subjectivities that dominate representations of young femininity in late capitalism: the "can-do girl," who is capable of self-invention, and the "at-risk girl," whose future is imperiled.[8] In media representations, both figures are used to justify an emphasis on individual responsibility that rejects the importance of social and economic forces. Although the young subjects of *16 and Pregnant* demonstrate that having a baby before finishing high school is disruptive, at another level, the series presents a makeover narrative in which successful subjects are capable of renovating their lives to accommodate (and excel at) the transition.

A postfeminist sensibility is also central to contemporary constructions of motherhood. Susan Douglas and Meredith Michaels coined the term *new momism* to describe the intense social expectations of mothering that have emerged as the "central, justifying ideology to what has come to be called 'postfeminism.'"[9] The label is an update on *momism*, a term used by pop psychologists in the 1950s to designate a phenomenon of "overmothering," in which attentive parenting supposedly had negative effects on child development. Douglas and Michaels argue that the contemporary ideal of motherhood requires a complete, selfless devotion to children. New momism reinscribes gender differences, positioning women as "natural," primary caretakers.[10] The authors argue that new momism "redefines each of us in relation to our children," aligning the individual sense of self with the mother role.[11] Significantly, they note that teen mothers have historically fallen into the category that Harris would identify as "at risk," because they are not fully employable and have been stereotyped as overly dependent on social safety nets.[12] In *16 and Pregnant* and *Teen Mom*, the social expectations of new momism frame the representations of teen motherhood as "can-do girls" and make parenting the central feature in their narratives of individual achievement.

The role of the individual young woman as a freely choosing, autonomous subject is meticulously formed in each episode of *16 and Pregnant*; neoliberal subjectivity is informed by the major constitutive features of postfeminist sensibility. MTV's teen pregnancy series construct a postfeminist neoliberal subject through discourses of individual choice and personal responsibility, the incorporation of a maternal role into adolescent identity, and the internalization of gendered social expectations of "successful" female adolescence and parenting.

"THEMES OF AFFIRMATION AND ACCOMPLISHMENT":[13] MTV AS PROSOCIAL PROGRAMMER

MTV claims a long history of encouraging involvement in social issues, but the cable channel's stress on political engagement and youth activism has increased since 2008, in response to declining ratings.[14] MTV's previous educational efforts have been characterized by direct, informational address to viewers. For example, Rock the Vote, a nonprofit organization designed to encourage political activism, has been promoted by the channel since 1990 with commercial announcements on how to register to vote and talk-show-style "Meet the Candidates" specials. The current trend of prosocial programming on MTV has expanded to include educational messages within entertainment-style programming, a strategy that shows the influence of the Sabido method innovated at Televisa, a private television network in Mexico, from 1975 to 1981.[15] Miguel Sabido, then vice president of research at Televisa, incorporated Albert Bandura's social learning theory into dramatic serials, with the intention of promoting women's status and family planning by encouraging viewers to learn from the behaviors they observed on television. *16 and Pregnant* was developed with an explicitly educational mission, during a time that MTV sought to shift its address to viewers.

Teen pregnancy is an issue of social relevance in every era, but it has become significantly more visible over the past few years, in part due to the success of fictional teen pregnancy narratives (examples include the 2007 film *Juno* and the ABC Family series *The Secret Life of the American Teenager*, 2008–present). The pregnancy prevention reality series on MTV bear a stronger mark of authenticity because they follow "average," often lower middle-class or working-class, girls. The style of series is distinct from more heavily produced reality series that appear on MTV, such as *The Hills* (2006–2010) and *Jersey Shore* (2009–2012), and clearly separate from popular fictional narratives about teen pregnancy. *16 and Pregnant* and *Teen Mom* arguably connect more powerfully with viewers because these series appear to be presenting reality as it unfolds, following young people who are strikingly similar to the target demographic in terms of age, family income, and life experiences. Lauren Dolgen and executive producer Liz Gateley claim that the documentary-style production is intended to motivate teenagers to practice abstinence or use birth control and that it encourages these behaviors by modeling the disruptive consequences of unintended pregnancy.[16] As of this writing, the original series has completed four seasons and has successfully spun off *Teen Mom* and *Teen Mom 2*, which follow the continuing stories of four young women featured in seasons 1 and 2, respectively. The National Campaign to Prevent Teen and Unplanned Pregnancy includes *16 and Pregnant* in its educational materials,[17] and it is being packaged for release to educational institutions by the Kaiser Foundation, along with a curriculum to facilitate its use in classroom instruction.[18]

Although *16 and Pregnant* is "unscripted," as in all reality programming, each episode is carefully formed by editors. A team of editors takes a large amount of footage, shot over a period of months, and develops it into an episode that is designed to be compelling, offer a sense of closure, and educate young viewers in line with the goals of the series. Each episode of *16 and Pregnant* begins with the subject's self-introduction, presented as voice-over narration that accompanies footage of the subject engaged in domestic and social activities. The striking similarities of these introductions (to be discussed in further detail) indicate that they are not extemporaneous. Each episode also includes a brief discussion of contraception, usually initiated by a friend or family member who asks the subject whether she was using birth control. The consistency with which each episode incorporates this same discussion indicates that it has been initiated by producers so that it can be captured on camera. The series avoids direct address to viewers, although the programs do include on-screen "bumpers" with additional information.[19] The intended educational "lessons" of family planning are emphasized by the repetitious episodic formula of *16 and Pregnant*, in which a pregnant teenage girl faces the difficulties of raising a child when she has not completed high school, is not financially independent, and, often, is not supported (emotionally or otherwise) by the father of her child. The systematic narrative structure, in which the subject faces and overcomes obstacles in her adjustment to motherhood, works to emphasize personal responsibility and self-discipline in the transformation from "teen girl" to "teen mom" in ways that engage with the contradictions inherent in dominant discourses of neoliberalism and postfeminism. The series and its spinoffs claim an educational mission to teach sexual responsibility by modeling the negative consequences of teen pregnancy, but they also present narratives of achievement that coincide with social expectations of "successful" female adolescence.

In Annette Hill's analysis of the educational potential of reality television, she argues that viewers may engage in a reflexive viewing process when reality programming is "designed to speak to viewers about issues that matter to them."[20] In a similar vein, *16 and Pregnant* producer Liz Gateley explains that by design, "this show doesn't preach; it doesn't teach. It just shows 'this could happen to you.'"[21] Laurie Ouellette has productively argued that "self-enterprising, neoliberal constructions of 'good citizenship' cut across much of popular reality television" and that such programming can work to "*construct* templates for citizenship that complement the privatization of public life, the collapse of the welfare state, and most important, the discourse of individual choice and personal responsibility."[22] *16 and Pregnant* and *Teen Mom* invite viewers to compare their own lives with those whom they see on-screen and to adjust their behavior to avoid the negative consequences of teen pregnancy. In this way, these series perform educational work without employing a top-down, didactic mode of address.

The young women profiled in *16 and Pregnant* model a specific set of behaviors for the viewing audience. Each episode is structured with the subject's voiceover narration. In a brief introductory segment, she introduces herself and describes her interests and activities at school, her plans for the future, and her relationship with her boyfriend. She then explains that "things are about to change" because "I'm pregnant." The casual introduction of the first episode provides an example:

> Hey, my name is Maci. I'm 16, I live in Chattanooga, Tennessee, and I'm a total overachiever. I get good grades, I play softball, and I'm even on the cheerleading squad. But don't let that fool you—I do have a wild side. I'm all about dirt bikes. My boyfriend Ryan started chasing me when I was a sophomore. . . . Eventually, he swept me off my feet. . . . All my friends are psyched for senior year, but I'm graduating early and moving in with Ryan because—I'm pregnant.[23]

These formulaic segments emphasize that it is the teen girl whose life is about to change (not her boyfriend's), and in each narrative, she must determine how best to alter her life and make sacrifices to take responsibility for the baby. Although the teen dads are often present, at least initially, no similar window into their interior lives is given, and the series places far less weight on what their lives were like before and what they must give up to become parents. Maci's introduction contrasts sharply with popular negative stereotypes of pregnant teens; it heightens the show's "this could happen to anyone" message but also prefigures neoliberal themes of individual achievement and success that play out in the series as a whole. In the next section, I discuss the relationship between the series's episodic formula and discourses of individualism and self-reliance.

"JUST PUT UP WITH IT":
CHOICE, AGENCY, AND PERSONAL RESPONSIBILITY

In her analysis of the intersections of postfeminism and neoliberalism, Rosalind Gill writes, "The notion that all our practices are freely chosen is central to postfeminist discourses which present women as autonomous agents no longer constrained by any inequalities or power imbalances whatsoever."[24] Each young woman featured on *16 and Pregnant* has already made the decision to carry her pregnancy to term by the time that her episodic narrative begins. The decision to have the baby is presented as freely chosen, even though some of the girls acknowledge the pressure from parents to consider alternatives and the uncomfortable disapproval or curiosity of peers. The depiction of each subject as a capable, autonomous individual masks the realities of adolescence. As a teenage girl, each subject is financially supported by adults (typically parents), has not completed high school, and is employed only part-time, if at all. Her autonomy is subject to the guidance and support she receives from the adults in her life. Many episodes offer a variation on the theme "You made a decision; you must take responsibility," but the participation of social welfare programs and, often, the contribution of the subject's parents (who share in the consequences) are rendered invisible. This emphasis on the role of the individual is evidence of what Rosalind Gill terms a postfeminist sensibility in media culture, and it is created through the elision of references to systems of support.

The series's engagement with the idea of "choice" is exemplified in the first episode by a conversation that occurs between Maci, visibly pregnant, and one of her classmates. Maci's classmate asks, "Did you ever like, think about, 'No, I don't want this, I don't wanna do this because I'm young and I'm not sure what I'm gonna do?' Or you just put up with it—just went through it?" Maci responds, "Just put up with it." She tells her classmate, "Every option crosses your mind," but she "never considered it."[25] This somewhat contradictory exchange reflects the complexity of claiming "choice." Maci wants to acknowledge that there are options, but they were not options for her. Her decision to "just put up with it" was simultaneously freely chosen and already made.

In the first episode of season 2, Jenelle's mother asks her to consider abortion and adoption, but a teenage friend of Jenelle's explains, "If you're responsible enough to have sex, you're responsible enough to carry a baby."[26] Here, a teenage girl's sexual activity is presented as freely chosen, and the consequences, becoming a teen mother, are presented as the natural result. In the series as a whole, the girls who acknowledge the availability of options almost never articulate a connection between their "choice" to have a baby and the political or religious beliefs held by themselves or their families. Valerie is one of the few subjects who states that her family does not approve of abortion. She herself was adopted and is the youngest in a family of eleven children. Although Valerie would like to return to high school after giving birth at age fifteen, the cost of day care makes it impossible. As her episode concludes, she says, "This is my choice, so this is what I have to do now . . . make the best of it."[27] The extent to which Valerie had legitimate options to consider is unclear, but she still claims the decision to give birth to and raise her child as a "choice."

The decision to keep the baby is based in each narrative on personal responsibility, rather than a result of socioeconomic status, available support of social institutions, or the inaccessibility of alternatives. As an example, Samantha explains, "I am a good girl. I just like made a decision to have sex, and it had consequences, and now I'm living with them."[28] In promoting the educational value of the series, MTV offers the statistic that three in ten teenage girls will become pregnant,[29] but it makes no connection between this startlingly high number and the rise of abstinence-only sex education in public schools, which expanded greatly under the George W. Bush administration.[30] Public relations materials distributed by MTV claim that the United States has "the highest rate of teenage pregnancy and teen birth in the entire developed world";[31] the series present each girl's experience of it as individual and personal. The responsibility for birth control falls on young women, and this is emphasized not just in the episodes themselves but through the postseason "Life after Labor" episodes hosted by Dr. Drew Pinsky, in which all of the featured young women meet in front of a studio audience. In the season 1 wrap-up, when Amber (featured in both *16 and Pregnant* and *Teen Mom*) explains that her boyfriend Gary did not like to use condoms, Dr. Drew tells her that "his pleasure cost you your childhood and your youth."[32] Gary, seated next to Amber during this exchange, receives no similar reproach from the medical authority, presumably because he does not bear the same responsibility for the choices that have created the couple's circumstances.

The illusion that young pregnant women are freely choosing, autonomous individuals is intensified by the series's lack of engagement with socioeconomic factors, including the significance of racial identity. Although financial obstacles are often discussed by the young parents, they focus on the relatively minor expenses of diapers and formula rather than on the cost of medical care and hospital bills. The young women featured on the series receive prenatal care and give birth in hospitals but never discuss the health insurance coverage or state aid programs that must contribute to making this possible. In place of an in-depth discussion of the high costs of day care, many episodes emphasize that "free" babysitting from family members (the availability of which differs for each individual) makes it possible for the young mothers to return to school, work, and, sometimes, engage in social activities. Three of the young women featured in the first two seasons are involved in interracial relationships,[33] but the show does not include discussions of racial prejudice or the potential impact that institutionalized racism will have on their children.

Ideas about choice and agency are made notably more complex in the narratives of two girls featured in the series who place their children for adoption. In season 1, Catelynn and her boyfriend Tyler choose adoption for their daughter to "give her a better life."[34] Their parents disapprove, but the couple is determined that they are not ready to raise a child, and their lower-income families are not equipped to help them. This is presented as a difficult decision and one that is clearly shaped by socioeconomic status and family histories of alcoholism and incarceration. In a more controversial season 2 episode, Lori is seemingly pressured by her parents into placing her baby for adoption when she and her ex-boyfriend cannot determine a plan of action for raising the child themselves. Lori's parents appear to be more than financially stable, but they argue that Lori lacks the maturity necessary to parent, and they do not want the responsibility to fall to them.[35] Unlike the other girls in the series, Catelynn and Lori are framed as beholden to their circumstances. Both indicate that they would keep their babies if they had the financial and emotional resources to care for them.

Although Catelynn, who is also featured in *Teen Mom*, consistently states that adoption was the "best choice" she could have made, in "Life after Labor," another teen mother comforts her by telling her, "When you get older and you do have a baby, you're going to be an awesome mom. You're just like us; you could do it."[36] The comment simultaneously denies the reality of Catelynn's experiences, in which she gave birth to a baby that she chose to place for adoption, and aligns Catelynn's self-sacrificing persona with that of the other young mothers featured on the series. It seems to indicate confidence that keeping the baby is the correct path and that Catelynn has demonstrated the requisite skills to achieve what the other girls have achieved.

The young fathers featured in the series are not presented as similarly responsible for the consequences of unprotected sex, and their choices are often discussed as limited by the "autonomous" decisions of the babies' mothers and the interventions of their parents. When Samantha and Eric, a Latino couple featured in season 2, discuss the possibility that Samantha could move in with Eric and his family, Eric tells her, "Whatever you pick, I don't really have a choice."[37] Kailyn, also featured in season 2, does move in with her boyfriend's family; Jo often refuses to speak to her, but he tells his mother that, nevertheless, he is "helping her out." Having the baby was "her decision," Jo explains, and that by virtue of his physical presence, "she's not a single mother."[38] Whether or not the fathers plan to be involved in supporting and raising their children, they often articulate a frustration with their perceived limited range of available options. Young women, as flexible, self-

regulating subjects, make the most significant choices and assume the majority of the responsibility; *16 and Pregnant* presents this as an inevitable,
"natural" gendered division of labor.

"IT'S MADE ME A BETTER PERSON": TRANSITIONING FROM "GIRL" TO "MOM"

The makeover subgenre of reality television focuses on individuals who
make changes to their appearance, habits, or households with the help of
"experts" and marketed products. Brenda Weber has carefully delineated the
generic markers of this type of programming, arguing that, ultimately, these
shows are about the conscious construction of the self.[39] These series generally emphasize the success of the alterations by structuring episodes around a
"before and after" formula that stresses how much the featured subject has
changed (presumably for the better). The episodic structure of *16 and Pregnant* is an atypical transformation narrative that would not strictly fit into
Weber's categorization but nevertheless shows the clear influence of the
common tropes of reality makeover shows. *16 and Pregnant* introduces pregnant teens (as exemplified in Maci's self-description) as subjects whose lives
are already in transition. The "before" picture is often rosy, emphasizing the
young woman's success in school and future aspirations; the "after" picture
is often vague, with episodes spending the most time on the transitional
period.

During the transition, problems abound. The pregnant teens worry about
money, where they will live when their babies arrive, and their relationships
with the fathers of their babies. Almost every episode devotes the majority of
narrative time to tensions between the teen parents. In some episodes, the
romantic relationship has already ended, and the couple must determine
what, if any, relationship the father will have with the child. More frequently,
the couple is trying to make their relationship work, and teen mothers express
frustration over the degree to which their lives and maturity levels must
change, while the fathers of their babies are not undergoing a similar altera-
tion. In the rare instances where teen fathers are depicted as supportive partners and parents, a narrative emphasis is placed on the couple's parents, who
worry about the teens' ability to handle the responsibilities of parenthood.

The arrival of the baby is part of the transition, and each episode emphasizes the difficulties of caring for a newborn. The baby functions as a cata-
lyst, and shortly after giving birth, each young woman establishes a new
course for the future that incorporates motherhood. The series formula constructs two main types of subjectivities that are consistent with what Anita
Harris identifies as "can-do" and "at-risk" girls. Can-do girls are self-confi-
dent and ambitious and capable of reshaping their goals and identities; in

contrast, at-risk girls lack the skills and self-determination to succeed. The series's engagement with these subjectivities is complicated by the fact that teen pregnancy has not previously been associated with ideals of adolescent achievement. As Harris defines it, postponing motherhood is "an intrinsic element of the can-do experience."[40] Within *16 and Pregnant*, can-do girls make themselves over into self-reliant, nurturing caregivers, while at-risk girls fail to mature and accept the responsibilities of parenthood.

Transitional narratives within these series demonstrate that before pregnancy, being an achiever meant being pretty, doing well in school, participating in extracurricular and social activities, and nurturing professional aspirations. After a young woman gives birth, the same requirements remain, but motherhood becomes the top priority. For example, before her son is two months old, Maci enrolls in college, returns to part-time work, and joins a dance team. Although she enjoys being with her friends again, she quits the dance team so that she can devote more time to parenting. She lives with her boyfriend Ryan, but he exhibits no interest in their son and continues the work and social routines he held before the baby's arrival. Maci's transitional period is complete when she determines how best to prioritize caring for the child, and that includes negotiating her tense relationship with Ryan.[41] This formula is present in each episode; successful subjects make their lives over to incorporate the baby, meaning that while they will still pursue school and career, these paths are now pursued as part of devoting their lives to their children.

As in any makeover narrative, not all subjects are successful. In season 2, Jenelle initially describes herself as a "party girl," which signifies that she is at risk; after she gives birth, she attempts to return to her old social life. Unlike the majority of the young women in the series, Jenelle says that motherhood is "like being in prison," and she frequently escapes to go to parties with her friends. Her mother, who becomes the child's primary caregiver, confronts Jenelle about her lack of responsibility but makes no headway. Jenelle fails to transform into an attentive parent, and although she voices her intention to complete her high school degree, the episode does not conclude on a note of optimism about her future.[42] The season 2 episode featuring Leah, who gives birth to twins, similarly breaks the "triumph over adversity" pattern of the series. When Leah returns to school shortly after giving birth, she attempts to recapture her adolescence. In the process, she alienates the babies' supportive father, and her concluding voice-over states, "I hate my life."[43] Leah's episode suggests that she is not a success because she does not embrace the responsibilities of her transformed identity. Leah and several other subjects who initially present themselves as "party girls" are depicted as individuals who do not take full responsibility for their choices.

The conclusion of almost every episode incorporates voice-over narration that offers some hint of what the future may hold. Often, as is consistent with the "message" of the series, the featured young woman expresses that she wishes she had waited to have sex, that she has made a lot of sacrifices, and that her life has been altered more than she ever thought possible. This is balanced, however, by notes of pride in the transition that has taken place. Farrah's episode concludes with her notes that "it's been a hard year but a good year. Everything that I went through—I would not take any of that back. Because it's made me a better person."[44] Giving birth is marked as a remaking of the self for can-do girls, and although many express regret over the adolescent experiences that they have missed, successful subjects embrace new identities and responsibilities.

"WAY 2B A GOOD MOM": SURVEILLANCE AND DISCIPLINE

The postfeminist sensibility of contemporary media culture encourages surveillance and discipline of both the body and the self, a facet that Rosalind Gill argues has intensified in relation to neoliberal subjectivity. Pregnancy affects physical changes that render the body "out of control," and the young women who successfully complete their transition into "good moms" bring their bodies back under strict disciplinary regimes as quickly as possible after giving birth. This is reflected in the laudatory *Us Weekly* coverage of Amber, referenced in the introduction to this chapter, which marvels that "she dropped 65 pounds from her 5-foot-4 frame!"[45] Many of the subjects of *16 and Pregnant* articulate fears about how pregnancy will change their bodies. Farrah introduces herself as a size 2 in her season 1 episode and asks a doctor if she can forego breastfeeding to limit the impact of pregnancy on her body shape. Ebony and Nikkole cry as they shop for formal dresses that will accommodate their expanding stomachs.[46] The level of surveillance that these young women experience is enhanced by their awareness that their actions are being followed by camera crews. Many of the subjects worry out loud about what they look like in the delivery room, embarrassed about their level of exposure to medical personnel and the cameras, even as they are in labor.

Teen pregnancy itself is a signifier of a lack of discipline, and many of the young women featured are fearful of the judgment of their peers. Whitney and Kailyn wear baggy clothes, insisting that other people do not know that they are pregnant and that they "just look fat." Whitney explains in voice-over that she has dropped out of high school to avoid the scrutiny of her peers. In a brief animated sequence, Whitney is pictured cringing in a high school hallway as other students point at her. Cartoon speech bubbles indicate the students saying, "She's pregnant!" and calling out, "Slut!" and

"Whore!" Although Whitney never states that she has encountered these particular charges and although she and her boyfriend are in a long-term committed relationship, the show's production team supplies the malicious judgment that she would face from other teenagers. When Whitney's friend arrives to take her on her first social outing in weeks, her grandmother attempts to reassure her by saying, "Bein' pregnant is a beautiful thing." Whitney's friend responds, "Not on the outside it's not."[47] A major aspect of the show's social behavior message reflects an awareness of the teenage female body as a commodity that is devalued by pregnancy.

Surveillance and discipline are in play not only with regard to the young women's physical appearances but also in terms of how the teen girls perform motherhood. Maci, who is a favorite among the viewers who post on MTV's message boards about the show, frequently states her desire to be a "good mom" and that everything she does has to be for the benefit of her son. When Jenelle's mother asks her to take more responsibility for her baby, Jenelle's friend counsels her to go to fewer parties for a while so that other people will think she's being a good mom. According to her friend, "people around the county" disapprove of Jenelle's behavior, and she advises Jenelle, "You need to prove it to 'em that you are a good mom and that you can do it."[48] Being a good mom requires self-sacrifice, and the assessment of a teen mother's performance comes from others (including the viewing audience).

As in any reality television production, each episode is constructed to highlight certain moments to create an orderly narrative. In Leah's episode, discussed as one of the few that does not end on a note of triumph, she is frequently shown fixing her hair and applying makeup, shortly after giving birth to twins.[49] Shots of Leah staring at herself in the mirror and applying mascara while balancing a baby in the crook of one arm invite the viewer to surmise that her commitment to a renewed high school social life is greater than her commitment to her newborn children. While the episode does not include the "expert" intervention that would be present in a traditional makeover series, the episode's editors have de-emphasized the time that Leah spends with her children to support an orderly narrative of her failed transition into motherhood.

Teen fathers are not subjected to the same level of surveillance and discipline. Chelsea attends the homecoming game with her friends when her baby is a few weeks old; upon returning home, she receives the following text message from the baby's father, Adam, who is not involved in the baby's life: "Hrd u went out. Way 2b a good mom." Adam sarcastically offers a negative assessment of Chelsea's parenting but feels no similar demands placed on him. Before the baby's arrival, Chelsea expressed sadness about missing the events of senior year, and Adam responded, "I can still go out and party."[50] The expectations of teen dads are not well defined and are far less restrictive than the expectations associated with being a "good" mom.

The series works to normalize this gendered division, which is present in almost every episode. Young women are aware that others are watching and judging them, and they attempt to monitor themselves and their behavior in accordance with perceived expectations.

CONCLUSION

Lizzie, featured in season 2, excels in school, loves marching band, and dreams of one day playing the flute in the Virginia Symphony. She quits band when she becomes pregnant to begin a home-schooling curriculum that will allow her to graduate from high school early. Although she misses interacting with her peers, she announces in voice-over, "I'm not just going to let having a baby stop me from doing what I want to do and what I love."[51] Lizzie enrolls in two college classes as her due date nears, but shortly after the baby arrives, she drops out of her program. Lizzie justifies this "choice" in terms of her daughter, saying, "I could do it perfectly fine. I just would rather be with her than go to class and have her." Lizzie is a can-do girl who describes her transition into a can-do mom as one of choice. Rosalind Gill explains that neoliberal construction of identity is gendered and "it is *women* who are called on to self-manage, self-discipline. To a much greater extent than men, women are required to work on and transform the self, to regulate every aspect of their conduct, and to present all their actions as freely chosen."[52] Lizzie's stance is that she could maintain her former adolescent identity as an achiever but because parenting takes precedence, she chooses to postpone her education and career goals. Lizzie makes no mention of educational costs, social services, or access to day care, and the viewer is left to take her at her word. The episode ultimately presents this as a positive choice by concluding with Lizzie's voice-over: "It's bummed me out a couple of times, but then I'll think about it . . . and in my mind, what I'm doing being a mom is far more important than just going out and having fun." Although Lizzie clarifies that she does not want her daughter to become a teen mother, she clearly draws motherhood into her own narrative of adolescent achievement.

As entertainment programming with an educational mission, *16 and Pregnant* and *Teen Mom* place far less emphasis on birth control and sexual health than they do on the consequences of teen pregnancy. By presenting pregnant teens who are smart, involved, and ambitious, these series may represent a significant intervention into widely held negative stereotypes that teen mothers are directionless, uneducated, and overly dependent on social welfare programs. The shows perform cultural work by aligning pregnancy with existing discourses of female adolescence and empowerment. These representational practices are troubling because they rely on false claims of individualism, choice, and autonomy that not only deny the necessity of social systems of support but consistently downplay the roles and responsibilities of teen fathers.

I would not suggest that every viewer watches these programs in the same way, but the repeated episodic formula and themes powerfully frame teen pregnancy as an individual consequence of personal choices, rather than as a social issue with myriad implications that stretch beyond the family unit. The responsibility for practicing birth control, sacrificing adolescence, and parenting is gendered female, and while the series do not always present this as a positive circumstance, its continual repetition serves a normative function. Whether or not *16 and Pregnant* and *Teen Mom* are effective in encouraging teens to practice family planning and avoid the negative consequences they see on television, these series operate as technologies of everyday life that shape postfeminist neoliberal citizenship.

NOTES

1. Grossbart and Abrahamson, "Teen Mom."
2. See Brooks, *Postfeminisms*; Lotz, *Redesigning Women*.
3. See Negra, "Quality Postfeminism?"; Projansky, *Watching Rape*; and Vavrus, "Putting Ally on Trial."
4. Gill, "Postfeminist Media Culture," 148–49.
5. Hennessy, *Profit and Pleasure*, 75.
6. Aapola, Gonick, and Harris, *Young Femininity*, 7.
7. Gill, "Culture and Subjectivity," 443.
8. Harris, *Future Girl*, 13–36.
9. Douglas and Michaels, *Mommy Myth*, 24.
10. Douglas and Michaels, *Mommy Myth*, 4.
11. Douglas and Michaels, *Mommy Myth*, 22.
12. Douglas and Michaels, *Mommy Myth*, 190–95.
13. In late 2008, MTV's president for entertainment used this phrase to describe the new direction for programming at the cable channel. He was introducing a slate of new reality programming that would premiere in 2009, including *16 and Pregnant*. See Frankel, "MTV Plans."
14. Arango, "Make Room, Cynics."
15. Brown and Singhal, "Ethical Dilemmas," 270.
16. Grigsby Bates, "MTV's *Teen Mom*."
17. Armstrong, "*16 and Pregnant* Delivers Big."
18. Grigsby Bates, "MTV's *Teen Mom*."
19. Every episode of *16 and Pregnant* and *Teen Mom*, for example, features the onscreen message: "Teen pregnancy is 100% preventable. To find out what you can do to prevent pregnancy, go to www.itsyoursexlife.org." The website is part of a public information campaign coproduced by MTV and the Kaiser Family Foundation.
20. Hill, *Reality TV*, 90.
21. Grigsby Bates, "MTV's *Teen Mom*."
22. Ouellette, "'Take Responsibility for Yourself,'" 232.
23. "Maci," *16 and Pregnant*, June 11, 2009.
24. Gill, "Postfeminist Media Culture," 153.
25. "Maci," *16 and Pregnant*, June 11, 2009.
26. "Jenelle," *16 and Pregnant*, February 16, 2010.

27. "Valerie," *16 and Pregnant*, March 2, 2010.

28. "Samantha," *16 and Pregnant*, March 23, 2010.

29. PR NewsWire, "MTV Chronicles."

30. Alesha Doan and Jean Calterone Williams write that funding for abstinence-only educa-tion was a George W. Bush campaign promise, and the Community-Based Abstinence Educa-tion program launched under his administration with initial funding of $20 million in 2001. See *The Politics of Virginity*, 41. The authors assert that one-third of American public schools have abstinence-only curricula.

31. PR NewsWire, "MTV Chronicles."

32. "Life after Labor," *16 and Pregnant*, July 23, 2009.

33. Season 1 features Ebony, who is African American; her boyfriend Josh is white. In season 2, Valerie is African American, and her boyfriend Matt is white. Kailyn is white, and her boyfriend Jo is Latino. Season 2 also features a Latino couple, Samantha and Eric.

34. "Catelynn," *16 and Pregnant*, July 16, 2009.

35. "Lori," *16 and Pregnant*, March 16, 2010.

36. "Life after Labor."

37. "Samantha," *16 and Pregnant*, March 23, 2010.

38. "Kailyn," *16 and Pregnant*, April 20, 2010.

39. Weber, *Makeover TV*.

40. Harris, *Future Girl*, 23.

41. "Maci," *16 and Pregnant*, June 11, 2009.

42. "Jenelle," *16 and Pregnant*, February 16, 2010.

43. "Leah," *16 and Pregnant*, April 6, 2010.

44. "Farrah," *16 and Pregnant*, June 18, 2009.

45. Grossbart and Abrahamson, "Teen Mom," 41.

46. "Ebony," *16 and Pregnant*, July 2, 2009; "Nikkole," *16 and Pregnant*, February 23, 2010.

47. "Whitney," *16 and Pregnant*, July 9, 2009.

48. "Jenelle," *16 and Pregnant*, February 16, 2010.

49. "Leah," *16 and Pregnant*, April 6, 2010.

50. "Chelsea," *16 and Pregnant*, March 9, 2010.

51. "Lizzie," *16 and Pregnant*, April 13, 2010.

52. Gill, "Culture and Subjectivity," 443.

Chapter Two

16 and Pregnant and the "Unvarnished" Truth about Teen Pregnancy

Letizia Guglielmo and Kimberly Wallace Stewart

Since 2009 MTV, in cooperation with the National Campaign to Prevent Teen and Unplanned Pregnancy,[1] has produced and aired *16 and Pregnant*, a documentary-style series that, according to program creators, allows "young women to share their story in their own voice" and offers an "unvarnished and honest portrayal of their experience" as pregnant teens.[2] In media accounts, the program has been touted as a "powerful public service," with the potential to influence teens' decisions about sex and contraception[3] and perhaps reshape the conversation created by government-funded sexuality education.

Over the last two decades, sex education across the United States has increasingly been dominated by a curriculum of abstinence-only programs and attempts to solve the "problem" of teen pregnancy. Often driven by conservative notions of morality and welfare reform and couched in the language of mitigating risk for our children and young people,[4] these approaches to sexuality education, many have argued, perpetuate gender, race, and class stereotypes as well as heteronormative marriage ideals and so result in a silencing of young people that leaves them voiceless in these initiatives and lacking sexual subjectivity. For young women—typically the sole targets of campaigns intended to eliminate teen pregnancy—discussions surrounding teen sexuality and sex education programs offer two versions of teen girlhood: a sexually naïve innocent—a "pure" and ideally submissive young woman who pledges her virginity to her father in a purity ball, perhaps—or a sexually experienced corrupting slut. More troubling is that within these running narratives, the authentic voices of young women are noticeably absent or deliberately silenced.

Feminist interventions traditionally foreground issues of race, gender, sexuality, and class. Specifically, they uncover the ways in which women—both their work and their experiences—have been excluded, deliberately ignored, and silenced. In the feminist tradition of consciousness raising, personal narratives have been powerful catalysts in prompting political action and fostering social change, reminding us that the personal is, in fact, political. For young women in particular—women whose voices are often further ignored because of age and perceived lack of experience—personal narratives offer opportunities to gain agency while intervening in essentialist descriptions of women's experiences. Beginning with six young women as part of season 1 in 2009, *16 and Pregnant* appears to offer a creative intervention through personal narrative, reinforced by voice-over and visual cues in each episode. In this chapter, we explore how the program simply reinforces stereotypes common in the rhetoric of teen pregnancy and sex education in the United States and facilitates the co-opting of the young women's narratives, often eclipsed by male voices. Drawing from individual episodes of the first season, online resources associated with the program, and educational materials prepared and distributed by the Kaiser Family Foundation, we question through our analysis the dominant narratives being retold and the extent to which the program and its supporting online materials simply reinscribe dangerous social norms.

NARRATIVES OF SEXUALITY EDUCATION

In her historical study of sex education within the United States, Alexandra Lord explores the intersections of medicine and morality, race, class, and religion at the heart of debates surrounding sex education since the beginning of the twentieth century and the extent to which these public programs were continually hampered by the threat of offending particular groups of citizens. Originally created within the purview of the Public Health Service, most early sexual health programs focused on controlling the spread of venereal disease—namely, syphilis and gonorrhea—with mixed success during the early to middle part of the century because of a lack of consistent sex education and understanding about sexual health. Although the focus remained on preventing the spread of disease in the first half of the twentieth century and not on reducing the number of "illegitimate births" (as they were then referred to), "during the early 1960s, federal officials became convinced that ending poverty also was 'feasible.' Believing that unwanted and out-of-wedlock pregnancies caused and exacerbated poverty, public health experts pointed an accusatory finger at Americans' limited understanding and use of birth control."[5] Yet, despite a recognizable need for comprehensive sex education by 1969, "concerns about offending the more conservative segments of American society . . . would continue . . . to plague federally funded efforts to promote sexual literacy,"[6] and the next thirty years brought continued cuts to sex education programs.

Following the presidency of George H. W. Bush, comprehensive sex education programs were systematically replaced by abstinence-only programs, and "by 2005, the United States had the highest teenage pregnancy rate of any nation in the industrialized world."[7] "Many of these programs," according to Lord, "endorsed outdated gender stereotypes," including the program "Choosing the Best."[8] Within the state of Georgia, for example, a state in which "Choosing the Best" has been in use,[9] state board of education guidelines for sexuality education require schools to "emphasize abstinence from sexual activity until marriage and fidelity in marriage as important personal goals [while promoting] high self-esteem, local community values, and abstinence . . . as an effective method of prevention of pregnancy . . . and sexually transmitted diseases."[10] Studies reveal that "teens in abstinence-only programs not only engage in sex, they are also less likely to use protection than their peers who receive comprehensive sex education."[11]

Further research on teen pregnancy and sexuality education programs reveals a number of recurring narratives and raises questions of concern for scholars in women's and girls' studies, including rhetorics of purity, risk, and "readiness" that impede discourse surrounding sex and sexuality; sexism regarding appropriate behavior for girls and boys, grounded in troubling dichotomies; and silencing on many levels. Dual narratives of "risk" and "innocence" are common within discussions of sexuality education across the United States, particularly those offered in defense of abstinence-only curricula: in other words, if we don't *talk* about sex, children won't *have* sex and everyone will remain *safe*. And apparently, within this equation, marriage mitigates all risk. In an attempt to maintain "a risk-free zone," school officials engage in a silencing of not only young people's voices but also their sexuality,[12] and in most cases, they deny young people accurate information on contraception should they choose not to abstain.

If impending risk is not enough to promote abstinence, then perhaps shame and ruin are. For example, Ed Ainsworth, an abstinence-only educator in Lubbock, Texas, suggested abstinence as a sure way "to avoid emotional and social ruin," and if that had not yet convinced students, he reminded them (read: young women), "You'll still be known as a slut."[13] Comments like these work to reinforce dangerous gender stereotypes that offer young men and boys the impression that safe sex, pregnancy prevention, and discussions about sexuality do not and should not include them and that pregnancy prevention begins and ends with the regulation of young women's sexuality.

When discussions of teen sexuality do take place, they often are dominated, as Catherine Ashcraft claims, by an "unexamined discourse of 'readiness'

[that] hinders teens' abilities to make sense of their sexual experiences."[14] If teens are led to believe that they should become sexually active when they are *ready*—presumably, that only *they* can make those decisions—their opportunities to engage in dialogue on the subject both with adults and with their partners are significantly limited. Without the opportunity to explore or to discuss readiness, young women may create "unrealistic expectations for sex and [engage in] self-blame if these expectations are not met."[15] Consistently, qualitative studies on sexuality education reveal a lack of agency among girls' stories that limits their choices and makes discussing birth control with their partners much more difficult.[16] When taken together, these recurring narratives suggest that sexuality education and pregnancy prevention programs certainly fail to operate with the interests of young women in mind.

According to Deirdre M. Kelly, outside the classroom "females remain the resounding targets for blame" in discussions of teen pregnancy and "are commonly portrayed as responsible for poor choices and 'wrong' decisions."[17] Furthermore, this discourse is reinforced through what Jessica Valenti terms "the purity myth," the skewed belief that all of a young woman's value is tied up in what is vaguely termed "virginity" and in the "sexual scripts," according to John Gagnon and William Simon, available to young women within the popular media.[18] For example, when we consider ongoing public discussions on contraception and abortion rights, most recently during the 2012 election year, and the eloquent words of legislators and public figures such as Rush Limbaugh—particularly when they are transmitted over and over again through social and digital media—these gender stereotypes are not only reinforced but become much more dangerous for young women and girls.

PROGRAM ANALYSIS

In the remaining sections of this chapter, we analyze season 1 of *16 and Pregnant*, and we pair this analysis of the six episodes with references to the program's website and to additional supporting resources prepared by national organizations affiliated with the series: the National Campaign to Prevent Teen and Unplanned Pregnancy and the Kaiser Family Foundation. A 2000 study conducted by the foundation "revealed that an overwhelming majority of Americans are still calling for more aggressive sex education,"[19] and it seems safe to assume that its involvement with *16 and Pregnant* has been connected to addressing that need. We focus on season 1 alone because it is being distributed as an educational resource, most notably with "3000 DVDs and guides to Boys and Girls Clubs of America chapters alone."[20] Whether described as a documentary series, reality television, or edutainment, it is clear that the creators of *16 and Pregnant* and their partner organizations intend for the series to hold educational value and to be used in classrooms and learning environments as supplements to, or perhaps in place of, sex education programs. In viewing and re-viewing the six episodes of season 1, as well as online materials included on the companion websites and in the *16 and Pregnant* kit distributed for educational purposes, we analyze the discourse of season 1 and the extent to which the series interrupts dominant narratives of teen sexuality and teen pregnancy and challenges ideological codes of behavior for the viewing audience, those ideological codes historically associated with teen sexuality and with sex education in the United States. In the following sections, we look at both the six episodes and the discussion materials, considering them individually and as complementary pieces in promoting teaching and learning as intended by program creators.

DISCUSSING "MISTAKES AND DECISIONS"

On the surface, *16 and Pregnant* offers a novel approach to the topic of teen pregnancy and pregnancy prevention through a network known for providing popular programming for teens and young adults. Over the last eight years, MTV has garnered sustained teen viewership with reality-style series such as *Laguna Beach*, *The Hills*, and *Jersey Shore*, programs that purport to show the "real lives" of young men and women. In keeping with this larger theme, the casting section of the *16 and Pregnant* website includes this description:

> This documentary series covers the journeys of young women during their unplanned pregnancy. We realize that this is a very sensitive subject for many, so our goal is to show what teen-aged pregnant women, from varying backgrounds, experience in their lives and relationships as a result of their unplanned pregnancies. From morning sickness to dealing with parents and boyfriends, as well as making challenging decisions and ultimately to the day of the baby's arrival and beyond, we would like you to let us document this exciting, life changing and complicated journey. This show seeks to allow young women to share their personal story in their own voice and how others could potentially learn from their mistakes and decisions. [21]

With this introduction, one might assume that the "mistakes and decisions" referred to here are those made before conception and those made by the pregnant teen and her partner, yet as we discuss in the following sections, *16 and Pregnant* includes little to no genuine discussion of these topics.

In 2000, a survey of teenagers by the National Campaign to Prevent Teen and Unplanned Pregnancy revealed that 88.1 percent of teenagers in the United States considered birth control an essential part of sexual activity, yet in spite of this fact, almost 38 percent of teens that did use contraception did not use it consistently. In the same survey, researchers asked teenagers, "Do you think one of the main reasons that teens do not use birth control is because their partner doesn't want to use any?" and 51.7 percent of teenage girls and boys responded "yes."[22] Given these findings and the fact that the young women on *16 and Pregnant* are facing unplanned pregnancies, one would assume that a discussion of the decisions that led to the teens facing this "mistake," as the program creators describe, it would be a central part of the program. Within this context, the topic of contraception is one that could be used to explore other aspects of teen sexuality and the young women's decisions to engage in sexual activity, whether "to experience pleasure, to gain popularity, to maintain a boyfriend, or to 'get it over with.' Each of these motivations might have different implications for the decisions girls make about disease protection and contraception, pleasure, and power"[23] and would serve as useful models of discussion for teen viewers.

Although the subject is introduced in a few episodes of the first season, often couched in the overarching question "How did this happen?" sustained discussions are never developed. In the fourth episode, for example, Ebony is given the opportunity by a counselor to listen to the experiences of other teen mothers in her school.[24] Though an opportunity for MTV to offer a creative intervention through personal narrative, allowing other teen girls to tell their stories and share similar experiences on camera, the scene lasts only one minute, during which three young women discuss difficulties with labor, caring for a baby in the first couple of months, and taking care of a baby while in school. Although these are important topics of discussion, particularly given Ebony's impending motherhood, the producers miss the opportunity to not only provide a forum for other young women regarding their decisions to have sex but also model these exchanges for viewers.

In the same episode, a conversation between Ebony and her fiancé Josh suggests some regret or, at minimum, some hindsight reflection on Ebony's part. Although it is not clear to viewers whether the two were engaged before the pregnancy, in this particular conversation, Josh suggests that he no longer wants to marry Ebony in the near future because they are "already seventeen and having a baby." Here the scene cuts away with Ebony's voice-over: "With Josh second-guessing our marriage plans now that I'm pregnant, I'm starting to wish we would have been more careful." This still image then shifts to an animated cartoon version of the scene—typical of the program as a whole—with a wedding ring turning into a condom. For viewers, this scene is confusing and abrupt. Although we are led to believe that Ebony may have agreed not to use contraception because she and Josh would marry anyway, this assumption is never confirmed for viewers. Without a sustained discussion on the topic, viewers are left to question how Ebony made the decision to engage in sexual activity and what kinds of discussions, if any, she had with her partner regarding contraception before doing so. Here again, we see another missed opportunity to discuss how and why teens make the decision not to use contraception, a discussion that may have been a useful resource for viewers to begin conversations with their partners.

In the third episode of the season, teen mom Amber displays a similar lack of agency when it comes to contraception.[25] In an exchange with her significant other, Gary, she exclaims, "You want to know why I'm pregnant? Because you don't like condoms, and I was too stupid to make you put them on." Here Gary responds, "I never said I didn't like condoms," and the scene cuts away from the conversation, with the topic of "not liking condoms" never addressed again in that episode.[26] This scene is significant in our analysis because it reinforces the findings of the National Campaign to Prevent Teen and Unplanned Pregnancy study that "the main reason that teens do not use birth control is because their partner does not want to use any"[27] and because it mirrors other "girls' stories," as Deborah Tolman, Celeste Hirshman, and Emily Impett discovered, that "lacked a sense of agency and clarity that would have enabled them to make active and unambiguous choices about their sexual behavior."[28] Again, without any further discussion of the topic, the program's producers fail to make any significant intervention into dominant narratives of teen sexuality and so normalize this lack of sexual subjectivity for their viewers.

Perhaps most striking in terms of agency is Whitney's story in the season's fifth episode and her final reflection: "When I'm feeling really overwhelmed, I will wonder how did this happen to me."[29] Like the other teen moms, Whitney's story does not include a discussion of "mistakes and decisions" as the program description suggests, and her words here—as well as her demure, often childlike presence on the screen—reinforce dominant narratives of sexuality education associated with "protecting children" and mitigating risk rather than inviting teens to engage in sustained discussions of their sexuality and sexual choices.

What the program does offer in terms of resources for viewers are frequent reminders during commercial breaks to visit itsyoursexlife.com (sponsored by the Kaiser Family Foundation) for more information on preventing teen pregnancy. Given the title alone, the message sent to viewers is quite clear: decisions about *your* sex life are *yours* alone. These related yet off-show resources send visual and verbal cues that these topics are personal and private, given that none of the teens' decisions regarding sex and contraception are discussed at length on the program. In an article for *Teen Vogue* reflecting on her experience with *16 and Pregnant*, teen mom Maci offers this insight: "When Ryan and I met the summer after my sophomore year, I was a virgin. A lot of my friends had made the decision to have sex, but their relationships didn't last. I didn't want to get hurt, but I fell in love with Ryan and decided that I could trust him. Four months into the relationship, we slept together. I hate to say it, but we didn't use protection."[30] Although we are given some insight here into Maci's decision—that choosing to have sex without protection was connected in some way to trust—these insights are never mentioned nor explored within her episode. It appears that Maci was faced, as are many teens, with making solitary decisions about "readiness" and engaging in the kind of "self blame" that Ashcraft describes.[31]

Maci offers additional insight on her decisions, again within the *Teen Vogue* article and not on the program, when she describes her work with high school teens: "I've been going to local high schools to speak to students too. I want them to know that if they've made up their mind to abstain from sex, they shouldn't feel pressured to change their decision."[32] In reflecting on Maci's story, we are left to wonder if she felt this kind of pressure and if that pressure came from Ryan, the father of her child. Similar to Ebony's and Amber's statements regarding condoms, we are reminded of Tolman, Hirschman, and Impett's findings that girls' agency and condom use are intimately connected, and "in longer-term relationships, girls said that asking a partner to use a condom was difficult because it brought up questions of trust."[33] Without these difficult discussions taking place on-screen or, at minimum, without any reflections on these decisions, young women watching the program are no better equipped to navigate them in their own lives.

DISCUSSION GUIDES AND ONLINE RESOURCES

For those viewers who do choose to consult the online resources connected to *16 and Pregnant* and in those cases where the six episodes of season 1 may be viewed and discussed within an educational context, discussion guides and other digital resources may create the potential for reflection among teens and discussion facilitators. Although three versions of the discussion guides are available, discussion questions are similar across them. StayTeen.org, sponsored by the National Campaign to Prevent Teen and Unplanned Pregnancy,[34] provides two-page guides accessible as PDFs on the *16 and Pregnant* program website, and each includes an episode summary, a section titled "Stuff to Think About and Discuss" that provides both statistics and brief facts on teen pregnancy and parenting, and discussion questions related to the individual episode. Readers are prompted to visit StayTeen.org and itsyoursexlife.com to "find out more." Through the National Campaign to Prevent Teen and Unplanned Pregnancy website, viewers will find a condensed version of the six discussion guides, with fewer questions and information; this booklet is also available as a PDF for easy download. A section titled "How to Use This Guide" is directed not at teens but those who might "watch the episodes with [their] teens." Readers are encouraged to "use the discussion questions inside to start conversations" and "to talk about the realities and consequences of teen pregnancy." Although this booklet is available through the website for download and use, visitors are reminded to contact the national campaign with questions or comments and to request "additional copies of the DVD and discussion booklet," suggesting that this booklet also has been distributed with the DVD of season 1.[35]

Finally, we encountered the third version of the discussion guide in the *16 and Pregnant* kit provided by the Kaiser Family Foundation for educational use. In addition to episode summaries and discussion questions (five per episode), the kit includes a DVD of the first season, as well as detailed handouts on contraception designed to engage teens with descriptions such as "Drag Factor" (the potential drawbacks of a particular method of contraception) and "Groovy Part" (the potential benefits). The inclusion of this information on contraception is particularly significant given that the potential exists for teens to view the program with these handouts and to engage in a facilitated discussion that may influence their decisions about engaging in unprotected sex. In this scenario, teens are provided with information not available through the program, rather than being expected to find it on their own. As with our analysis of the individual episodes, however, we are interested in how the discussion guides facilitate interruption of dominant narratives, and in the following sections, we discuss recurring themes within the guides that also appear within the program episodes. Again, given that the questions are similar among the guides, we draw most of our examples from the individual episode guides available on StayTeen.org because they are most comprehensive.

REINFORCING GENDER INEQUALITY ON- AND OFF-SCREEN

Although we have identified a number of important conversations that do not take place on the program, perhaps more notable are the voices that we do hear and the recurring stereotypes regarding women's sexuality reinforced for viewers. Given the novel foregrounding of young women's voices, *16 and Pregnant* has the potential to serve as a feminist intervention in ongoing debates on sex education and teen pregnancy. Instead, what we see and hear and what is reinscribed by discussion guides are appropriate behaviors for women and girls grounded in patriarchal values, silencing of women's voices, normalized public shaming of those whose behaviors fall outside these rigid expectations, and reinforcement of assumptions commonly associated with teen pregnancy and sex education.

The Virgin-Whore Dichotomy

Self-described as a "country girl from the southern town of Rome, Georgia" who "[loves] to gossip and shop," sixteen-year-old Whitney becomes for viewers the ideal of angelic purity.[36] Whitney lives with her mother, who also is expecting a child (within a few weeks of Whitney's due date), and her grandmother. The episode opens as she rides a carousel horse and states that she "feels like a little kid," adding later that she hopes "to live happily ever after with Weston" (her boyfriend). She is soft-spoken, timid, and unsure of her actions throughout the episode, and editing reinforces this positioning as a naïve innocent, with descriptions of Whitney as "a baby," with discussions and images of Whitney not able to tie her own shoes, and with Whitney's own statement that she does not understand "how this happened to [her]." Furthermore, Whitney becomes the example of heteronormative conservative sexuality (likely Southern Christian conservative sexuality given that she is from Rome, Georgia): she loses her virginity to her first boyfriend, the young man she now plans to marry because the sexual act led (as it should, presumably) to pregnancy. Later in the episode, we see Whitney reflecting on the pregnancy and what viewers are led to believe are "the consequences."

In the voice-over for this scene, Whitney states that she and Weston considered both abortion and adoption, yet no additional details are offered to viewers regarding these decisions. Instead, we hear her grandmother describe Whitney's first doctor's visit after deciding to keep the baby: "You looked so excited, like an angel had kissed you." Quickly, however, Whitney's voice-over clarifies for viewers that this moment of excitement was followed by shame and fear of what others would think and, ultimately, her decision to drop out of school as a result. The cameras then show Whitney at home eating a sandwich alone and explaining that she is now too embarrassed to leave the house.

Although this scene closes with Whitney and her friend Eerie leaving Whitney's home for an outing, there is no questioning of her decision to drop out of school and lock herself in her home because she is ashamed and fearful of how others will judge her. In fact, these feelings are reinforced in the storyline when she accompanies her friend to the mall in the next scene for what seems to viewers like a public shaming, with classmates staring and whispering. Here program producers clarify for viewers precisely how Whitney should be judged, with a cartoon image of a pregnant Whitney called a "slut" and "whore" by classmates, who point and stare. In a story for *Slate*, *16 and Pregnant* creator Lauren Dolgen had this to say about the program: "A key component is that it doesn't have our opinions in it; it's completely from the point of view of the girls who are going through it."[37] Yet in this scene, although Whitney never uses the words *slut* and *whore* to describe herself, it seems important for program producers to reiterate these social stereotypes visually for the audience. The larger message here is clear: girls may occupy one of two roles, virgin or whore, and viewers are offered a clear illustration of the devastating consequences of the latter.

Within the discussion guide for Whitney's episode, her decision to drop out of school is never questioned but is used as an opportunity to reinforce the "consequences" of teen pregnancy: "Teen parents have a hard time keeping up with friends and activities like they did before the baby. Whitney dropped out of school and is losing touch with her friends."[38] Although the reference here is to "teen parents," the very next statement focuses on Whitney alone and not Weston. Similarly, the discussion guide for Farrah's episode notes that "when she becomes the subject of high school gossip she leaves school and starts spending a lot of time with her mother."[39] Here too, there is no questioning of Farrah's decision to leave school, and the shame and gossip are normalized on the program and through the supplementary resources.

Women and Girls Preventing Pregnancy, Men and Boys Enforcing These "Policies"

Gender stereotypes are most evident in the brief scenes in each episode during which family and friends discuss with the teen moms how the pregnancy occurred in the broadest terms possible. In their analysis of public discourse surrounding the pregnancies of teens Bristol Palin and Jamie Lynn Spears, Bute and Russell note that blame is often placed on the mothers of pregnant teens, particularly in the case of Jamie Lynn's mother.[40] It is not surprising then that in each "how did this happen" scene, the teen girl's mother becomes an important focus of the discussion—whether or not she is present—and quite often, she is blamed for not providing her daughter with the right kind of guidance in terms of pregnancy prevention and is accused of being irresponsible or reckless in how she has raised her child. Within Maci's episode, for example, during a scene in which Maci, Ryan, and Ryan's parents are discussing just how the two conceived a child, it is Ryan's father who asks Maci, "Didn't your mom talk to you about . . . ?" a statement followed by awkward laughter among the group.[41] While Ryan's presence in this discussion offers a visual reinforcement of his presumed involvement in the pregnancy, the statement made by Ryan's father—"Didn't your mother talk to you?"—effectively absolves Ryan and his father of responsibility. Given that it is Maci who is questioned and expected to offer an explanation suggests that she alone is to blame, and with Ryan's father directing the questions while implicating Maci's mother, he asserts his innocence and his power, the innocence of his son, and indirectly, the innocence of Maci's father. When the attention turns briefly to Ryan, at the end of the scene, it is Ryan's mother who repeats her son's response for the audience: "Don't go there now, Mom." Ryan is not expected to explain his choices, nor is he prodded any further on the topic on-screen, reinforcing the social norm that "boys are generally not held responsible for their sexual actions" and that girls are "responsible for controlling boys' sexuality as well as their own."[42]

Earlier in the same scene, Ryan's father expresses disbelief upon hearing that his son was Maci's first boyfriend. He then states, "Well, he really ruined you." Although it is Ryan who is named the active agent here, the scene as a whole is focused on Maci, her blame, her consequences. Particularly important is the use of "ruined" to describe Maci, suggesting that she is perhaps damaged goods, precisely the kind of "ruin" referred to by abstinence-only educators. [43] The messages in these scenes, as in sexuality education, are clear: women and girls are responsible for preventing pregnancy, and they alone will suffer the consequences.

The introduction to the season 1 discussion guides references the "difficulties of being a teen parent," yet the focus is largely on young women throughout the television program. In fact, the next paragraph of this introduction specifically references women's sacrifices, not young men's: "these girls are forced to sacrifice their teenage years and their high school experiences." Within the discussion guide for Maci's episode, readers learn that "Maci has to put her own interests aside to care for Bentley." [44] Although the discussion guide creators do acknowledge Ryan's lack of involvement, a discussion question for this episode again suggests that Maci is to blame: "Why do you think Ryan is so slow to pitch in and help? Is there anything Maci could do to get Ryan to be more focused on the baby?" Although this topic presents an opportunity for helping teens to interrogate these gender norms, the question, as it is phrased, works instead to reinforce them and to do so without also questioning Ryan's verbal abuse of Maci throughout the episode.

Discussion prompts for Whitney's episode express many of the same sentiments: "Having a supportive partner makes a big difference. Can you imagine how difficult parenthood would be for Whitney if Weston weren't so committed to being a father?" [45] Again, the assumption reinforced for viewers is that responsibility would fall on Whitney. Unlike Weston or Ryan, she does not have the option "not to be committed" as teen fathers do. Although the discussion guides suggest, over and over again, that "becoming a teen parent means putting other dreams on hold," *teen parent* here is read as *teen mother*, as it is the young women who are expected to table these dreams, whether graduating from high school or otherwise. As the discussion guide for Ebony's episode explains, "Ebony doesn't graduate from high school and she isn't able to join the military like she wanted to." [46] Her fiancée, Josh, however, is still able to fulfill his dream of joining the air force.

Deviant Women Will Be Subject to Shaming by White Men

In Ebony's episode, viewers see her and Josh in a personal health class during one of the only school-centered discussions on teen pregnancy during the first season. Before class, a very pregnant and smiling Ebony gives a few of her friends invitations to her baby shower and then walks into a scene involving what viewers are to conclude is a discussion on teen sexuality and pregnancy. Two young men speak in this scene, namely as bookends for Ebony's statement, during which she speaks clearly and with agency: "I know she [her daughter] wasn't a planned pregnancy, but I think things happen for a reason, and I'm planning to have my baby because I want to have her."[47] A young man offers this response: girls who "have enough respect for themselves" should keep their "legs closed," which is followed by laughter from the other students in the class. The camera then shifts from the young man to Ebony, who hangs her head in what viewers are to conclude is shame. Earlier in the same scene, a young man echoes what viewers heard in Maci's episode, explaining that pregnancy "ruined" his sister's life—that is, the teen *mom's* life, not the teen father's. Again, while the teen mom faces "ruin," there appear to be no consequences for the teen father.

This classroom scene, though brief, is troubling on many levels given that it again privileges the voice of men and places the responsibility of pregnancy prevention solely on the teen girl. The comments suggest that young women who choose to engage in sexual activity do not respect themselves and, as viewers might conclude, do not deserve respect. Given that this discussion is not interrupted or redirected in any way—at least on-screen—by the white male educator present in the room, viewers are to assume that these cultural assumptions constitute popular opinion and that this kind of public shaming of young women is acceptable. For young women watching the program, these "lessons" are also reinforced, as we note in previous sections, by current debates on access to contraception and abortion rights, as well as by repeated public shaming of women by (white) men.

A Final Word from Dr. Drew

Following the format of many reality-style programs, particularly those on MTV, each season of *16 and Pregnant* closes with a reunion special, during which the teen moms and, often, the teen fathers or other family members join Dr. Drew Pinsky—MTV's resident expert on everything from love and relationships to drug and sex addiction and, within this context, teen sexuality—for an update and surface-level reflection. This special episode typically includes a live audience and, presumably, an opportunity to hear the unedited voices of the young women. However, a similar gendered and raced power distribution and policing are evident in the after-show, given the positioning of bodies on the stage and who is directing the majority of the conversation. All of the young women sit on one couch, and Dr. Drew is seated in the traditional "talk show host" chair. He asks nearly all of the questions, and this questioning often turns to interrogation. None of the gender stereotypes that we explore in this chapter are interrupted or revisited by Dr. Drew in what has the potential to be a teachable, reflective discussion. Furthermore, in keeping with previous references throughout the season, Dr. Drew directs viewers before nearly every commercial break to itsyoursexlife.com, reinforcing once again that real discussions of sexuality and contraception lie outside the scope of the broadcast episodes. Particularly relevant to our analysis in this chapter is that the reunion special, despite being a part of every season, is not included in the DVD distributed by the Kaiser Family Foundation nor referenced in the discussion guides, and so we limit our analysis of the episode. However, this omission is one worth exploring in future work given the shift in format when compared to the other season episodes and the opportunity for collective dialogue among the young women.

CONCLUSION

These examples, from the season 1 episodes of *16 and Pregnant* as well as the companion discussion materials, cause us to question the larger impact of the "personal stories" shared by the young women on *16 and Pregnant* and the extent to which they simply reinscribe social and cultural assumptions regarding sexuality and gender roles. Given what we have argued here, we have to ask ourselves to what extent this program meets the creators' stated goals: that viewers will learn from the teens' mistakes and decisions. What is the intended learning, in other words? Furthermore, what are the added dangers of the reinforced stereotypes that we highlight with regard to what we are terming the current "war on women," and what does it mean to sell these narratives as the *real* stories of girls in their own words? According to program supporters, "the shows aren't merely great television; there is evidence that young women who watch narrative drama about teen pregnancy are more likely to use contraception, and research shows that viewing these MTV shows is positively correlated with support for abortion rights."[48] And while these findings may be true in the case of *16 and Pregnant*, we must ask, what are the larger costs of publicly shaming young women and reinforcing social norms regarding their sexuality as a method of preventing teen pregnancy? Given that the aforementioned statement addresses "young women who watch narrative drama," who is responsible for influencing the decisions of young men?

Although we see great potential for *16 and Pregnant* to disrupt current conversations on teen pregnancy and teen sexuality when used with a critical lens—one that helps teens to identify and interrogate gender inequality, lack of agency, and patriarchal values—on its own, the program simply offers teens more of the same with few opportunities to consider their sexuality within a context of reproductive justice. Without sustained discussions about *decisions*—discussions that are potentially awkward and uncomfortable—*16 and Pregnant* falls dangerously short of the public service that program producers claim it to be.

NOTES

1. This organization claims to work "with over 100 major media leaders and now works with every major television broadcast network and with many of the top cable networks most popular with teens and their parents." This group purports to send out "key messages" that will "shape attitudes and behavior" about teen pregnancy. National Campaign to Prevent Teen and Unplanned Pregnancy, "Accomplishments."

2. Grose, "Does MTV's *16 and Pregnant*?"

3. Grose, "Does MTV's *16 and Pregnant*?"

4. Lord, *Condom Nation*; Fields, "'Children Having Children'"; Fields and Tolman, "Risky Business."

5. Lord, *Condom Nation*, 116.

6. Lord, *Condom Nation*, 125.

7. Lord, *Condom Nation*, 181.

8. Lord, *Condom Nation*, 182.

9. Lieberman and Su, "Impact of the Choosing."

10. Georgia State Board of Education, "Comprehensive Health."

11. Lord, *Condom Nation*, 183.

12. Fields and Tolman, "Risky Business."

13. Quoted in Fields and Tolman, "Risky Business," 66.

14. Ashcraft, "Ready or Not . . . ?"

15. Ashcraft, "Ready or Not . . . ?" 340.

16. Tolman, Hirschman, and Impett, "There Is More to the Story."

17. Cited in Bute and Russell, "Public Discourses."

18. Cited in Kelly, "Virginity Loss Narratives."

19. Lord, *Condom Nation*, 186.

20. Hoffman, "Fighting Teenage Pregnancy."

21. "MTV's *16 and Pregnant* Is Casting Now."

22. National Campaign to Prevent Teen and Unplanned Pregnancy, "Risky Business a 2000 Poll."

23. Tolman, Hirschman, and Impett, "There Is More to the Story," 10.

24. "Ebony," *16 and Pregnant*, season 1, July 2, 2009.

25. "Amber," *16 and Pregnant*, season 1, June 25, 2009.

26. At the beginning of this conversation, Amber relays her unease of having a baby to Gary, and Gary replies, "It's your fault," which sparks the brief interplay between the couple of "not liking condoms."

27. National Campaign to Prevent Teen and Unplanned Pregnancy, "Risky Business: A 2000 Poll."

28. Tolman, Hirschman, and Impett, "There Is More to the Story," 11.

29. "Whitney," *16 and Pregnant*, season 1, July 9, 2009.

30. Davis, "Baby Mama."

31. Ashcraft, "Ready or Not . . . ?" 340.

32. Davis, "Baby Mama."

33. Tolman, Hirschman, and Impett, "There Is More to the Story," 12

34. According to the "Accomplishments" section of its website, the National Campaign to Prevent Teen and Unplanned Pregnancy has "distributed more than 7.6 million publications and related resources through sales, complimentary copies, and website downloads." National Campaign to Prevent Teen and Unplanned Pregnancy, "About Us."

35. National Campaign to Prevent Teen and Unplanned Pregnancy, "*16 and Pregnant* Season 1 Discussion Guide."

36. "Whitney."

37. Grose, "Lauren Dolgen, Creator of *16 and Pregnant* and *Teen Mom* Talks."

38. "Episode 5 Whitney Discussion Guide."

39. "Episode 2 Farrah Discussion Guide."

40. Bute and Russell, "Public Discourses," 716

41. "Maci," *16 and Pregnant*, season 1, June 11, 2009.

42. Tolman, Hirschman, and Impett, "There Is More to the Story," 8, 11.

43. We had the opportunity to attend one of Maci's speaking engagements at Kennesaw State University, where she discussed many details that were not featured in the program, including the reason why she had unprotected sex with Ryan. She claimed that she had to "talk him into having sex," that her school's sexual education program did not offer information about how to get protection, and that she "now wished they had."

44. "Episode 1 Maci Discussion Guide."

45. "Episode 5 Whitney Discussion Guide."

46. "Episode 4 Ebony Discussion Guide."

47. "Ebony."

48. Grose, "Lauren Dolgen, Creator of *16 and Pregnant* and *Teen Mom*, Makes."

Chapter Three

Teen Moms Negotiate Desire

The (Re)Production of Patriarchal Motherhood in MTV's
Teen Mom

Anastasia Todd

We do not think of the power stolen from us and the power withheld from us in the name of the institution of motherhood.—Adrienne Rich

I'm not a kid. Well I am a kid, but . . .—Amber Portwood

Historically, teenage mothers have been positioned as "a homogenous group of immature, irresponsible, single, benefit dependent, unfit parents."[1] This monolithic positioning in the collective social imaginary has shifted, in part, because of the hypervisible representation of teenage motherhood in MTV's *Teen Mom*.[2] Although *Teen Mom* attempts to present the lived experiences of teenage mothers and, as such, disrupts the homogenous positioning of teenage mothers, I argue that *Teen Mom* functions as a technology that aids in (re)production of the hegemonic discourse of institutional/patriarchal motherhood. In examining the (re)production of institutional/patriarchal motherhood, I critically interrogate a new late-modern subject position: the ideal teenage mother, which, like institutional/patriarchal motherhood, is characterized by the mother's willingness to forgo all selfish desire. This selfish desire includes teenage sexual desire, which is already constructed as inappropriate and "dangerous" by the larger discourse of teenage girls' sexuality. As such, the series's inherent elision of representation of "teen mom" sexual desire effectively buttresses the current discourse of teenage girls' sexuality, which denies teenage girls sexual subjectivity and sexual desire and legitimizes increased surveillance due to their positioning as dangerous citizens, teens, and mothers. In this chapter, I ask, how does MTV represent the ways in which girls negotiate sexual desire and motherhood, and what are the implications of those representations? In doing so, my analysis begins to answer Michelle Fine's persistently relevant question: "In what arenas do we still encounter a roaring silence about female adolescent girls' sexual desire?"[3]

TEENAGE MOTHERHOOD IN LATE MODERNITY

The discourse of teenage motherhood has been largely constructed through academic literature, specifically scientific and economic literature, and it has positioned teenage motherhood as a social or public health problem, cleverly couching it within scientific and economic discourse.[4] Thus, while scholars have examined how teenage motherhood has been framed as a moral, social, and public health problem, I would like to frame this chapter in terms of how it has been problematically constructed and represented as a threat to the ideals that characterize late modernity:[5] responsibility, freedom, autonomy, and choice. Indeed, as Anthony Giddens argues, within the psychosocial worldview of late modernity, "we become responsible for the design of our own bodies."[6] As such, I argue that under late modernity, there emerges a new ideal subject: the ideal teenage mother. The ideal teenage mother is constantly making/remaking herself, and through shouldering the burden of "personal responsibility" and attempting to follow the prescriptive narratives set forth by the discourse of institutional/patriarchal motherhood, she "chooses" to forgo all selfish desire.

When an adolescent girl becomes pregnant, her normative biosocial life course is interrupted. As such, teenage motherhood creates a rupture in the already slippery transition from adolescence to adulthood and is presented as a threat to the teenage mothers' "project of self." In other words, because teenage mothers are already constructed as deviant and in some ways "unfit" vis-à-vis their age, they are constantly negotiating making/remaking their own subjectivities as a method to disrupt these negative characterizations. Within the work of Ulrich Beck and Giddens, "risk acts as a key organizing principle. . . . More particularly, late modernity is an era imbibed with 'ontological insecurity' or anxiety."[7] There is a movement toward a "risk society," in which an individual must manage risk by "reflexively constructing [his or her] own biography."[8] Thus, individuals within a risk society experience a process of "individualization," in which the construction of subjectivities is privileged through self-monitoring and choice. Discourses of risk can act as "technologies of the self,"[9] which "offer possibilities for both self-liberation and for increased technologization and regulation of self construction."[10] Henceforth, a "new politics of citizenship" is created, where responsible citizenship is measured by an individual's ability, through self-surveillance and self-help, to self-manage risk.[11] In many ways, teenage motherhood has become a "risky" identity for young women, and as such, those who identify as teenage mothers must engage in managing their own risky subjectivities.

Elizabeth McDermott and Hilary Graham, in their study of working-class teenage mothers in the United Kingdom, illustrate how the young mothers "positioned themselves within the regulatory framework of 'normal mothering'" as a method to construct "good" maternal subjectivities.[12] The teenage mothers in McDermott and Graham's study engaged in a project of reflexively creating their own subjectivities and life narratives through following already established scripts of institutional/patriarchal motherhood.[13] Andrea O'Reilly argues that these scripts contain several tenets: the notion that a child can be properly cared for by only its biological mother, the idea that a mother must put the child's needs before her own, and the requirement that the mother must shoulder the burden of motherwork, without any outside help. Thus, by following these scripts, the mothers are actively engaging in managing their risky identities through the process of constructing a "good" maternal self, which leaves no room for "selfish desire."[14]

SEXUAL DESIRE AND THE INSTITUTION OF IDEAL TEEN MOTHERHOOD

Emma Renold and Jessica Ringrose's theoretical appropriation of Rosi Braidotti's Deleuzian-inspired concept the "schizoid double-pull" helps us to understand the contemporary discourse of adolescent girl sexuality. This is a concept that "is used to articulate how gender and sexual norms can be simultaneously displaced . . . *and* refixed."[15] As such, in late-modern society, subjects have to navigate these pushes and pulls of contradiction. Within this schizoid double-pull, the body is "ambiguously positioned in the reproduction of social habits, requirements, and regulations (e.g. through girls' often contradictory sexual regulation of themselves, of one another, and by others)."[16] Teen girls must therefore navigate contradicting narratives within the discourse of sexuality, one that presents them as passive victims who are harmed in this era of "hypersexuality" and one that presents them as agentic "knowers" who are capable of navigating a changing sexual terrain. My intent is not to frame the discourse of teen girl sexuality as one that activates a renewed binary, "where girls' sexuality is always risky/at risk." I am merely pointing out the slippery and messy reality that teen girls have to navigate in regard to sexuality.[17] That is, "becoming" in regard to sexual subjectivity is an iterative (and infinite) process informed by contradictory and competing sexual scripts.

Further complicating this notion of a schizoid double-pull is the reality of teenage mothers and their sexual subjectivities and desires. On one hand, as

adolescent girls, they are subject to the same pushes/pulls and sexual regulation that all adolescent girls must navigate. Unfortunately, their status as
mother points to the fact that they "failed" in successful navigation of "age-
appropriate" sexuality. On the other, now that they are mothers, they are
subject to the pushes and pulls that all mothers are subject to in terms of the
discourse of motherhood and sexuality.[18] Shannon Trice-Black argues that
there is a strong schism between motherhood and sexuality: good mothers
are not supposed to be sexual.[19] Within the discursive confines of institution-
al/patriarchal motherhood, it is not a surprise that a mother's sexual desire is
characterized as "selfish desire" that detracts from her singular focus on her
child. Thus, the teenage mother must navigate interlocking and co-constitut-
ing pushes and pulls in regard to her sexual subjectivity. As such, the teenage
mother is constantly trying to "make sense" of herself through conflicting
narratives/discourses, which restrict the potential for constructing a sexual
subjectivity that privileges sexual desire and pleasure.

MEDIATED REALITIES AND THE "SPECTER OF DESIRE": TAKING A DISCURSIVE APPROACH

In late modernity, the television is positioned as a site that functions as a
"symbolic resource" that teenagers use to make sense of their lived experiences, conveying cultural scripts for a variety of social norms.[20] Teenagers,
living in a mediated reality, construct their subjectivities, in part, by and
through the media. As such, because subjectification is informed, in part,
through media, an examination of *Teen Mom* starts to fill in and clarify the
gaps and recesses within the discourse of teenage motherhood.

Because of the difficulty of locating sites where teen mom sexual desire[21]
was represented within the series, I watched the first three seasons of *Teen
Mom* and examined each episode, paying particular attention to what I characterized as referencing sexuality, anything of a sexual nature, or the "specter
of desire."[22] I evoke the metaphor of a specter, a ghost or apparition that
could be considered dangerous or a source of anxiety, as a method of articu-
lating the sexual desire represented within *Teen Mom*: one that may lie bur-
ied within the recesses of a personal narrative or gleaned from a subtle
suggestion of sexual desire through body language or tone of voice.[23]

In taking a discursive approach, my position is one that is locatable as a
theoretical position, one that is "post-structuralist, social constructionist,
oriented to processes and concerned with material conditions."[24] Thus, I
understand the study of "*all* systems of signification, the processes by which
they operate, their effects and, critically, their conditions of possibility."[25]
Specifically, I am focusing on a mesolevel, one focused with various "texts"
from a specific location. Although it is impossible to isolate discursive

(re)productions and although *Teen Mom* is only one "text" that works to inform the larger discourse of teenage motherhood, discourse construction is an interwoven, ongoing process. Thus, an attempt to examine one piece of a particular discourse can offer a sense of "what is being discursively reproduced in particular domains."[26]

"YOUR NUMBER ONE PRIORITY IS YOUR CHILD": SEXUAL DESIRE AS ABDICATION OF MOTHERLY DUTIES

In season 1 of *Teen Mom*, Farrah Abraham is the only single mother. Throughout this season, the show highlights her struggles in negotiating the construction of a "good" maternal self and her own desires for a partner. In the first episode of the season, "Looking for Love," Farrah resumes dating after her pregnancy. At a model casting, Farrah meets Cole, another model, and right away she says that he is the "first guy she's been interested in since Sophia [her daughter]."[27] Farrah quickly decides that she would like to pursue Cole romantically, and she agrees to go out for ice cream with him. When Farrah's mom, Debra, discovers that Farrah is going to meet Cole, she immediately becomes suspicious. She asks Farrah, "Are you having ice cream, or are you going on a date?" She then remarks, "You're taking time away from Sophia and your schoolwork."[28] Although Farrah did not explicitly state that she was romantically or sexually interested in Cole, her mother quickly condemns her for taking time away from her "motherly duties."

By expressing her desire to go on a date with Cole, Farrah bumps up against the discursive bounds of ideal teenage motherhood. Her mother insists that Farrah's priorities are to spend time with Sophia and focus on schoolwork, which are both privileged as duties necessary for the construction of a "good" maternal self. First, the discourse of institutional/patriarchal motherhood dictates that Farrah is obligated to provide all necessary motherwork and that she must shoulder the burden of caretaking. Second, as a subject governed under late modernity, Debra's concern with Farrah's schoolwork resonates with the reigning capitalist ideology that equates success with economic self-sufficiency and autonomy. Schoolwork functions as a method for Farrah to manage risk and make/remake herself into an ideal teenage mother, one who reaches her "full potential" (maximization of human capital) to produce capital for the purpose of economic reproduction, which plays out as Farrah's "personal responsibility" to her daughter Sophia.

After Farrah goes out for ice cream with Cole, she meets with her sister Ashley, who agrees with Debra's framing of the situation. Ashley argues that

> there are other things more important than boys right now. If you were a normal eighteen-year-old, then I understand, but you're not. Guys get their little motors running in their head. When you're out on a date with a guy,

wouldn't you rather be with Sophia? When you have a child, your number one priority is your child.[29]

Ashley's comment illustrates that Farrah is subject to surveillance from multiple agents. Her mother and sister both reinforce the notion that a good mother is one who always desires to be with her child. Although Farrah's interest in Cole is not represented as explicitly sexual, her sister brings up that he could "get his little motor running." One could argue that Ashley is discussing the possibility that Cole would want to have sex with Farrah, which again is framed as a dangerous situation.

Looking closely at the scene in which Farrah is on her ice cream date with Cole, we get a glimpse of the specter of desire, which manifests itself through flirting and a flirty body comportment. Thus, although desire is not specifically mentioned, we understand there to be a specter of desire that looms over Farrah's plot. Furthermore, there is a constant unexplained anxiety within Farrah's family surrounding Farrah's desire, and tension is present when anything about Farrah's desire for Cole is discussed or alluded to. This anxiety manifests most visibly in "Looking for Love," when Cole meets Farrah's parents and Debra interrogates him about his past relationships: "What . . . is important to you?" When Cole responds that he believes that physical attraction is important in a relationship, Debra offers her opinion:

> I would hate to think that the only reason that you would be interested in Farrah would be for physical attraction and a physical relationship. I understand being young, alright, but I don't go for being ruled by your crotch. I will never go for that because I don't want any more Sophias. I don't need that. . . . With our religious background we believe in abstinence until you get married. That's where we're from.[30]

Debra's anxiety about Farrah's sexual desire and a possible reciprocation of desire from Cole manifests itself through her terse answer and irritated tone. Within this scene, Debra acts as a disciplining agent, effectively regulating Farrah's sexual desire. Furthermore, Debra's use of "we" and "our" when discussing abstinence finds Farrah's sexual agency silenced and subsumed by a constructed "Abraham family" standpoint on sex. Farrah's desire for Cole is automatically foreclosed because of her positionality, in this instance, as someone who was unable to navigate discourses of "age-appropriate" sexuality successfully and as someone who, as a mother, must forgo "selfish" sexual desire. As such, because Farrah is actively pushing against the discursive confines of ideal teenage motherhood, her mother, like her sister, functions as an agent of surveillance, attempting to regulate Farrah.

At the end of the episode, Farrah comes to the realization that Cole had been cheating on her the entire time they were dating. After this realization, Farrah decides that dating Cole was "a bad decision" on her part.[31] Her declaration represents a sense that Farrah is attempting to position herself into the regulatory framework of "normal mothering," by resisting the negative discursive construction of sexual desire. Thus, as a method to construct a "good" maternal self, she comes to realize that her selfish desire is potentially distracting from her duty as a mother, and she attempts to draw herself back within the discursive regime of ideal teenage motherhood. [32]

After Farrah's encounter with Cole, she meets Shaq, a colleague from work. After dealing with the backlash that she received from her family for dating Cole, she decides that because she "really likes this guy," she's "not going to tell her mom."[33] Because Farrah understands that she is under surveillance, her decision can be read as an attempt to discipline herself in regard to her sexual/romantic desire. She now seeks to construct a façade of good motherhood because she believes that she is acting outside the prescriptive discourse of ideal teenage motherhood. Once Ashley discovers that Farrah is dating again, she remarks, "You're acting too single, too unmotherly, too irresponsible. How much time are you giving up for Shaq, time when you could be spending with Sophia?"[34] Farrah's trepidation in regard to voicing her desire was warranted, and she is again framed as a "bad mother."

Furthermore, Ashley's claim that Farrah is acting "too single" is another instance in which Farrah is subject to discipline and regulation as method to control her "excessive" sexual desire. First, Farrah is single, so how can she act *too* single? Second, how does that play out in the context of sexual desire as opposed to romantic desire? Although Farrah does not explicitly voice her sexual desire, her flirting and body language on the ice cream date with Cole and on her mini-golf date (in "How Many Chances")[35] can be read as potential sites of visible sexual desire. As such, her sister's claim that she is acting *too* single could be read as a warning—*too* single is *too* dangerous because of her position as a teenage mother—thus her excessive sexual desire must be contained. The idea that she has already disrupted the normal trajectory of adolescence/womanhood because she was already *too* sexual is constantly used as a reminder: that is, first she was unable to navigate the terrain of sexuality "successfully" and because of that she is now a mother; second, now that she is a mother, she has another reason to abstain because any and all sexual desire is now rendered selfish.

"BE A KID": SEXUAL DESIRE AS AGE INAPPROPRIATE

As Sarah McClelland and Michelle Fine argue, adolescent girls' sexuality "captures cultural attention and collects cultural . . . anxieties. . . . Although the sex they want and the sex they have are *typically* intended to be decoupled from reproduction, they are seen as too young to reproduce; too young to know anything about their bodies and their capacity; too young to be sexually pleasured and pleasurable."[36] Although teenage mothers have already reproduced and thus have already engaged in sexual intercourse, heightened anxieties regarding age-appropriate sexual desire are represented on *Teen Mom.*

Catelynn and Tyler, the only couple who chose to place their baby for adoption, are the focus of age-appropriate disciplining in several episodes. In the Valentine's Day episode, Tyler wants to take Catelynn on a Valentine's date to a romantic hotel room. When Tyler and Catelynn talk to Tyler's mother about their idea, she immediately retorts, "What would you do there? That's something adults do. Be a kid. I thought that was one of the reasons why you gave up Carly for adoption."[37] Tyler's mother's reaction and her statement that going to a hotel room is "something adults do" exemplify the notion that there is no age-appropriate teen sexual desire.

Although Catelynn is a hypervisible representation of a "birth mom" and, as such, is not a teenage mother in the same way that the three other teen mothers are, she is still subject to similar disciplining in regard to her sexuality. Nevertheless, she considers herself to be a teenage mother, and her subjectivity is constituted by and through the discourse of ideal teenage motherhood. Complicating MTV's representation of Catelynn is the fact that because she placed her child for adoption, she has actively resisted the reigning discursive bounds of ideal teenage motherhood, which in part are characterized by the notion that a child "can only be properly cared for by the biological mother."[38] Catelynn is thus constructing a counterhegemonic ideal teenage mother subjectivity. Furthermore, MTV portrays her decision to place her child for adoption and forgo motherwork as a positive one and is thus forging new conditions of possibility for the subject of the ideal teenage mother. This is played out by the representation of Catelynn as having an endless amount of opportunities—her whole life ahead of her—because she made a "responsible" decision. She successfully managed her risky identity through choosing adoption. Although Catelynn was "responsible" enough to place her child for adoption, she is not "responsible" to make decisions regarding her sexual desire.

Furthermore, when Catelynn makes the decision that she must move into Tyler's mother's house or face homelessness (because of problems at her mother's house), she is extremely nervous when approaching Tyler's mother about the situation. Although Tyler's mother lets Catelynn move in, she agrees with a stipulation: "There's going to be some rules. . . . My main thing is that you guys are staying in separate bedrooms, and there will be issues if I find you guys in the same room."[39] Tyler's mom "doesn't want the same thing to happen twice" to Catelynn,[40] thus implying that no sex is safe sex and that sexual desire and acting on that sexual desire are inappropriate. Again, Catelynn is disciplined in regard to her sexual desire despite her framing as responsible.

Another instance of desire being cast as age inappropriate is when Farrah decides to go on birth control because she "is still looking for the right guy and wants to be prepared when he comes along," and she makes the decision to hide it from her parents.[41] In "Moving On," she goes to see her gynecologist and decides to begin using NuvaRings as a form of contraception, which she has to store in the refrigerator. She notes that she is "not talking to [her] mom about it because she will freak out."[42] Unfortunately, Farrah's dad discovers her NuvaRings when he is cleaning out the refrigerator and lectures her:

> You shouldn't even have a need for birth control. Didn't we learn eighteen months ago? The bottom line is this—we've been through this thing and we got a beautiful gift out of a mistake. You need to focus yourself on your baby and all of the things you need to do to make a beautiful life for your child and you.[43]

Instead of being applauded for taking responsibility for her reproductive health and sexual well-being, she was condemned for even contemplating engaging in sexual behavior or desiring sexual intercourse. Thus, she is constrained by virtue of her position as a teenage mother. Her age and previous "mistake" foreclose any potential for an appropriate sexual desire. Because an ideal teenage mother is one who "must always put children's needs before her own," Farrah's role as a mother is in direct conflict with her sexual desire.[44] Furthermore, although Farrah is capable of mothering a child, because of her age, she is still seen as unable to negotiate her own desire. To be a good mother is thus represented as foregoing "selfish" sexual desire, and to be a good young woman is to forgo "risky" sexual desire.

"SOMETIMES YOU JUST DON'T THINK IN THAT MOMENT": SEXUAL DESIRE AND PROCREATIVE CONSEQUENCES

Although all the teens featured on *Teen Mom* have admitted to engaging in consensual sexual intercourse, their sexual desire and activity are consistently framed by procreative consequences rather than pleasure. Amber, arguably the most controversial member of the cast, encounters another pregnancy scare at the beginning of the second season. She admits to her cousin that she is beginning to feel sick and have irregular periods, which is what happened with her previous pregnancy. She also states, "In the heat of the moment, there was only one time we didn't use a condom."[45] Note Amber's rhetorical use of the phrase "heat of the moment." This implies that she was acting on her sexual desire. Although this is one of the only moments in the three seasons that I viewed where desire is explicitly mentioned, the focus of this episode was on Amber's potential pregnancy and how she and her boyfriend Gary would not be able to support the potential child.

This focus on the negative and unintended consequences of sexual desire reinforces how teenage mothers produced under late modernity must navigate several overlapping discourses. First, because the episode was so heavily framed around the concept of "not being able to support" another child, we can see how the late-modern ideal of personal responsibility is reinforced. Second, we can see how the overarching discourse on teenage sexuality is reinforced as constraining—focusing on the risks inherent in choosing to act on sexual desire. Therefore, as represented, there is no space carved out for sexual desire that does not end in negative repercussion. Furthermore, through the potentiality that she could be pregnant again, she is positioned as not adequately managing her risky identity, as well as not properly managing risk in a more general sense. Amber is outside the discursive bounds of ideal teenage motherhood and, as such, is consistently framed throughout the series as a "bad mother."

Likewise, "Looking for Love" features Catelynn and her experience with acquiring an IUD. Catelynn's gynecologist asks her if she has been "intimate since she had her last period" and if she used protection.[46] Although the gynecologist was just asking a routine set of questions, Catelynn seemed visibly uncomfortable and ended up lying about using protection.[47] If there were any possibility that she could have been pregnant, the gynecologist would not have inserted the IUD. When Tyler confronted Catelynn about lying, she said that she felt like the gynecologist would have judged her, and she really wanted the birth control. She also remarked that "sometimes you just don't think when you're in that moment [regarding sexual intercourse]."[48] As with Amber, this is one instance in *Teen Mom* where sexual desire is explicitly voiced. Her acknowledgment of being an active agent in "that moment" is her admitting to possessing sexual desire and actively enacting it. Not only is the whole episode framed like Amber's—that is, about the procreative consequences of having unprotected sex—but we encounter another instance of self-regulation in regard to sexual desire. When Catelynn denies having sexual intercourse when seeing her doctor, she is actively engaging in the construction of an ideal teenage mother subjectivity. Because she understands that "good" teenage mothers do not engage in sex, she constructs the façade of ideal teenage motherhood by positioning herself as not having engaged in sexual intercourse. Furthermore, Catelynn's desire to not be "judged" can be read as her recognition of potential disciplining (by the gynecologist). Although it is critical to acknowledge the importance and applaud MTV's representations of contraception, it is peculiar that any and all sexual desire is framed in light of negative repercussions.

TEEN MOM:
REWORKING AND REINSTATING TIRED NARRATIVES

Among familiar critiques of the "hypersexualization" of girlhood and the "potentially dangerous sexual scripts" that adolescent girls are learning from their favorite television shows, *Teen Mom* focuses almost exclusively on "sexual risk and responsibility themes."[49] Thus, *Teen Mom* can even be read as a response to the recent heightened anxiety surrounding adolescent girls' sexuality, another way to discursively confine adolescent girls' sexuality by presenting itself as an overly moralistic cautionary tale. I argue that *Teen Mom* at least makes an attempt at presenting itself as tenuously "pro-sex." Take, for example, the commercial frequently aired during the show for MTV's website itsyoursexlife.com: "It's your sex life—take control at itsyoursexlife.com." This website deals with sexuality and the decision to have sex, and it implores the viewer to "take control," thereby presenting an option for agency in regard to sexuality. Also, the fact that the television show at least touches on contraception attests to a focus on "arming" teenagers with the knowledge that is necessary for them to navigate ambivalent sexual situations that they may encounter.

However, the total absence of acceptable teen mom sexual desire enables moral boundaries to be drawn around "(hetero)normative and age appropriate notions of . . . sexuality, isolating and regulating what is acceptable and unacceptable desire and practice."[50] This "boundary drawing" reinforces already confining and limiting narratives of sexuality that are informed by overlapping discourses, thus reworking and reinstating tired narratives found within the reigning discourse of institutional/patriarchal motherhood that function to position teenage mothers who act on sexual desire as deviant and that showcase heightened anxieties surrounding the contradictions and tensions within the larger discourse of adolescent girl sexuality. Unfortunately, this results in the teen moms being forced to navigate the mythology of ideal teenage motherhood, which includes forgoing any/all sexual desire as a method to construct an acceptable/ideal subjectivity. Furthermore, because we understand that media is an important component "in the construction and reconstruction of sexualities for young people," we can see how there are implications of this portrayal with regard to the lived realities of teen mothers and their construction of their own sexual subjectivities.[51]

Karen E. Dill argues that "media constantly program the way we think of ourselves."[52] So although we understand that the teenage mothers who are watching *Teen Mom* are not passive receptacles of knowledge—they make sense of the portrayals of sexual desires and use the information that is presented to help construct their own subjectivity—I would conjecture that the risk/protectionist narratives that are found within *Teen Mom* effectively support the prevailing discourse that forecloses the acceptability of sexual subjectivity/agency for teenage mothers. Unfortunately, teenage mothers that attempt to disrupt this proscriptive discourse, by voicing their desire or even thinking about their desire, are positioned as "bad mothers." This type of positioning is even more detrimental for many teenage mothers because they are already considered "bad mothers" vis-à-vis their age. In this reading, their sexuality is deemed even more dangerous to others and to themselves. They must regulate themselves in regard to sexual desire for the sake of constructing a subjectivity that coincides with the proscriptive ideals espoused by the discourse of ideal teenage motherhood. Unfortunately, this relegates the notion of teen mom sexuality as one that is unacceptable and inappropriate.

TEEN MOM SEXUAL DESIRE: TOWARD A (RE)CONSTRUCTION OF AN ACCEPTABLE SEXUAL SUBJECTIVITY FOR TEENAGE MOTHERS

MTV's *Teen Mom* does little to counter the "roaring silence" in terms of teenage motherhood and sexual desire. As feminists, we are faced with tangled discourses of teenage motherhood that are steeped in years of heteropatriarchal ideology, and we must work to give voice to those knowledges and experiences that are pushed to the margins. My attempt is to begin to look at a gap in scholarship and give voice to an underresearched topic—that of teen mom sexual desire. Mapping the different narratives regarding sexual desire in *Teen Mom* exposes the discursive bounds and "the conditions of possibility—the discourses which prescribe not only what is desirable, but what is recognizable as an acceptable form of subjectivity" that work to exclude teenage mothers from the project of constructing an acceptable sexual subjectivity.[53] As such, my attempt is to denaturalize and reveal how teenage mothers are immersed in discursive economies of what it means to be an ideal teenage mother. As such, I want to highlight how there are some teen moms who temporarily resist the notion that they cannot construct an acceptable sexual subjectivity, like Farrah, when she decides to date Shaq and keep it a secret from her mother, or Amber and Catelynn, who speak of being "in the heat of the moment."

Despite these brief and ephemeral displays of resisting and reworking tired narratives, there is a visible lack of a "more explicit integration . . . of positive aspects [of sexual desire and sexuality] and risk management and how they develop in tandem or dialectically."[54] There is a history of critique of the "lack of viable discourses of desire or erotics for teen girls," but what about the lack of viable discourses of acceptable sexual desire for teenage mothers?[55]

NOTES

1. Yardley, "Teenage Mothers' Experience," 671.

2. Although some may disagree with my claim, citing that *Teen Mom* and *16 and Pregnant* "glamorize" teenage pregnancy and motherhood, Bill Albert, a chief program officer at the National Campaign to Prevent Teen and Unplanned Pregnancy, argues, "While MTV is not in the teen pregnancy prevention business, we firmly believe they have developed two shows that are probably among the most powerful interventions you're likely to see" (quoted in Rochman, "*16 and Pregnant*: Tuned-In Teens"). Furthermore, in a study conducted by the National Campaign to Prevent Teen and Unplanned Pregnancy, 82 percent of the group of teens that watched *16 and Pregnant* said that the program "helped them better understand the challenges of teen pregnancy and early parenthood and how to avoid getting into such a situation" (quoted in Rochman, "*16 and Pregnant*: Tuned-In Teens"). I am not trying to argue that there are not current narratives within the popular discourse of teenage pregnancy and motherhood that position teenage mothers as unfit, irresponsible, and immature parents. However, I do believe that *Teen Mom*, for many, has discredited the static trope of a "teenage mother" because of the presentation of the lived realties and intersectional subjectivities of real teenage mothers. As such, the "teenage mother" is (for some) no longer a singular discursive figuration, and is now an intersectional subject.

3. Tolman, "Found(ing) Discourses of Desire," 6.

4. Wilson and Huntington, "Deviant (M)Others," 62.

5. Gonick, "Between 'Girl Power.'" In this chapter, I use the term *late modernity* to characterize a historically situated economic and political shift that is discursively constructed by a broader shift in psychosocial worldview. Historically speaking, many scholars identify the rapidly changing political terrain and economic rationality that rose to prominence under the Reagan administration in the 1980s, marked by a rolling back of social services, deregulation, and privatization. Furthermore, it is often framed as a shift in relations between the state and its citizens, in which a focus on state building "through the development of government programs in support of citizens," morphs into a "concern for *making the individual responsible*" (see Gonick, "Between Femininities," 5). The subjects that are produced under late modernity are inculcated with the notion that they possess freedom, autonomy, and choice. This focus on personal responsibility disregards the forces that constrain many lived realities.

6. Giddens, *Modernity and Self Identity*, 102.

7. Mitchell et al., "Situating Young People's," 219.

8. Mitchell et al., "Situating Young People's," 219.

9. Mitchell et al., "Situating Young People's," 220. In this chapter, I use the term *technologies of the self* to characterize, what Foucault argued, was a shift from "spheres of existence traditionally characterized as personal or natural, such as body shape" to a privileging of "interventions via human agency rather than beyond human risk calculations."

10. Mitchell et al., "Situating Young People's," 220.

11. Mitchell et al., "Situating Young People's," 220.

12. McDermott and Graham, "Resilient Young Mothering," 71.

13. O'Reilly, "Outlaw(ing) Motherhood." O'Reilly argues that institutional/patriarchal motherhood is characterized by several tenets. First, "children can only be properly cared for by the biological mother"; thus, in this study, teen mothers are represented as responsible for shouldering the burden of caring for their children, even if they have support from family or a partner. Second, the mothering must be provided twenty-four hours a day, seven days a week, which bleeds into the third characteristic: "the mother must always put children's needs before her own." The teenage mother is expected to be available to her child at all times, thus foreclosing any potential of her own needs apart from her child's needs. Fourth, the mother must value expert's knowledge. In terms of my own research on *Teen Mom*, the "experts" are often framed as parents. The fifth characteristic is that "the mother must be fully satisfied, fulfilled, completed, and composed in motherhood." This rule, like the third, reinforces the notion that a mother is selfish if she desires anything apart from her child and her role as a mother. Sixth, mothers must spend inordinate amounts of time and energy on their child. Seventh, "the mother has full responsibility but no power from which to mother." In terms of

this study, teenage mothers have full responsibility to mother, or "raise," their children, but they are constrained by outside forces. So, for many of the teen moms, they are not allowed full agency in regard to mothering, because of their age. They are not seen as fully capable and thus are constantly under surveillance by a disciplining agent (parents, a partner, etc.).

14. O'Reilly, "Outlaw(ing) Motherhood."
15. Renold and Ringrose, "Schizoid Subjectivities?" 393.
16. Renold and Ringrose, "Schizoid Subjectivities?" 393–94.
17. Renold and Ringrose, "Schizoid Subjectivities?" 391.
18. Kidger, "Stories of Redemption?" 492.
19. Trice-Black, "Perceptions of Women's Sexuality," 154.
20. Van Damme, "Gender and Sexual Scripts," 80.
21. Smith, "Scripting Sexual Desire." There is much difficulty in defining what sexual desire is, but I find Smith's definition to be useful in understanding the concept. She argues that sexual desire is the cognitive, physical, and/or emotional want for embodied sexual interaction and/or activity. Sexual desire is commonly conflated with romantic desire, and it is often hard to uncouple the two when examining representations of teen girl desire in the media, but in my analysis I attempt to focus on sexual desire.
22. The fourth, and final, season was airing while I was going about my analysis, so I focused on the three previous seasons.
23. McClelland and Fine, "Writing on Cellophane," 233.
24. Cherrington and Breheny, "Politicizing Dominant Discursive Constructions," 91.
25. Cherrington and Breheny, "Politicizing Dominant Discursive Constructions," 91.
26. Cherrington and Breheny, "Politicizing Dominant Discursive Constructions," 92.
27. "Looking for Love," *Teen Mom*, season 1, December 8, 2009.
28. "Looking for Love."
29. "Looking for Love."
30. "Looking for Love."
31. "Looking for Love."
32. McDermott and Graham, "Resilient Young Mothering," 71.
33. "How Many Chances," *Teen Mom*, season 1, December 14, 2009.
34. "How Many Chances."
35. Farrah's date with Shaq can be read as another instance in which we get a glimpse of the specter of her desire. Farrah's flirty tone of voice when she is offering to cook chicken for Shaq, after she finds out that it is his favorite food, and her voice-over at the end of the date scene, "I think I like this guy," both allude to her desire for him ("How Many Chances").
36. McClelland and Fine, "Rescuing a Theory," 89.
37. "Valentine's Day," *Teen Mom*, season 2, August 3, 2010.
38. O'Reilly, "Outlaw(ing) Motherhood," 5.
39. "Moving On," *Teen Mom*, season 1, December 14, 2009.
40. "Moving On."
41. "Moving On."
42. "Moving On."
43. "Moving On."
44. O'Reilly, "Outlaw(ing) Motherhood," 5.
45. "Not Again," *Teen Mom*, season 2, July 20, 2010.
46. "Looking for Love."
47. "Looking for Love."
48. "Looking for Love."
49. Cope-Farrar and Kunkel, "Sexual Messages," 75.
50. Renold and Ringrose, "Schizoid Subjectivities?" 390.
51. Smith, "Scripting Sexual Desire," 322.
52. Dill, *How Fantasy Becomes Reality*, 167.
53. Davies et al., "Becoming Schoolgirls," 172.
54. Tolman and McClelland, "Normative Sexuality Development," 251.
55. Ringrose, "Are You Sexy, Flirty, or a Slut?" 112.

Chapter Four

Othering the Mothering

Postfeminist Constructs in Teen Mom

Jennifer A. Fallas

The wrongness of oppression isn't contingent on the sweet demeanor of the oppressed. [1]

INTRODUCTION: REINING IN THE WAYWARD

Potential exists for MTV's *Teen Mom* and *Teen Mom 2* to be sites of critical feminist intervention in a time of neoconservative backlash against feminist gains and politics—especially in regard to reproductive health and rights for all women. *Teen Mom* and *Teen Mom 2 could* serve as valuable entry points for viewers to enter discussions about teen sexual autonomy. [2] Arguably, these shows *could* be useful modes (at least in terms of popular culture) through which to inform young women about maintaining healthy active sexual lives and include ideas about safe sexual practices, sexual pleasure, emotional fulfillment, and reproductive health. In response to the fact that the girls have been acculturated by, and exist within, a patriarchal culture that is completely devoted to maintaining the gender status quo, the series addition-ally *could* offer a much-needed critique of delimiting roles and acceptable behaviors for young women. And by featuring the all-female casts of Farrah, Maci, Amber, Catelynn, Kailyn, Leah, Chelsea, and Jenelle, the shows *could* highlight the strength and power of these teen moms, the trangressive pos-sibilities of female agency and bodily sovereignty they represent, and the unique spaces they carve for themselves (and, by extension, other young mothers in general) within public discourses. [3]

However, MTV—the same network that unilaterally promotes the sexually available (read: "hot") young white female as ideal throughout many of its other reality shows—situates the girls of *Teen Mom* and *Teen Mom 2* as immoral and reckless for the same exact behaviors exhibited by females of the same age on its other shows. The key differences are the pregnancies and maternities in the *Teen Mom* programs; in fact, the *Teen Mom* series relies on preexisting dominant forms of white femininity to frame its portrayals of young women who have become "other" by virtue of their pregnancies and subsequent motherhoods—clear violations of normative social structures guiding white female youth.[4] Through various measures throughout *Teen Mom* and *Teen Mom 2*, any semblances of sexual agency that the girls have are nearly completely quashed. Patriarchy via the *Teen Mom* series insists that young women are doomed due to the independent sexual choices they have made, and it thereby successfully disarms the challenges that such young women represent to its power structures. To remonstrate with the girls (and, by extension, all teen girls), it utilizes postfeminist rhetoric and ideology to control young women—first with increasingly narrower gender norms and then by vitriolic attack when they do not wholly (and *cheerfully*) meet those norms. Through a sustained focus on prescriptive and fixed notions of appropriate femaleness, the *Teen Mom* series extends stereotypes about female youth and reinforces ideas of spatially fixed female subjectivities.

Teen Mom and *Teen Mom 2* expand postfeminism's aims by appropriating the conditions of young motherhood and by increasing scrutiny of the primacy of young female*ness* in social discourses. In centralizing teen motherhood, patriarchy drives and maintains public scrutiny of young females, especially in terms of their sexualities; in effect, young maternity is used as fodder and justification as to why teenage girls in general ought to be surveilled and *ideally* controlled. In developing scare tactics (for young women watching the shows and to amplify existing social anxieties about teen mothers), MTV's series stress how young white women face marginalization (as evidenced by a heavy emphasis on the teen moms' "otherness" throughout the shows) as a result of acting on their sexualities and sexual desires. Thus, the shows further widespread public anxieties about young female culture with those additions.

In this chapter, I confine my analyses to all four seasons of *Teen Mom* and both seasons of *Teen Mom 2*.[5] I address the patriarchal-informed and postfeminist-enforced social processes that depict the teen moms as gendered and sexual as beings. I utilize a broad survey approach (versus analyzing the texts episode by episode) to capture the most salient examples from the shows that explicate the postfeminist themes and constructs I examine. In this chapter, I look at the young mothers' "otherness" as it is highlighted in relation to their differences from dominant culture's concept of appropriate young womanhood, as well as how the depictions of their otherness are supported by their separations (literal and figurative) from male partners and by their distinctions from their peer groups (i.e., other mothers and age peers). I look at both to illustrate how the two *Teen Mom* shows represent teen girls and, in those representations, reiterate existing stereotypes about young women in general, as they supposedly currently are and as they ideally *should* be. The broader functions of portraying the girls in these ways are to extend the shows' narrative focus on young women's fear of social death. Likewise, the series destabilizes female relationships (and thereby any hope of solidarity) and turns the girls against and away from other females by its insistence on individualization. In doing so, *Teen Mom* and *Teen Mom 2* reinforce postfeminist focus on individualization versus solidarity and naturalize separation as part of the results of teen sexuality and maternity.

COMPULSORY HETEROSEXUALITY AND INCIDENTAL SEX

The postfeminist context is rife with young female sexuality, yet it insists that young women maintain all semblances of sexual purity and innocence.[6] As such, in *Teen Mom* and *Teen Mom 2*, teen sexuality is centralized and simultaneously made invisible. Postfeminist discourses dictate that the girls cannot be trusted with their sexualities, *period*, and that being active agents—acting on or gaining knowledge about sexuality—is inherently dangerous. Thus, as part of postfeminist ideology that continuously reinscribes dominant gender and sexual standards, the girls' sexualities are not necessarily freely chosen and autonomously actualized. Rather, heterosexuality is implicit insofar as it is the only sexuality represented in the shows, and it is compulsory as part of normative, young femininity discussed throughout this chapter.[7] In part, all the girls have cemented their viability as young white women by virtue of the fact that they engaged (at least once) in heterosexual sex and likewise by the fact that they have had children. The irony is, of course, clear—the show lambastes and crafts the girls as "other" because of their past sexual behaviors, yet these same "expressions" of their sexualities (i.e., their children) provide a reassuring safety net. Still, they must necessarily be "punished" for demonstrating any sort of sexual agency. Through the constant theme that they "should have known better," the shows imply that the girls need constant supervision, most typically from older family members but also exemplified through reminders about the dangers of sex from peers and partners. Because of this surveillance, viable white girlhood requires that the girls be placed into an idealized state of total nonsexuality.

To some extent, the girls have internalized this postfeminist ideology that they *cannot* admit to having had sex for their own pleasure or as part of their normal sexual development. Despite the ability to inform young women about reproductive and sexual health choices, including the choices to have mentally and emotionally healthy relationships with their sexual identities, the girls of the *Teen Mom* series are produced in ways that reinforce historical representations of young women as subjects to be monitored closely. In season 1 (episode 1), Catelynn lies to her gynecologist about her current sexual behavior, to avoid a scolding. Also, in the same episode, Maci and Amber describe the coitus that resulted in, or took place before, their pregnancies as a sort of happenstance. The former states, "I lost my virginity to my high school boyfriend. . . . Before I knew it, I was pregnant," and the latter says, "I didn't mean to get pregnant instead of finishing high school; it just happened." Farrah frames her first sexual encounter within a larger narrative about how she would not have had sex with anyone before Derek, thus proving she was a "good" girl.[8] Similarly, *Teen Mom 2*'s Leah focuses on the length of her relationship, rather than the frequency of engaging in sex, when she states in season 1 (episode 1), "My boyfriend Corey and I had only been dating for a month when we found out we were going to be parents." Of course, such portrayals further stereotypical perceptions of girls as flighty— because the teen moms did not execute forethought and because they did not refrain from sex, the girls can fulfill neither expectations of them as young white females, nor can they fully actualize any real sense of agency (sexual or otherwise).

Likewise, throughout the shows and seasons, the young women are portrayed as being unable (typically framed to make it seem as if they are not mature enough or, more likely and more fittingly, that they are ashamed) to pursue options for sexual and/or reproductive health.[9] *Teen Mom* and *Teen Mom 2* continue the associations of reproduction, birth control, and parenthood as sole domains and responsibilities of females. These ideas continue the traditional identification of women's worth solely in terms of their bodies. This patriarchal-informed bias posits female sexuality and discussions about female reproductive health as entirely shameful and utilizes a narrowly framed discourse to purposefully obscure the potentialities for sexual health and pleasure. Catelynn outright lies to her gynecologist in season 1, stating that she has been using condoms when she has not and that she has not had unprotected sex since her last menstrual period (both lies are revealed in the same episode, after her appointment is over). In season 2 (episode 1), Amber details that the "one time" she did not use birth control resulted in "pregnancy scare," a comment meant to make the audience feel some measure of sympathy for her (and perhaps excuse her sexual behavior), considering the additional burden that a second baby would heap on her life. *Teen Mom 2*'s Chelsea states that she was on the pill but that its purpose was "just to be ready." Therefore, because she makes it seem that sex was not a certainty in her mind, it cannot be counted as a definite plan that would necessarily take away from her goodness.

SUSTAINING THE GOOD MOTHER–BAD MOTHER DICHOTOMY

In the face of female sexual agency and for the purposes of reinforcing the concept of the girls as "other," postfeminism resurrects long-held archetypes (in the case of this section, good and bad mothers) and morphs them into contemporary versions that offer convenient categorizations of and assessments for the girls. To reinforce the postfeminist construct of motherhood as a naturalized trait and inherent desire of all females yet to simultaneously ensure that the girls do not step beyond the preset bounds of otherness, the *Teen Mom* series elevates the figure of "the good mother." Although motherhood is not an *ideal* form of young white girlhood, the series reframes the conditions of maternity to suit its aims of keeping young women in check. *Good* mothers (such as Maci, Catelynn, and Farrah of *Teen Mom* and Chelsea, Leah, and Kailyn in *Teen Mom 2*) are made accessible and agreeable through qualities such as submissiveness and acquiescence and through their generally quiet affects toward most people (but especially male partners) with whom they come in contact. And because they largely follow these normative guidelines (which can also be conveniently applied to *all* "good girls"), they are more tolerable as young mothers than their "bad" *Teen Mom* counterparts (discussed later).[10] Season after season, Catelynn patiently endures April's (her mom's) emotional and mental abuse of her. While Farrah typically disputes her mother (Debra) and has received some audience criticism for doing so, both women are afforded "good mother" status. Debra is portrayed (via Farrah's voice-over interpretations of her mother's actions) to be a constant, nagging, intrusive nuisance. Yet, Farrah's frequent and loud objections, if not excusable, become somewhat understandable and relatable to the targeted audience because her protestations echo popular portrayals of teenagers contesting parental figures.[11] Similarly, in season 1 of *Teen Mom*, Maci faces and is the subject of several dinnertime discussions about her by Ryan's family. Kailyn, in *Teen Mom 2*, is present and puts up with similar discussions by Jo (Jonathan) and his parents. In both cases, the girls remain in the room while the families discuss what ought to be done to better their lives and provide for the babies. In these instances, the girls are not only admonished but admonished in front of their male partners, who often join in on the discussions. Given their physical proximity to the conversations and the fact that they join in the dialogues, the males are clearly given permission (and are expected) to join in the policing, while the girls are expected to simply remain silent. At the same time though, Ryan's mother (Jennifer) and Jo's mother (Janet) demonstrate the good mother in adult form and through their ever-present concern for their sons now fathers. The two women, like Debra, while easily identifiable as nuisances (in these instances) toward the teen moms, behave according to postfeminist scripts of the ideal mother (hereby grandmother as well) insofar as their insistence that their children and grandchildren take precedence over all else. Furthermore, despite the fact that Debra was arrested for assaulting Farrah (season 2, episode 1), Debra arguably emerges as a good mother because (as she maintains) her intrusions into Farrah's parenting stem from a concern for her granddaughter and daughter. According to postfeminist emphasis on separation, MTV's portrayals of the women and girls in these scenes establish that motherhood is not a community but an institution that inevitably pits mothers against one another.

The good mother subjectivities are also based on the girls' altruistic natures and their sole focus on the children.[12] These figures usually stipulate that all their efforts (employment, schooling, maintaining relationships) are for their children's benefits.[13] Farrah and Catelynn are posited in such ways. In the first episode of season 1, the former is the "good" mother because she details that she juggles work, school, and modeling for the benefit of her daughter. Throughout all the seasons of *Teen Mom*, Catelynn is a good mother in that, while she does not parent her birth daughter Carly, she frequently mentions her as the motivation for her life choices (i.e., finishing high school as opposed to just skating by, getting a job, applying to colleges). Leah of *Teen Mom 2* is also portrayed as self-sacrificing. When she notices that her daughter Ali has physical and developmental abnormalities, she is individuated by this task of her daughter's difficulties in addition to being frazzled by having *two* children. The audience is meant to have sympathy for her, especially when she notes that her preoccupation with Ali's appointments is affecting her wedding planning. In a voice-over (season 1, episode 10), she states "My wedding's two weeks away but because I've been so focused on Ali's health issues, we're nowhere near ready."

Good mothers are marked also by family support. In season 1 of *Teen Mom 2*, Kailyn is allowed to live in Jo's parents' house (so long as she does not date anyone or have male friends).[14] In the first season of *Teen Mom*, Ryan's mother (Jen) offers to help pay for Maci and Ryan's wedding as her form of support. In a remarkably similar instance in the eighth episode of *Teen Mom 2*'s first season, Leah's mother (Dawn) pays for Leah's wedding dress despite the excess cost and even though it is clear to the audience that she is wary of her daughter marrying at such a young age. Chelsea is evidenced as good insofar as her father (Randy) supports her financially (by securing and then paying for a house for her to live in with her daughter Aubree). In season 2 (episode 8), Farrah, too, secures housing in a rental property house owned by her mother. What is more, in season 3, Farrah's parents (though they totally disagree with her desire to move) go with and drive her around several states in search of suitable communities in which to live.

Contrastingly, "bad" mother figures Amber and Jenelle cement not only that what the teen moms have done (in terms of having sex and children) is wrong but also that without a properly reticent attitude, they are "doomed" to failure and their otherness is amplified even more than the other girls.[15] Portrayals of Jenelle and Amber are so far outside civilized human behavior, let alone normal teen girlhood.[16] In short, they deserve the punishments they eventually receive—from public scrutiny infused with moral judgments to their respective stints in rehab (where they must ultimately fail by way of relapse) and, in both cases, losing custody of their children. From the earliest episodes, it is clear that both young women are to be disliked for a number of reasons. In stark contrast to the other six teen moms, these two are shown on camera as caustic and antagonistic. Amber constantly baits and then berates her on-again/off-again partner Gary throughout all the seasons of *Teen Mom*.[17] As opposed to Farrah's contentious interactions with her mother that are usually short-lived, in nearly every interaction with her mother (Barbara), Jenelle is featured as a petty, deceitful, downright nasty, and totally irrational girl. Despite the fact that Barbara (as another good mother figure) allows Jenelle to live with her and is portrayed as patiently permitting Jenelle to return to living with her several times (even in light of several brushes with the law), Jenelle continuously abuses her mother. In the first episode, she yells at her mother, "Obviously you're not a good mother either because I'm the one who got pregnant at sixteen." And after their fights, her reactionary statements (to Barbara and in voice-overs) are clearly resentful. For instance, in an episode when Barbara confronts her about her drug use, Jenelle complains to her boyfriend Keifer that someday she will have more money, a bigger house, and a bigger car than her mother. As a result of this, Jenelle states that her mother will then be sorry for not believing in her. Obviously, the audience is meant to understand that Jenelle simply does not recognize the foolishness of her ways and the dangerous situations in which she places herself. Postfeminism, through its commodification of teen girlhood and teaching girls to desire material goods as a means for empowerment, makes it seem that Jenelle's priorities are askew, a notion furthered by her distractions (noted later). So while she is following the "script" of postfeminism, she is made to appear entirely ridiculous by doing so.[18]

In opposition to figures such as Maci and Leah, neither Amber nor Jenelle maintains a steady and sole focus on her child or perceived "duties" and place as a teen mother. Although Jenelle and Amber suffer from emotional disorders and chemical imbalances that require treatment with medication, these facts are not disclosed until well into both series and only after the girls have several volatile incidents (Jenelle with her mother and Amber with Gary). As such, Jenelle's and Amber's mental illnesses merely end up reinforcing the spectacle of teen motherhood and function as the *ultimate* warning against parenting at what patriarchy deems too young of an age and, by extension, against young females having sex at all. MTV portrays the two teens—regardless of their lived realities that are clearly affected by their disorders—as totally irrational toward people in their lives and entirely detached and uncaring toward their children. Both are commonly shown lying down and not directly interacting with their children—clearly illustrating their laziness (as opposed to Kailyn having two jobs, Farrah working extra hours as a cook, and Leah constantly negotiating how to transport her twins between locations as well as how to achieve all of her daily tasks while caring for them). Many times throughout *Teen Mom 2*, Jenelle chooses partying and going out with friends over staying with her son Jace. She even states her awareness in episode 1 of the first season by saying, "I know I should go home," clearly demonstrating that partying takes precedence over her son. And whereas in season 1 when Farrah states that she works to support Sophia and when Maci is shown as being annoyed by the hectic pace of her job and by the fact she cannot be at home with her son, Amber claims in season 2 that work is a welcomed "break" from daughter Leah. During periods when she is with Leah, she implies that it is wholly unpleasant, as in season 2 (episode 4) when she states, "This is no spring break." Therefore, as with the punishments listed earlier (jail and rehab), viewers are led by producers of the shows to conclude that the girls "deserve" to lose custody of their children. *Teen Mom*'s fourth season opens with Leah becoming a ward of the state. In the second episode of the first season of *Teen Mom 2*, Jenelle "signs over" custody of her son to her mother (Barbara) and thereby reinforces, yet again, her status as an ambivalent mother. Although both girls make statements claiming that they want to be with their children (through voice-overs and during discussions with others), neither girl can be shown to directly parent her child, because each lacks the supposedly innate "mothering" qualities that are evident in all the other teen moms. In fact, their struggles with the expectations and demands of parenting are not shown as normal difficulties that many people may face but are rather framed as personality deficiencies in these girls.

U.S. patriarchal ideology maintains that family support marks good mothers; if this is so, then it is no wonder that Amber's family is rarely ever shown. It is not until season 4 when her mother (Tonya) is seen on a somewhat regular basis. In such cases, it is only to help transport Amber to and from court hearings or to help clean her house before Amber arrives home from rehab. Even more so, Jenelle is shown to have almost no family support at all. The one family member she has, her mother, is (as noted) the one person with whom she fights the most. In a particularly violent moment toward her mother, Jenelle yells, "Do you know I could punch you in your [fucking] face?"[19] Therefore, as with the aforementioned punishments, the show's creators imply that because Jenelle disregards her son and abuses her mother (Barbara), then she is unfit to have any type of family at all. Although Amber is able to secure her own housing, in opposition to the good mothers who are able to find housing with others if they are not immediately able to find and afford their own homes, Jenelle relies on temporary housing, whether living with friends or her mother; in both seasons, Jenelle is kicked out of Barbara's house and her friends houses for a number of reasons. She is portrayed as being unstable not only because she is focused on material goods and getting high over taking care of her son but also because she is totally unappreciative of the fact that people are willing to house her despite her commonly known erratic and outright violent behavior.

Patriarchal ideology, as its normal course of action, repudiates femininity; motherhood, as a part of feminine identity, requires careful navigating. Yet, MTV's portrayals of the teen moms (and the now grandmothers as well) dictate that regardless of whether they are good or bad mothers, they have zero agency of their own. They, as good or bad mothers, are made recognizable only through MTV's use of long-held historical tropes and dominant discourses of mothers. Like the girls' sexualities that are not freely chosen, neither are their versions of motherhood freely constructed. Because of the portrayals of them as "either/or," their motherhoods are not autonomously negotiated; as with their sexualities, females, according to MTV, cannot be trusted to forge any sort of nuanced versions of motherhood or a middle ground within its established dichotomy.

MALE PARTNERS

Postfeminist rhetoric maintains that gender parity is assured yet female dependence is natural. As such, the *Teen Mom* shows remind the audience that the girls' worth as females depends on their attractiveness and desirability to males. According to the series, the girls' relationships with the fathers of their children are what initially cause most of the difficulties in their lives. Yet, their happiness depends on successful relationships with these males. This is evidenced by their constant attempts to maintain their "worth" as females to the males in their lives by proving themselves as good mothers to the males' children and as potentially good "wives" by constantly striving to construct happy families with the children's fathers.

To the first point about their roles as good mothers, as part of its insistence that *everything's equal*, postfeminism never explicitly addresses the clearly unequal sexual relationships between males and females. According to the series, by virtue of the fact that they are females, motherhood is somehow an innate quality, and the teen moms are expected to care for the children no matter what. The good teen moms maintain full-time custody of the children, in terms of while they are apart from the babies' fathers (e.g., Chelsea and Adam, Farrah with the deceased Derek, Maci with Ryan in season 1, and Leah when Corey works all the time), or providing nearly all the care when the fathers *are* present and/or remain in relationships with the girls.

Furthermore, the girls attempt to stay with the father (e.g., Leah with Corey in season 1, Maci with Ryan in season 2) or return to the father (Kailyn to Jo in season 2, Amber to Gary several times) and, thereby, the ideal of what "could have been."[20] Thus, because of having sex with the babies' fathers and because of the couples' continuing attachment to each other through the baby, the girls are "other" because they cannot possibly date anyone else, as they are now of no worth or interest to any other male. To emphasize this point, *Teen Mom* seeks ways to "punish" or reprimand the girls if dating seems successful or, at the very least, likely to occur. To enhance the intended audience dislike for her, early in her dating relationships Amber is shown bringing a variety of men (in the second and third seasons) around Leah. Farrah's date in season 1 cheats on her with a previous girlfriend, leaving her feeling dejected. And in the fourth season, another of Farrah's dates ceases their relationship because of her demonstrably intense desire and efforts to be in a stable romantic relationship with him. Kailyn gets kicked out of Jo's house because she dated Jordan while living there. And most striking, Leah's marriage falls apart in season 2 because she cheated on Corey a few days before their wedding. In all of the cases, MTV means for the audience to understand that the girls are driven to align themselves with males their own age. It is advantageous to do so, yet because they have had children, it is markedly more difficult than it would be for girls who are not mothers.

What's more, the *Teen Mom* shows further pull the girls back "into line" closer to appropriate femininity by making it clear that it is wrong at various levels to not be with the children's fathers.[21] As part and parcel of its constant attempts to delimit the girls according to their gender, *Teen Mom* dredges up historical stereotypes of the happy family, shown by a frequent emphasis from the girls' statements that they are driven by a desire to remain with their male partners. This supposedly illustrates a commonly held desire of all women to secure the idealized (and clearly ironic as it appears in both *Teen Mom* shows) nuclear family. All of the teen moms (save Jenelle) are shown at some point trying to remain with or return to the fathers of their children (or, in Catelynn's case, remaining with Tyler throughout all seasons). Even when a relationship is obviously dysfunctional (e.g., Jo's berating of Kailyn in season 1, Adam's emotionally abusive behavior toward Chelsea in episodes 6–8 of the first season, or Amber's clear abuse of Gary in all seasons), the girls make every attempt to maintain nuclear family structure because, as the girls tout, having normative families for their children is most important.[22]

The series' portrayals divest the girls of feminist politics and gains through the productions of the girls who cannot possibly be or ever become normal (read: appropriate) teenage girls. Through MTV's depictions of the teen moms, postfeminist ideology maintains the idea that all things in terms of gender are equal. In light of the girls' attempts to have stable romantic and sexual dating relationships with males, the shows illustrate that it is inherently dangerous to do so because of the strong possibility of rejection and/or failure. Like the versions of motherhood that the *Teen Mom* shows offer, the girls are afforded two options for "happiness": they must either return to the fathers of their children (as discussed) or remain single (read: isolated and nonsexual).

CONCLUSION: SEPARATING FROM THE HERD

The postfeminist cultural space that surrounds *Teen Mom* and *Teen Mom 2* and in which the girls live dictates that young women's obedience to normative expectations takes precedence over all other aspects of their lives and identities and at the expense of their autonomy. Seemingly, postfeminism offers young women a prescriptive method to follow for them to be "successful" as young women. The series warns against female liberation, empowerment, and success run amok, all of which emerge in the shows' attitude that the girls were not being watched closely enough. In various ways, the series consistently lambastes Catelynn, Amber, Farrah, Maci, Kailyn, Jenelle, Chelsea, and Leah for being sexually active. The girls are featured in situations and contexts where their differences (resulting from their maternity) are amplified.

As a purposeful part of systematic efforts that are in place to restrict women in every way possible, patriarchy (via the *Teen Mom* series) is able to counter, nullify, and disarm the potential subversive possibilities of young female sexuality by appropriating and commodifying teen maternity. To offset the autonomy that teen motherhood *could* represent, *Teen Mom* and *Teen Mom 2* increase public scrutiny and anxiety of young mothers, by separating the featured girls from other females in their age group. Because the girls have violated acceptable forms of young white femininity, the *Teen Mom* series frames them in ways that consistently emphasize their otherness from their other young white female friends. Usually, they are featured in ways that attempt to bring them back to acceptable female roles and behaviors. The girls are shown seeking to return to the rituals and meaningful engagements with peer groups. But as they struggle to be "normal," the shows highlight how it is nearly impossible for the girls to do so. Chelsea, throughout the first and second seasons, tries to get her GED to go on to beauty school (where others her age and gender would be). Because she never achieves this goal, the show illustrates the near impossibility for her to rejoin the ranks of other females who are engaging in gender-appropriate activities. Correspondingly, in episode 8 (season 1), Farrah goes to a parent-child music class with her daughter but is the only person her age and without a partner at the event. In the same episode, Farrah states that her current friends (of her own age group) do not understand her because she is now a mother; she is effectively caught in an amplified "otherness"—both from age group peers and from other mothers. Similarly, Catelynn is rarely shown spending time with other females her own age (save her prom dress shopping excursion in season 2), and when she is, it is during retreats with other adoptive mothers. In her case, Catelynn is othered from peer groups in high school by the pregnancy (as all the other girls from *Teen Mom* are) and by her codecision to place her baby for adoption.

Against the backdrop of a long history of social change and liberation for women, MTV's *Teen Mom* series completely divests the featured girls (as they traverse their roles as mothers, as friends, as lovers, as partners, as daughters, as workers, as students, and as young women) of feminist politics and gains through various means and depictions. To recapture its featured girls, the series utilizes a postfeminist framework to portray Farrah, Catelynn, Maci, and Amber of *Teen Mom* and Leah, Kailyn, Chelsea, and Jenelle of *Teen Mom 2* as having violated forms of viable young white femininity. MTV's series provides a cultural means by which genderizing social processes are bolstered. The potential for transgressive points of view or *true* feminist perspective is undone by the dominant concept, which highlights the problematic nature of unchecked female sexuality.

Patriarchy's end objective is to regulate female sexuality and keep women, who are lawfully equal to men in society (in terms of economic, political, and social parity), as secondary citizens and complacent within their subjugation. Throughout its postfeminist messages that saturate most areas of media, young women are socialized by patriarchy's ideas that are geared to keep them in place; more concretely, patriarchal agendas are structured to prohibit them from exemplifying control over their own thoughts, lives, or physical well-beings. In practical terms, young females are taught not only that their bodies are their primary worth (insofar as their sexual availability and attractiveness to males) but also that their reproductive abilities are sources of anxiety and punishment. In short, to be the "good" young white female, being "sexy" is key, but bearing the markers of *actual* sexual engagement (i.e., becoming pregnant) is to become something less. The girls of this series thus become tropes and emerge at a time when media hypersexualizes them and simultaneously holds them subjects to delimiting neoconservative public discourses. This exacerbates the idea that teenage female sexuality (and, in the case of the shows, teen maternity) represents a national crisis. By virtue of scare tactic messages and narratives, *Teen Mom* and *Teen Mom 2* attempt to rein in female sexuality after it has gone "awry." According to the series, motherhood takes precedence (or *should*) over all else. The series warns how "hard" (arguably, the girls' most-oft used description throughout their narrative voice-overs and dialogues with others) motherhood is. In fact, motherhood becomes a monolithic identity and is their *only* identity. Postfeminist culture merges a narrative about what viable young women *should* be and simultaneously binds them with its single analytic about young womanhood. As a result, girls are othered (and effectively "doomed") by these conflicting ideological constraints.

NOTES

1. Twisty, "Blaming XPress."
2. Before the *Teen Mom* divinations is MTV's *16 and Pregnant*, wherein one episode is devoted to a girl's pregnancy, delivery, and first few days and weeks of motherhood. In order, the girls' individual shows aired as follows: Maci, June 11, 2009; Farrah, June 18, 2009; Amber, June 25, 2009; Catelynn, July 16, 2009; Jenelle, February 16, 2010; Chelsea, March 9, 2010; Leah, April 6, 2010; and Kailyn, April 20, 2010.
3. For a useful discussion of postfeminist aims and potential disruption and containment discourse within popular culture, see Projansky, "Mass Magazine Cover Girls," 66–69.
4. A 2011 Centers for Disease Control and Prevention report ("U.S. Teen Birth Rate Fell") notes, "Contraceptive use is lowest and teen childbirth is highest among Hispanic/Latinos and non-Hispanic blacks. Rates also are high among youth of all races and ethnicities who are socioeconomically disadvantaged. Black and Hispanic teen girls are about 2–3 times more likely to give birth than white teens." So, despite a marked difference in pregnancy rates between young women of color and young white women, *Teen Mom* deftly constructs solely white casts. The featured teen girls in *Teen Mom* and *Teen Mom 2* represent and sustain postfeminist idealized teen girlhood characterized by class and race exclusions. *Teen Mom* makes it seem that being female (or at least being white, young, and female) is something that all teen girls might identify with. This assumed universality neatly avoids intersectionalities and multiplicities of identity and completely sidesteps the issues of race, socioeconomic class, and education levels that also affected teen pregnancy rates and stats.
5. This chapter provides a broad overview of the shows' content, themes, postfeminist framework, and constructs. I do not examine other content from tabloids, the shows' websites or blogs, or any fan-based/produced materials.
6. For details regarding the impacts of contradictory messages of widespread abstinence-only education within a larger social culture of hypersexualization, see Valenti, *The Purity Myth*.
7. Tasker and Negra (*Interrogating Postfeminism*, 19) argue that postfeminism can likewise consolidate queerness into its rhetorics. However, there are no LGBTQ-focused concerns, identities, or articulations in either *Teen Mom* show (i.e., lesbian, gay, bisexual, transgender, queer). Queerness simply does not exist in *Teen Mom* world.
8. In part, she notes, "After two hours of him saying how much he cared about me, I gave in and lost my virginity. Everything was so dramatic, with the rain, and my perfect hair and makeup. In the past when guys pressured me about sex, I stopped talking to them. But I really didn't want to break up with Derek" ("Relationship Details").
9. Jessica Valenti states, "Sex is not framed as a deliberate choice, but rather as something that just occurred, thus freeing . . . young women—from the judgment that's heaped upon those who actively choose sex. The lack of protection . . . 'proves' that the encounter wasn't premeditated; this allows the participants to absolve themselves of guilt." Valenti, *The Purity Myth*, 194. The other part of the absence of sexuality and discussion thereof is that postfeminist discourse in *Teen Mom* and *Teen Mom 2* illustrates that the "worst" thing to happen to females is potential pregnancy. There is never a mention of protection against sexually transmitted diseases; such would imply premeditation of sex and demonstrate sexual agency.
10. Rachel E. Dubrofsky ("Fallen Women in Reality TV," 357) argues that postfeminism traps women in such portrayals (positive and negative) insofar as their "behavior is consistent

with how the series constructs her wanting to present herself and it is in line with the image the series has already constructed of her."

11. A fact further substantiated in season 4 when Farrah's sister Ashley echoes many of Farrah's thoughts on how annoying Debra is to her as well.

12. See also, Douglas and Michaels, *The Mommy Myth*, 15, 22. The authors state that popular/postfeminist constructions of motherhood dictate that it "is the most important thing a woman can do." According to them, the good mother always illustrates "boundless, unflagging and total love."

13. The focus of this chapter is on the teen moms. However, the shows often posit the girls in juxtaposition or contrast to the now grandmothers. Jo's mother, Janet, in *Teen Mom 2* and Tyler's mother, Kimberly, in *Teen Mom* allow Kailyn and Catelynn (respectively) to live with them when the girls' families disavow (usually temporarily) them. Even though she is usually acerbic regarding Maci's sexual behaviors, Sharon allows Maci to live with her, as does Farrah's mother, Debra, and Jenelle's mother, Barbara. Debra even goes so far as to "give" her daughter an entire house to live in, and Barbara continually brings Jenelle back into the home despite her daughter's various brushes with the law and volatile nature.

14. Episodes 2 and 8 in season 1.

15. Reality shows often "frame the emotional behavior of some women as excessive, and therefore dangerous and threatening, barring them from 'having it all'" (Dubrofsky, "Fallen Women," 353). To be clear, I do not disregard that both young women are known to have substance abuse problems alongside mental health issues. My focus in this chapter, though, is on how their roles as mothers take precedence. Additionally, just as the good-mother trope extends to the now grandmothers, so too does the bad-mother figure. This is most prominently seen in Catelynn's mother, April, who, throughout all four seasons, verbally and emotionally abuses her daughter at every turn. Her substance abuse problems, like Jenelle's and Amber's, clearly split her focus, thus rendering it impossible for April to be a mother *period*. For a discussion regarding what typically qualifies one as a good mother, as well as what ensures "bad" mother status in terms of "race, class, age, marital status, sexual orientation and numerous other factors, millions of mothers have been deemed substandard," see Ladd-Taylor and Umansky, *" Bad " Mothers*, 6.

16. MTV programming chief David Janollari stipulates that the targeted core audience for *Teen Mom* is "12 - to 34-year-olds . . . looking to not only have fun but have their lives reflected back at them in a heightened way." He continues about *Teen Mom*, saying that "it's a dramatic look at a real situation amplified by a baby in the mix" (Rose, "MTV's David Janollari Opens Up"). Susan J. Douglas (*Enlightened Sexism*, 193) stipulates, "Reality TV . . . [calls] us in as active participants to serve as judges and juries of 'ordinary' people, to bring to bear our own social, moral, and gender norms on predicting what should, should not, and will happen next." Obviously then, postfeminilism, by way of reality television, negotiates its footing in its portrayals of the young women but also its hold over audiences of younger people (especially women). The intended effect is clear: to keep women trapped in social norms, it crafts portrayals of young women (as seen throughout *Teen Mom* and *Teen Mom 2*) and simultaneously reinforces the messages by requiring audiences to repeat back its tenets through their judgments of the teen moms.

17. Eventually, in season 3, Amber is arrested for domestic battery. And at the beginning of the first episode of season 4, Amber notes that her house was vandalized and "bad mom" spray-painted on her car. Her daughter becomes a ward of the state, and she is on several medications to help her cope with her daily life.

18. I offer as contrast Farrah, who undergoes breast enhancement surgery and has braces put on her teeth, both of which she admits to getting to improve her chances for a successful modeling career. However, Farrah is made to seem logical in her choices to want to look good to have a better career. Jenelle, though, is clearly meant to be understood as foolish for her attempts to obtain the same types of empowering material goods that Farrah does.

19. Episode 1, season 1.

20. In some ways, this likewise applies to Farrah and the deceased Derek.

21. Males, however, can leave at any time, without consequence or reprimand. For example, Adam comes and goes in Chelsea's life (as her on-again, off-again boyfriend), as well as in and

out of her home at will and without excuse; when asked to account for his behavior and poor attitude toward her throughout season 1, Adam typically exclaims that Chelsea needs to "change" herself and her views.

22. In the same episodes, Adam not only emotionally manipulates Chelsea, with the constant fear that he will once again cheat on her, but verbally abuses her by calling her names and by virtue of his antagonistic behaviors, which separate and alienate her from her friend Megan. Similarly, in episode 8 of season 1, Jo's mother, Janet, tells Kailyn (despite Kailyn's description of his abuse toward her, as well as Janet's observations of such behaviors) that she should try to spend more time with Jo as a couple (to reaffirm their relationship). Furthermore, Janet tells her that the housing support will be withdrawn if she's no longer with Jo.

Part II

"The Personal Is Political":
Teen Pregnancy and Hegemony

Chapter Five

"100% Preventable"

Teen Motherhood, Morality, and the Myth of Choice

May Friedman

The young women of MTV's *16 and Pregnant* and *Teen Mom* are presented as unfolding disasters: stripped of autonomy, with limited opportunities and all future promise taken away by their own poor choices. Both the popular imagination on young motherhood and the social supports provided to young mothers begin from the same fundamental oversimplification: that the specific challenges faced by young women who choose to parent are individual difficulties, evidence of bad choices or bad values or both.[1] Yet an honest examination of these young mothers shows that the difficulties of their lives may be much more complicated.

For many young women and young families portrayed on the shows, the decision to parent results in a compromised life—social and educational choices are both curtailed, and the future is presented as grim and lonely. Many of the young women on the show experience violence and verbal abuse, from both their partners and their own parents. This violence is shown as problematic, yet the specific political context of violence against women is oddly minimized. Violence is thus divorced from its structural roots and instead viewed as an inevitable consequence of the poor choice to indulge in promiscuous behavior and thus welcome a life of young motherhood.[2] Likewise, poverty is seen as an inescapable outcome for young mothers. The show does not allow for the possibility that the limitations on supports offered to young mothers and young families could contribute responsibility to the poverty and violence that many such women experience. Instead, these women are seen as getting what they deserve. By presenting these shows as morality plays, *Teen Mom* and *16 and Pregnant* force audiences to confront their ambivalence about sexuality, youth, and motherhood.

This chapter considers the ways that two dominant themes of the shows—poverty and violence—are presented as logical conclusions to the perceived moral failings of the shows' protagonists. As a result, the shows are considered as evidence of a moral panic around young motherhood. Coming from a social justice framework, this chapter considers the messages that come from these shows and the possibilities for alternate ways of telling the stories of young mothers. Before we can consider alternatives, however, we must begin by looking at the story as it is already told.

DISCOURSES OF MOTHERHOOD: "BABIES HAVING BABIES"

How do we know what we know? Through what mechanisms do we learn about the world around us? The contemporary feminist lens through which I view the world reminds me that we are all held by dominant discourses, commonsense "truths" that provide generalized (though often incorrect) knowledge about people, groups, situations.[3] As a scholar of motherhood, I have long grappled with the dominant discourses of motherhood, the expectation that mothers shape-shift into Betty Crocker–June Cleaver hybrids immediately upon giving birth.[4] Yet when I consider the dominant discourses about young mothers, I hit a dissonance—young mothers are set apart from other mothers, from what we often think of as *motherhood*—the Hallmark card version of "mom" that stabilizes maternity as associated with stability, strength, and selflessness[5] is often withdrawn from young mothers who are viewed instead as distinctly unstable, weak, and selfish.[6] As Nicole Bailey et al. suggest, "motherhood is something that all women are expected to do, but only in the 'right' social, economic and sexual circumstances."[7] These messages about teenage motherhood are strongly reinforced by MTV.

16 and Pregnant begins by conveying a paradox: young women can be teenagers, or they can be mothers, but they are unable to reconcile these two discursively opposed positions. The formula of the show begins with a narrative of a young woman's life as a carefree teen but with the somber end point "Because . . . I'm pregnant," reminding the viewer that her life as a teenager will shortly come to an end. The show then meanders through relatively mundane teenage realities before arriving at the apex of each episode: the delivery, followed by requisite footage of teary and sleep-deprived young women tending to inconsolable infants. In this respect, the show portrays the slaying of one identity—teen—with the imposition of another—mom. The dissonance between the expected routines of carefree adolescence and the emergent realities of parenthood is thus shown as an inevitable recipe for disappointment and sadness. As young mother Mackenzie responds to her partner's expectation of enjoyment or pleasure, "you screwed yourself out of being happy when you got me pregnant."[8]

This narrative of childhood lost to young motherhood is puzzling given the dominant narrative of maternity as the biological imperative of all females.[9] If older mothers are assumed to seamlessly transition from independent and occupied women to caring and courageous mothers, why are young mothers not held to the same (impossible) standard? Amy Middleton suggests that young mothers are not held to high standards because they are "overtly mothering against the societal standard of 'good mother.'"[10] This conundrum may expose deeply held beliefs about the sanctity of childhood.

In a society that reveres childhood, mothers are meant to be selfless and immediately put their children's needs above their own. For young mothers, this expectation necessarily curtails their own childhoods. Yet many young people who are childless experience adversity that requires rapid maturation: illness, poverty, and other challenges limit the capacity for many young people to elude responsibility. Indeed, other life difficulties are viewed as impressive efforts by courageous youths. Young mothers, by contrast, are met with derision and scorn[11] because they have done the unthinkable: they have sacrificed their own childhoods, and they have done so by engaging in sexual activity. The discourses of *16 and Pregnant* and *Teen Mom* thus mirror broader societal understandings: that childhood is sacrosanct (necessitating sacrificial mothering)[12] and that sexual desire and activity (especially by young women) are abhorrent. The sex that led to these women becoming mothers thus makes them incapable of meeting the requirements of "good" motherhood. Bailey et al. note that "the legal and social concept of the 'child' which has developed in modern society became divorced from sexuality and this has meant that it is particularly difficult to acknowledge the emotional and physical capacity of teenagers for sexual activity."[13]

Despite the hegemonic supposition that young mothers are de facto bad mothers, many young mothers flourish. Young mothers, like all mothers, may be more or less patient, may parent with more or less creativity, may have an equal share of good and bad parenting moments. Yet young mothers, in many cases, do not have the same experiences as their older counterparts. Many young mothers, and especially those portrayed on *Teen Mom* and *16 and Pregnant* parent under conditions of considerable adversity, conditions that limit their potential and that of their children.

VIOLENCE AND ABUSE

While the show aims for a sassy upbeat vibe, drama is key. Set alongside other MTV shows, such as *Jersey Shore*, *16 and Pregnant* aims to ensure that the formula still results in shocking and compelling viewing. Thus, arguments as well as physical altercations, between young women and their partners and, sometimes, between young women and other family members, are foregrounded. Likewise, infidelities, arrests, and other extraordinary challenges are given a lot of airtime, with no fewer than three of the young mothers of the first two seasons experiencing pregnancy at the same time as their own mothers. The women of the show are thus presented as naïve, unstable, and at risk.

Many of the young women in *Teen Mom* and *16 and Pregnant* experience abuse, both physical and emotional, from people around them. This abuse manifests in a number of ways. Interestingly, while young male partners of protagonists are often seen behaving negatively, intimate partner violence by young men toward young women is the least represented form of violence on the show. Notably, young women are increasingly seen punching and hitting their partners. Amber, for example, a young mother from *16 and Pregnant*'s first season[14] who became a protagonist of *Teen Mom*, hits and punches her partner Gary on multiple occasions.[15] Confronted with her boyfriend's infidelity, young mother Markai swats him repeatedly while weeping, "I hate you."[16] These "attacks" are met by a somber voice-over at the commercial break intoning, "If you or someone you know has experienced violence, get help."[17] There is absolutely no discussion of the disparities in physical size and cultural capital that take place within these heterosexual partnerships and that young women hitting their male partners *should* make different choices, but simultaneously, such behavior does not stand in as an exact corollary for the poor choices made by the young men of the show.

While the show is virtually silent on the topic of male violence against women, the young fathers of the show are presented as a rotating bunch of ineffectual and emotionally abusive morons. Infidelity abounds. Young men fail to consider the ways that their partners' lives have been transformed, and they do not coparent equitably. There is a lot of emotional abuse, name-calling, abandonment. On season 2 of *16 and Pregnant*, Chelsea is repeatedly left by her daughter's father, Adam. He sends her texts calling her a "fat bitch" and telling her that he never wants to see "that mistake" again. Yet moments later, Chelsea and Adam reconcile. She wants him to be part of her daughter's life. Her anguished father looks on.[18] This behavior does not warrant the public service announcement of the physical violence referenced earlier. Instead, the emotional abuse inflicted by young men toward young women on virtually every episode is seen as par for the course, a necessary by-product of young women making poor choices and allowing themselves to get "caught."

Young women also encounter violence and abuse in their families of origin. Farrah, in season one of *16 and Pregnant*, is screamed at and slapped by her mother[19] and, in a later altercation on *Teen Mom*, is punched in the face by her mother, leading to criminal charges being laid.[20] Even as Farrah's mother is in jail, Farrah, out of necessity, still lives in her mother's home. In many other cases, young women experience emotional abuse and the withdrawal of both emotional and tangible supports from their families. Again, such behavior is normalized within the show as a necessary by-product of young motherhood, rather than problematic behavior in its own right.

As young mothers, the women of *16 and Pregnant* are caught in a unique vulnerability: in most cases, they are still deeply dependent on their families of origin, yet for many of the women, they still hope to coparent with their children's fathers. The tension, especially between the mothers of the young mothers and their young partners, is often explosive. Such was the case with Nikkole, whose mother and boyfriend Josh are literally fighting over her as she delivers her baby on *16 and Pregnant*. After a particularly hostile interaction by Nikkole's bedside, her mother and Josh demand to hear from her which relationship is more important.[21] This emotional manipulation is emblematic of the incoherent supports that many young women on the show receive: they must pick and choose their allies, and they are often left silently and passively suffering while others decide their fate.

POVERTY

Teen Mom and *16 and Pregnant* portray significant violence and abuse yet in a context that divorces violence from its structural roots. Young mothers consistently return to conditions of abuse and violence, and MTV would have viewers believe that these are inevitabilities of young motherhood. Yet there is never a consideration of ways that violence might be prevented: by allowing young women more choices and, specifically, by funding those choices to allow for better social supports. Instead, poverty is seen as an inconvenience of young motherhood rather than something that forces women into untenable situations.

The biggest reason that young women experience violence (and significant other difficulties) as young mothers is poverty.[22] Poverty is the looming message of the show, never explicitly articulated yet nonetheless present. Young women are seen at Walmart buying diapers and looking frantically at the cash register. Parents ask young mothers how they will afford child care, when they will return to work, how they aim to support themselves. Boyfriends are scolded for failing to support young families, for working too little or, paradoxically, for failing to support within the home, for working too hard. The overwhelming message about teen motherhood is about the absence of choices, yet the biggest reason for the removal of these choices is never made explicit—the omnipresence of poverty for women who choose to parent at a young age.

Young mother Samantha will be the first member of her family to graduate high school—yet now must figure out how to complete her schooling with her new baby and with a boyfriend who must now work multiple low-paying jobs.[23] Ebony must give up her lifetime dream of joining the air force, since her "dependent" daughter renders her ineligible—even more problematically, Ebony must marry her boyfriend to follow him through his progress through the armed services since dependents are not acknowledged by the air force outside formal marriages.[24] Jenelle, notoriously portrayed as a party girl in both *16 and Pregnant* and *Teen Mom 2*, finds herself unable to contest her own mother's bid for custody of Jenelle's son because she cannot afford a lawyer.[25] Jenelle's poverty forces her to give custody to her mother and to live in her mother's home: as a result, she must now parent to her mother's standard while having no autonomy over her child or herself. In an especially troubling episode of *16 and Pregnant*, young mother Kailyn, abandoned by her family of origin, moves in with her boyfriend's family, who treat her as its own.[26] When Kailyn wants to break up with her boyfriend, however, she finds herself potentially facing homelessness and the loss of her child. She quietly gets back together with her boyfriend.

While the shows aim to reveal these scenarios as cautionary tales of the perils of young motherhood, in fact in all these scenarios the helplessness experienced by young mothers can be traced to a lack of financial and other support. If Kailyn could afford a caregiver while she attended college, she could make a true decision about whether she wanted to stay in her relationship or not. Perhaps Jenelle is not yet ready to parent, but her choice to allow her mother to take over custody is borne of desperation and coercion, rather than deliberation. If Samantha's boyfriend could provide caregiving instead of working at McDonald's, she could complete her high school diploma, and they could figure out a strategic plan to move forward with their young family. The show presents the limited educational opportunities as obvious outcomes of young parenthood, never acknowledging the presence of potentially successful supported learning contexts for young parents[27] nor advocating for further such opportunities. Instead, poverty is seen as a choice and an irresponsible choice at that, especially for young mothers who, by choice or otherwise, part from their babies' fathers. As Tanya Darisi compellingly suggests, "in addition to a characterization which strongly implies 'not good mothers,' single young mothers are also presented as not good adults. They are expected to fail as contributing members of society."[28] Of course, to acknowledge the role that poverty plays in the narrative of young motherhood is to suggest that, as a society, we have a responsibility to support young parents, something that we are, as yet, reluctant to do.

Young mother Felicia realizes that she can afford only diapers or a stroller for her daughter Genesis. After buying the diapers, she wistfully muses, "I do need a stroller for Genesis—but I only have money for diapers. I wish Alex would put more money into baby supplies instead of spending it with his friends."[29] Alex comes home with $80 sneakers, and Felicia is angry and disappointed. Yet the exchange highlights the problem facing many young mothers—the baby is viewed (emotionally and structurally) as their responsibility and their problem. In many instances, young fathers, by contrast, continue to act as the young teenagers they are. This presents a difficult conundrum: do we hold these young men (with their extremely limited earning potential) accountable, or do we, as a community, have a responsibility to support young mothers? Perhaps in a context in which young families are subjected to less stigma and young parents are set up to succeed, the disparities between partners would be less stark and the lives of young parents, male and female, less bleak.

If Felicia could afford reasonable child care, rather than having her elderly grandmother care for her daughter, she would graduate high school more readily and be in a position to earn more. If she was supported through college, her earning potential (and tax contribution) would increase. It would seem that a relatively limited investment of social support would result in a healthier family, enhance Felicia's decision-making capacity, and best support everyone involved. Furthermore, ensuring her financial independence allows Felicia (and other young mothers) to set her own limits on her partner's involvement in her life and empowers her to demand his support, financial or otherwise. So why does the show present poverty as an inevitable consequence of teen motherhood—and one, more importantly, that young mothers deserve? To consider this, we must examine the show's third key theme: promiscuity.

PROMISCUITY

These are not subtle shows. For all the flashy marketing and MTV hype, the shows enter many commercial breaks with a public service announcement intoning, "Teen pregnancy is 100% preventable. For more information, go to itsyoursexlife.com." Nearly every episode of *16 and Pregnant* ends with a weepy and remorseful young mother tearfully admitting that she should have waited longer, made better choices. And while *16 and Pregnant* is fairly explicit on the topic of birth control (young mothers are routinely queried in the first quarter of the episode, with most admitting shamefacedly that they did not use any protection), the overall message of pregnancy as "100% preventable" is clear: to avoid the tragic outcome of the women profiled in the show, there's only one sure thing—stay abstinent. The shows maintain that teen pregnancy and parenting are tough because they are natural consequences of teen sex. On some level, the women of *16 and Pregnant* are thus seen as having gotten what they deserve.

The shows take little care to parse out the nuances between the instrumental challenges of young parenting and the shame and stigma that many young mothers experience. In effect, the shame is seen as yet another natural consequence of poor choices. Young mother Kayla suggests, "I always grew up thinking I had to be the perfect pageant queen with brains, beauty, and good values. So when I found out I was pregnant I was really afraid everyone would judge me. . . . JR was raised really traditionally, and now that I'm showing, I know he's uncomfortable being out in public with me so pregnant and us not married."[30] Judgment is presented as yet another inevitability, and the shows do not begin to consider the possibility of defiant young parenthood that responds to social shaming by presenting the positive characteristics of teen mothers. In this context, the notion of an entitled consciousness that allows the show's protagonists to demand social supports seems absurd.

If poverty and violence are the consequences of promiscuity, motherhood is seen as a natural end to any sexual relationship. Parents of the shows' protagonists are routinely shown scandalized by their daughters' expectations that they might want to date again after parting from their (often abusive) baby daddies. For example, Jenelle is presented as irresponsible, not only in her refusal to take a greater hand in her son's care, but also in her casual dating. The shows repeatedly portray young women being told by parents, in-laws, guidance counselors, and other concerned "adults" that they are no longer in a position to date since they have chosen to parent. Nowhere is the message of a difficult life as a natural consequence for bad choices made more clear than in the show's casual acceptance of the expectation that young mothers have ended their romantic and sexual lives.

The judgmental tone of the show is interestingly suspended for young people who make adoption plans. Young parents who choose to place their children for adoption are celebrated as having unusual reserves of bravery and strength. While the show does a surprisingly good job in considering the very real challenges of birth parenting, it nonetheless presents adoption-choosing parents as redeeming their slutty behavior, in contrast to the "selfishness" of young women who choose to parent. This is especially true for Catelynn and Tyler, who in season 1 of *16 and Pregnant* choose to place their daughter for adoption.[31] Their subsequent experiences as birth parents, profiled in *Teen Mom*, show their pain over living apart from their daughter but also celebrate the "selflessness" of their choice. Significantly, they are also one of the few couples that are presented in a respectful and loving fashion.

The choice to profile both parenting and adoption-involved teens, however, makes the near total silence on the third choice available to all pregnant women even more baffling: in a candid show about teenage sexuality and its outcomes, the topic of abortion is notably and suspiciously absent. Teens who parent are seen as suffering; teens who place their children for adoption are likewise shown grieving and experiencing considerable emotional trauma. If the show is meant to suggest that motherhood compromises young people, then why is the possibility of abortion largely ignored? Fundamentally, the curtailing of any dialogue on abortion reveals the shows' unambiguous moralizing: young sexually active women are presented as deserving of suffering. The show does not just cast a light on the "real lives" of real teens: it sends a very clear message on the loathsomeness of young women who are sexually active.[32]

The message that young women should avoid sex and that those who do not are destined to suffer a deservedly miserable fate is, of course, in stark contrast to the presence of increasingly sexualized accounts of girls of younger and younger ages. As one anonymous contributor to Deborah Davis's 2004 anthology on the topic of teen motherhood eloquently states,

> Why did my culture push me to be sexy, to obsess about my weight, my hair, my skin, my breast and ass size and shape, taunt me to be beautiful, skinnier, sexier—and then not expect me to act on my body's hormonal imperative? It is so confusing to live in a culture that values women's sexiness and chastity but not women's sexuality. It is so confusing for me to live with a popular culture that expects me to look like a teen forever, a culture that plasters pictures of half-naked, teenage-looking women everywhere and then punishes me for acting on my sensuality, for having sex and no longer being chaste.[33]

The young mother quoted makes explicit the links between gender and sexuality and the specifically contradictory public distaste for the intersection of youth and femininity with respect to sexual behavior. The young fathers of *16 and Pregnant* and *Teen Mom* are not held to the same standard, nor are they judged with the same ferocity as the young mothers profiled in the shows. The message is thus that boys will be boys but that girls really ought to know better. This messaging is emblematic of a broader understanding of the roles of fathers and mothers, in which "to father" means establishing paternity while "to mother" involves nurturing and caring labor.

The notion that promiscuity is the chief social problem identified by the show masks dismaying structural inequalities and curtails any useful analysis of the limitations of a choice-based framework. As Rickie Solinger asks in *Beggars and Choosers*, "How can users of such a term avoid distinguishing, in consumer-culture fashion, between a woman who can and a woman who can't afford to make a choice?"[34] Deirdre Kelly expands on this point, arguing,

> The common understanding of the word choice tends to mask the circumstances under which people make decisions. . . . For example, the barriers to access to contraception and abortion services, mixed messages about sexuality, and the pervasiveness of poverty, child abuse, and unequal power relations based on age, race, class, gender and sexual orientation all shape the lives of young mothers profoundly.[35]

By shifting the stage to a tacit condemnation of young women's sexuality, *16 and Pregnant* and *Teen Mom* thus distract us from a need to grapple with the very real structural limitations faced by young mothers and young families.[36] In particular, the show's limited diversity skews heavily toward young mothers who come from conditions of poverty, and this initial lack of class privilege is never acknowledged as a contributing factor to the limitations placed on young mothers. In the realm of schooling, the show never presents a young mother advocating for effective assistance to maintain her schooling, never suggests that young mothers motivated to continue their educations deserve supports. Rather, the show is a never-ending parade of the beaten and the broken, a miserable cautionary tale.

MAYBE PARENTING IS JUST HARD (FOR EVERYONE)

If viewers can somehow look past the heavy-handed moralizing of the show, *16 and Pregnant* actually has commonalities with other reality shows that showcase early parenthood, such as TLC's *Bringing Up Baby.* New parents are often overwhelmed; relationships are taxed; finances are strained; and the sharp learning curve and identity shift of new motherhood are overwhelming. For the older parents of other television shows, however, such growing pains are shown as endearingly comical. For the young mothers of *16 and Pregnant*, by contrast, these rough spots are meant to serve as a warning to other teenagers of the perils of young motherhood. Without minimizing the very real systemic difficulties experienced by young mothers, perhaps the reason that the teen mothers profiled by MTV are portrayed in desperation is, at least in part, because the early stages of parenting are very difficult for many people. As the dreadful Dr. Drew intones on the "Life after Labor" special for season 4 of *16 and Pregnant,* "When you're sixteen and pregnant, your whole life changes in an instant. But for many the reality doesn't set in until you're alone, exhausted, feeding their [*sic*] newborns in the middle of the night." Yet it is easily argued that the same could be said of many new mothers of thirty-five.[37]

And now I must confess: These thoughts were in the front of my mind as I sat nursing my third baby while watching these young women. When I gave birth to a very colicky infant, I found myself trapped on the sofa, terrified to move for fear of unleashing my screaming baby, and I began a sustained relationship with the young mothers of MTV. I was myself overwhelmed, despite my advanced maternal age, despite my two older children, despite my freshly minted *doctorate* on the topic of mothering—in fact, I was chagrined to see how much *better* many of the young mothers of the show were faring than I, despite their *terrible choices*, despite their *risky lives*.

All of this got me to thinking about *why* teen motherhood is meant to be so intrinsically problematic. It curtails choices, no doubt, but it may provide a degree of autonomy in later life that many of my peers, first-time mothers in their late thirties, are sorely missing. The mothers of the show are, in many instances, better playmates to their children, more energetic and more genuinely delighted by play than some older mothers—or at least me. Yet I was appalled by the violence and poverty that these women were experiencing. I wonder what a feminist version of the show would look like and whether a show that fails to mention the word *abortion*—beyond some muttered "not a choice I could make, not for me"—can ever be considered feminist. Yet a show about young mothers that sees teen parenting as yet another legitimate and challenging path to family—one with its own unique pitfalls but also some very real assets—would force us to rethink a feminist agenda toward young motherhood that is truly pro-*choice*. We see the seeds of this revolution in collections such as Davis's *You Look Too Young to Be a Mom* and Ariel Gore's *Breeder*, but it is tempting to believe that these texts merely preach to the feminist converted. Furthermore, empowerment is not achieved solely by recording the success stories of young mothers while disguising the real difficulties that such women face. Rather than attempting to shift discourses solely by showing that young mothers can be good mothers, young mothers must explore the impossibilities of good motherhood for all mothers, must explore alliances with other normative and nonnormative families that acknowledge motherhood in the midst of the "ambivalence, confusion, and turbulence that may characterize its practices."[38]

16 and Pregnant and *Teen Mom* show the need for an empowered message about teen motherhood in popular culture, a strong voice to shift the ubiquity and taken-for-granted logic of shame, stigma, and despair surrounding young mothers. As Kelly exhorts, "if young mothers (and their allies) are to succeed in rewriting young motherhood, they must look to various oppositional discourses and social movements for pieces of new scripts, pieces that help them name their experiences and link these to the ongoing quest for various forms of social justice."[39] The shows of MTV, sadly, merely reinforce existing scripts rather than allow for the rewriting of young motherhood.

Young motherhood does not, despite the shows' best efforts to convince us otherwise, result in disaster. Poverty, violence, shame, and lack of choice, however, make young mothers' lives much more complicated. Instead of viewing the shows as a gleeful reckoning for women who have made bad choices, perhaps we must resist their heavy-handed moralizing and see them instead as examples of the pathetic social supports afforded to young mothers, of the obligations that we have to build a society that will honor their efforts and struggles. Perhaps we must see how impressively young mothers flourish despite being left to flounder.

NOTES

1. Rock, "The 'Good Mother.'"
2. Bailey et al., "'The Baby Brigade.'"
3. Baxter, "Feminist Post-structuralist Discourse Analysis."
4. Douglas and Michaels, *Mommy Myth*; Hays, *The Cultural Contradictions*; Maushert, *The Mask of Motherhood*.
5. O'Reilly, *Mother Outlaws*.
6. Kelly, "Stigma Stories"; Rock, "The 'Good Mother.'"
7. Bailey et al., "'The Baby Brigade,'" 102.
8. "Mackenzie," *16 and Pregnant*, season 4, March 27, 2012.
9. Douglas and Michaels, *Mommy Myth*, 4.
10. Middleton, "Mothering under Duress," 78.
11. Rock, "The 'Good Mother'"; Kelly, "Stigma Stories" and "Young Mothers."
12. O'Reilly, *Mother Outlaws*, 4.
13. Bailey et al., "'The Baby Brigade,'" 102.
14. "Amber," *16 and Pregnant*, season 1, June 25, 2009.
15. "Moving On," *Teen Mom*, season 1, December 14, 2009.
16. "Markai," *16 and Pregnant*, season 2, November 16, 2010.
17. Amber's behavior on the show led to charges of domestic violence. She is currently incarcerated for drug-related offenses.
18. "Chelsea," *16 and Pregnant*, season 2, March 9, 2010.
19. "Farrah," *16 and Pregnant*, season 1, June 18, 2009.
20. "Not Again," *Teen Mom*, season 2, July 20, 2010.
21. "Nikkole," *16 and Pregnant*, season 2, February 23, 2010.
22. Berman, Silver, and Wilson, "'Don't Look Down on Me."
23. "Samantha," *16 and Pregnant*, season 2, March 23, 2010.
24. "Ebony," *16 and Pregnant*, season 1, July 2, 2009.
25. "Change of Heart," *Teen Mom 2*, season 1, January 25, 2011.
26. "Kailyn," *16 and Pregnant*, season 2, April 20, 2010.
27. Kelly, *Pregnant with Meaning*.
28. Darisi, "'It Doesn't Matter,'" 34.
29. "Felicia," *16 and Pregnant*, season 2, November 2, 2010.
30. "Kayla," *16 and Pregnant*, season 2, December 7, 2010.
31. "Catelynn," *16 and Pregnant*, season 1, July 16, 2009.
32. It is an interesting feminist thought experiment to consider how a show that involved abortion, in all its ambiguity and emotionally variable permutations, could be presented. An example of one medium that attempted to take on this challenge is the 1996 documentary "If These Walls Could Talk," which profiled three fictionalized accounts of women who chose abortions in different eras. Although the pregnancy of Briana in season 4 is juxtaposed against her sister's simultaneous pregnancy, which ended in abortion, the episode's treatment of abortion is problematic. Brittany, Briana's sister, is shown as a party girl who refuses to change diapers but also is traumatized by her choice to abort. The episode thus reinforces the show's emphasis on teen sexuality as irresponsible and selfish and the challenges of parenting as necessary punishments for young sexually active women. Significantly, however, Briana ends the episode confiding that she is envious of her sister's choice, stating, "I would trade places with my sister any day."
33. Quoted in Davis, *You Look Too Young*, 86.
34. Soliger, *Beggars and Choosers*, 6.
35. Kelly, "Young Mothers," 10.
36. Ahola-Sidaway and Fonseca, "When Schooling Is Not Enough"; Shoveller et al., "'Aging Out.'"
37. Darisi, "'It Doesn't Matter.'"
38. Kinser, "Mothering as Relational Consciousness," 123.
39. Kelly, "Young Mothers," 12.

Chapter Six

Teen Sex:
An Equal Opportunity Menace

Multicultural Politics in 16 and Pregnant

Clare Daniel

MTV's "reality" series *16 and Pregnant* has been listed as one of the "most dangerous shows your kids are watching" because it is thought by some to glamorize teen pregnancy, though at the same time being credited by others with informing and dissuading teens from sex and pregnancy.[1] While the direct effects of the show on teenagers' decisions regarding sexuality and reproduction are difficult to determine, the series is clearly helping to shape the dominant construction of adolescent pregnancy and the public identity of the teen mom. In this chapter, I use visual and discursive analysis to examine the racial, sexual, gender, and class politics of the first two seasons of MTV's *16 and Pregnant*.[2] I argue that the show helps to consolidate a shift in the dominant discourse of adolescent reproduction, from an issue primarily associated with societal "ills," such as welfare dependency and urban decay in the 1990s, to one marking the personal and moral perils of teen sexual activity in the first decades of the twenty-first century. The episodes illustrate the transforming racialization of teen pregnancy and parenthood, where images of the generational poverty of poor black and Latina single-parent households give way to a multicultural teen motherhood, in which race and class are largely empty categories.

Seasons 1 and 2 of *16 and Pregnant* participate in two broad and interrelated trends within the current neoliberal moment. First, they engage and further the role of reality television, laid out by Laurie Ouellette and James Hay, of cultivating personal and intimate citizenship in the face of a scaled-back public welfare apparatus.[3] They do this by instructing teenagers in the characteristics of proper and improper adolescent sexual behavior, consumption, and recreation, elucidating the path to suitable adulthood. Second, in setting forth an analysis of reproductive choice that is almost wholly personal, the episodes obscure the complexity of structural forces through which people's reproductive behaviors are produced, enabled, regulated, and prevented. In stark contrast to the heavily racialized and class-based problematic of teenage pregnancy in the 1990s, in which concerns about national economic and social decline at the hands of teen welfare queens of color provided some of the most salient imagery in the drive to end welfare, *16 and Pregnant*'s critique of teen parenthood sidesteps race and class and draws on a revamped rhetoric of "cycles" of "broken families" and early pregnancy.

Questions of who makes a proper mother, one who can rear desirable citizens, cannot be understood separately from dominant paradigms of racial, class, gender, and sexual difference. As a survey of scholarship on motherhood and social policy shows, from the colonial period forward, notions of motherhood have been shaped by a white middle-class heteronormative ideal in ways that have differentially affected the social, political, and economic realities of people engaged in the activities of mothering.[4] Widespread concern about adolescent motherhood is a relatively recent development in this long history, emerging fully into the public consciousness as a social problem in the mid-1970s and coming to embody a central aspect of the perceived looming racial and economic disaster posed by the welfare state in the early 1990s.[5] As Kristin Luker suggests, in the growing sense of urgency around teenage pregnancy through the 1970s and 1980s, age became a politically acceptable index for concerns about race and class.[6] A focus on the universality of the category of teenager, paired with racially coded language and racially skewed imagery, allowed representations of teenage pregnancy within welfare reform debate to remain outwardly racially neutral while utilizing and forwarding racist stereotypes.[7] As this chapter shows, although the discourse of teen pregnancy has transformed, teen motherhood remains an important category for the differential regulation, discipline, and prevention of sex and reproduction according to race and class.

While the welfare reform legislation of 1996 represents the defining biopolitical approach to teen pregnancy of that decade, with its focus on dictating the household, familial, and labor arrangements of impoverished teen moms of color, *16 and Pregnant* is part of a dominant biopolitical approach to the reformulated social problem in these first decades of the twenty-first century. The Foucauldian theory of biopolitics holds that the modern state simultaneously operates on both the level of the individual, disciplining behavior, and the level of the population, regulating the national body based on notions of desirability and undesirability.[8] These efforts to cultivate the optimal citizenry follow a eugenic logic, encouraging and cultivating the lives and reproduction of some while discouraging, neglecting, or preventing others. Understanding modern state power as diffuse, flowing through public as well as private institutions that are sanctioned and supported by the dominant political logic, *16 and Pregnant* can be seen as an important element of a new biopolitics of teenage pregnancy.

16 and Pregnant, along with its spin-off series *Teen Mom* and *Teen Mom 2*, is part of a collaboration between the private nonprofit National Campaign to Prevent Teen and Unplanned Pregnancy and the cable television channel MTV. The national campaign (originally the National Campaign to Prevent Teen Pregnancy), "inspired" by the Clinton White House, was founded in 1996 and receives a portion of its funding from the Department of Health and Human Services.[9] It is further enmeshed in the formal governmental apparatus in its role as major participant in advocacy and policy debate about teen pregnancy at the congressional level.[10] The national campaign's partnership with MTV, owned by media conglomerate Viacom, engendered these programs as part of a long-standing goal of using media as a "force for good," showing that "sex has consequences," and presenting "teens making the case to each other that postponing sexual involvement is their best choice for many reasons."[11] Meanwhile, the show's unscripted and heavily edited format, use of nonactors, and emphasis on apparently unpredictable real-life drama follow a current template of successful MTV programming. *16 and Pregnant* is thus a product of a complex intersection of public, private, philanthropic, and profit-driven interests aimed at influencing its young audience. This chapter focuses on only the first two seasons of *16 and Pregnant* as result of practical concerns about length and because, although the series transforms in certain ways during later seasons and differs somewhat from *Teen Mom* and *Teen Mom 2*, these episodes exhibit important themes occurring throughout the three series.

THE MULTICULTURAL CRITIQUE:
TEENAGE FRIVOLITY SACRIFICED

While the makers of *16 and Pregnant* may have multiple, sometimes conflicting aims producing various intentional and unintentional representations of sex, teen motherhood, and proper adolescence, its explicit cautioning against teen sex, "premarital" sex, "unprotected" sex, and pregnancy is present in the episode narrations, intermittent public service announcements, and finale specials with "Dr. Drew" Pinsky.[12] This discourse of prevention differs significantly from the urgent warnings typical of 1990s welfare reform debate in which teen pregnancy, coupled with a lenient welfare system, would be the downfall of American civilization.[13] In this post–welfare reform moment, a lack of evidence that welfare reform has successfully reduced teen pregnancy or poverty might suggest that welfare policy and its relationship to the status of adolescent reproduction as a problem should be revisited.[14] Instead, teen pregnancy is taking on a new identity as a problem that is forwarded and exemplified by *16 and Pregnant*, in which it is an individual more than a national conundrum, and race and socioeconomic class no longer appear as factors in its occurrence.

In these episodes, teen pregnancy and parenthood are problematic for reasons entirely separate from poverty. There is no mention or depiction of welfare or urban decay in the entire first two seasons. Financial hardship is represented only by teen parents who are unable to purchase luxury items and live separately from their parents or grandparents. Rather than being a one-way ticket to lifelong poverty and dependence in a crime-ridden inner-city setting, teen pregnancy is presented as an unnecessary curtailment of normative adolescence and all its sanctioned frivolity. Teens who become parents can no longer participate in the carefree, narcissist consumption, social life, and recreation that are apparently integral to a proper teenage life. Many of them lament that they are missing their prom or cannot fit into their desired prom or homecoming dress. For example, in the "Unseen Moments Special" episode of season 2, Dr. Drew says, "It's hard for a woman of any age to accept the way her body changes when she's pregnant, but it's *really* hard for a teenager, especially when she wants to be a part of *normal* teenage life," as the show cuts to a sequence of clips in which one pregnant teen, Megan, "agonizes," in Dr. Drew's words, over finding a homecoming dress to fit her swelling body.[15] Next, teen mom Kayla is shown trying on a dress one week after her baby is born and being unsatisfied with it. The show then skips to three weeks later when she is wearing the dress she eventually chose, and Dr. Drew says, "At least for one night, Kayla could still be a teenager. Well, almost," as a shot of her baby flashes on the screen.[16] In this way, the show defines an apparently definitive experience of all women's pregnancies—struggling with bodily changes—while opposing that experience to "normal" adolescence. Teenage motherhood thus appears to exacerbate the automatic burdens of motherhood and counteract the joys of being a teen.

The show also emphasizes the monetary, bodily, and time constraints that reproduction puts on other appropriate teen activities. Some teen moms emphasize their ability to "grow up" in an instant, while their babies' fathers continue to spend money on unnecessary things as normal teens.[17] Most episodes emphasize the teen mom's favorite extracurricular activities (e.g., Farrah and Leah are cheerleaders, Jenelle likes going to the beach, Brooke races cars, Lizzie plays in marching band) and the ways that being a teen mom infringes on these endeavors.[18] Likewise, the shows repeatedly stress the havoc that teenage pregnancy and motherhood wreak on a girl's social life.[19]

Whereas the dominant 1990s critique of teenage pregnancy drew on racialized discourses of poverty and welfare, *16 and Pregnant*'s class- and color-blind critique attributes undesirable characteristics to adolescent child-bearing in whatever racial and class context. Twelve of the sixteen pregnant teenagers followed in the first two seasons appear unambiguously white and the majority middle class. Their pregnancies are therefore presented as unsettling and burdensome in a way that affects all teenage girls with the same basic consequences—by ruining their lighthearted innocence and disrupting their life course. This is well illustrated by Kayla's episode in season 2. Kayla lives in rural Alabama. She and her boyfriend JR appear to be white and middle class. Although a major source of drama throughout the series is the apparent irresponsibility of teenage fathers, JR has a high school diploma and a steady (while perhaps low-paying) job as a mechanic. He is portrayed as committed to Kayla and their baby Rylan. Kayla and JR each appear to live with their parents, who are married to each other and accommodating of the pregnancy (although Kayla's mom does talk about being sad about the news at first). Both Kayla's and JR's parents appear to provide emotional and material support to them.

Nonetheless, Kayla's life is not free of turmoil. One major source of conflict in the episode is that JR wants to marry Kayla and move into a house (which appears spacious and has "brand new cabinets and appliances in it") that his parents own, but Kayla is not "ready" to move away from her mother.[20] Kayla is also portrayed as somewhat distraught over having to sacrifice apparently crucial high school experiences and go to community college instead of the university that she had planned on attending with her friends. As Kayla puts it to JR, "You got to have your senior year, but I had to miss out on a lot of stuff, like me moving off with all my friends and going to college."[21] Although her mother tries to reassure her that the community college is a "wonderful" school, that she will still be able to pursue the career as a nurse that she had planned, and that she will make new friends, Kayla cries over these changes in her life. Despite Kayla saying repeatedly, "I love being a mom," having no cause for concern over providing for the material needs of herself and her baby, and being fully able to complete high school and go to college to pursue the career she had planned (her mother and JR's mother have agreed to provide child care), Kayla's story is presented as a cautionary tale against teenage pregnancy.

While the episodes of *16 and Pregnant* produce many different and contradictory meanings, the authoritative prevention message of Kayla and most of the other episodes in the first two seasons is typically as follows: Do not get pregnant as a teenager if you want to continue participating in *normal* teenage activities, such as playing sports, looking thin and fashionable, attending a regular high school, buying trendy nonessential goods, and moving away to college to live in a dormitory with your friends. Whereas the social science and political discourse that propped up teen pregnancy as a social problem in the 1990s held it to be a dire symptom of a larger culture of poverty that accepted early childbearing as the norm due to welfare incentives and/or the decline of family values, Kayla and many of the other *16 and Pregnant* teen moms are portrayed as enduring social ostracism due to the precisely nonnormative status of their actions.[22] In one of the animated illustrations that punctuate and highlight certain moments throughout the episodes, Kayla is depicted as being back at school pulling formula bottles out of her locker while her schoolmates stand by discussing a party, "cheer practice," and going to "the game." They then walk away, leaving her standing alone and dejected (her head hanging) next to a wall of lockers.[23] Kayla does not live in a pathological community—in which "babies" are commonly "having babies" to get a welfare check while "deadbeat dads" are always shirking their responsibilities—but rather in an apparently normal setting in which teen pregnancy is alienating.

Not only is she "growing apart" from her friends as a result of becoming a teen mom, but she is also no longer able to participate in beauty pageants, a previous pastime of hers. She is shown calling a local pageant director to ask why girls with children are not allowed to participate and being told, "This is for kids who just don't have children."[24] In another segment, an animation depicts her standing in a line of pageant contestants while her belly grows and knocks them all over like dominoes. This is similar to an illustration that shows her pregnant belly growing until it breaks the school desk in which she is sitting. As Wanda Pillow points out, pregnant teenagers do not "'fit' literally and figuratively into educational research, theories, policies, and practices."[25] The exclusion of pregnant/mothering teens' from their desired extracurriculars and social circles, as well as from the educational politics and practices that Pillow discusses, is reflected and reinforced in Kayla's episode as a way of demonstrating the wrongfulness of teen motherhood.

Social exclusions, relationship turmoil, and decreased freedom of recreation and consumption are shown affecting almost all teen moms of the first two seasons (perhaps with the exceptions of Catelynn, Lori, and Ashley, who place their babies for adoption, which I discuss later). In the final segment of Kayla's episode, she states, "When I had unprotected sex, I really wish I had thought it through more, because even though I had all the love and support in the world, the emotional struggle that you have to go through along with being pregnant is really really hard and I just wanna slow down my life a little bit."[26] As some of Kayla's final words, these help solidify the notion that the problem with teenage motherhood is not that it might lead to poverty, crime, or generational welfare dependency but that it interferes with the natural and logical course of life. As such, no structural factors, such as social policy, racial inequality, economic structure, reproductive politics, or health policy, appear to be at play. Rather, teenage motherhood is universally a personal failure that comes with personal sacrifices. As I illustrate further, the first two seasons of *16 and Pregnant* draw on a neoliberal version of multiculturalism to problematize teen pregnancy. By presenting a somewhat diverse cast—*mostly* white, *mostly* middle class, but with some exceptions—in which diversity is left to speak for itself, in other words, nothing is explicitly made of these differences and the social inequalities they represent and engender—the show upholds the white middle-class norms that structure citizenship.[27]

BREAKING "THE CYCLE" AND REGULATING SEX

A defining aspect of the "epidemic" of teen pregnancy that helped drive social reformers to overhaul welfare in 1996 was its purported self-perpetuation.[28] "Babies" were having babies who would have babies as babies and so on, due to a lack of proper role models and the perverse incentives of Aid to Families with Dependent Children. The intersecting racialized tropes of the culture of poverty, generational welfare dependency, and teenage pregnancy were enough to paint a harrowing portrait of U.S. economic and social decline at the hands of misguided inner-city adolescents of color, whose actions were part of a cascading snowball of degeneracy. The "cycle" of teen pregnancy needed to be broken, and welfare reform, with its monetary "carrots and sticks," was an important strategy in doing so.[29] Although teenagers currently can still draw on public assistance in many forms when they become parents, the perils of early pregnancy appear to have nothing to do with poverty or cyclical dependency on the government in *16 and Pregnant.* In fact, in the first two seasons, while there are some instances of relative poverty and some discussions of cycles, being poor is not a constitutive aspect of the discourse of cycles. Instead, the new cycle of teen pregnancy results from inadequate familial relationships, with the regulation of sex as a clear solution.

While most cast members in seasons 1 and 2 appear far removed from the stereotypical teen mom of 1990s discourse, Catelynn comes the closest. Although she and her boyfriend Tyler are white (something true of a large portion of actual teen parents but obscured by the racialized discourse of the late twentieth century), they describe their lives as "unstable," an apparent euphemism for growing up in relatively impoverished households with emotionally unsupportive parents.[30] Catelynn's mother struggles with substance abuse and gave birth to her when she was nineteen. Tyler's dad has been "in and out of prison" throughout his life. In this way, Catelynn and Tyler's situation bears the most resemblance to the cycle of teen pregnancy that Republicans and Democrats mutually concerned themselves with in welfare reform debate. As the story goes, a child of a teen mom grows up in a poor dysfunctional home and becomes pregnant at sixteen as a result of that dysfunction, as will her own daughter. Catelynn's episode, however, forecloses that possibility by depicting the difficult process that she and Tyler go through to place their daughter for adoption so that she can have a "better life."

As Catelynn and Tyler choose adoptive parents for their child, rather than continuing the purported pathological cycle, their actions consolidate a heteronormative ideal. Per Catelynn and Tyler's preferences, the adoptive mother will be a "stay-at-home mom" with a husband who is "a provider." The couple they choose explains that they met at church and that Brandon, the adoptive dad, works as a financial planner while his wife Theresa has a job at a "private Christian school" that she presumably plans to quit when the baby arrives. This married white Christian middle-class couple (their large brick house with white pillars and lush manicured lawn is pictured) is attributed by Catelynn and Tyler with the ability to give a child a "stable household" and a "better life" and to make her "so happy."[31] Catelynn and Tyler name emotional stability as their primary hope for their daughter's adoptive household, defending their decision not to raise her to Tyler's father, who appears to take offense at the implication that their household "is not good enough." However, the episode does little in the way of explicitly describing what emotional stability might look like. Instead, as Catelynn and Tyler thumb through Brandon and Theresa's portfolio from the adoption agency, visual imagery of Brandon and Theresa's apparent material wealth—their house, dress, and disposable time and income channeled toward recreation—is accompanied by Catelynn and Tyler's exclamations about these things and how "perfect" they would be as parents. In this way, an "emotionally stable household" is equated with being a middle-class nuclear family with traditional gender roles.[32]

Catelynn and Tyler's decision to place their daughter with this couple is unambiguously promoted and celebrated by the moral and psychological authority of the series, Dr. Drew. In all of the "Life after Labor" finale specials, Dr. Drew speaks with the teen moms about their sex lives, struggles in their relationships, and other hardships attributed to being a teen mom. He probes into their personal lives, providing counseling about contraception, healthy romantic partnerships, and parenting. In speaking with Tyler and Catelynn, he repeatedly refers to their "strength and courage" in making the choice that was "natural" to them and "right" for their daughter.[33] Out of the six pregnant teenagers of the first season, Catelynn is the only one to receive this kind of praise and admiration from Dr. Drew. Her choice of adoption is presented as the best and most logical choice that a pregnant teenager can make, not just because of her "unstable" household, but also because of the option of postponing parenthood until she and Tyler are "ready."[34] Catelynn and Tyler can reach the heteronormative ideal, regardless of their apparent disadvantages, if they just time their parenthood appropriately. In this way, Catelynn and Tyler's story helps the series negate the consequences of social inequality while also dismantling the links between teen parenthood and poverty.[35] As Catelynn discusses with Dr. Drew why she is not currently living in her mother's household with "drunks, loud music and partying," he commends her on her ability to recognize that she could and should "break the cycle." Rather than leading her to become a teen mom, Catelynn's apparent lower socioeconomic status and familial "instability" seem to have spurred her on in her decision not to parent her child, presenting an opportunity for a celebration of the universal accessibility of white middle-class ideals.[36]

The trope of the "cycle," however, rather than disappearing in the absence of substantiating evidence in the series, becomes redefined in accordance with the broader shift in the problematic of teen pregnancy. Rather than being tied to class status, cultural norms, or welfare policy, this newer version of the cycle of teenage pregnancy is understood in purely intimate, familial terms. As Dr. Drew interviews each teen mom, he utilizes the term *cycle* liberally and sometimes in the absence of any apparent cycle of poverty, dependency, or teen pregnancy. For example, Dr. Drew prompts Kailyn to talk about her "rocky" relationship with her mother (who has never been identified as a teen mom herself). When Kailyn says that she is afraid that Jo, her son's father, might leave her because "everyone just leaves," referring presumably to her father (whom she met for only the first time during filming of her episode) and her mother, Dr. Drew says that she can "hang in" with her son, adding that she has the ability to "change that cycle."[37] In this case, he uses the term *cycle* to refer to one generation's worth of behavior.

At times when he does use the term *cycle* to discuss what could be considered a generational pattern of behavior, it is nonetheless stripped of its associations with theories about poverty and welfare. Dr. Drew says to Samantha that there is a "cycle of teen pregnancy we see here in your family system," and he wonders how she plans to help her daughter break that cycle, when Samantha's parents tried and failed to do so with her. Samantha answers that she will talk to her daughter and give her birth control and, when prompted by Dr. Drew, that she will try to get her to delay sex. Samantha is the daughter of apparently middle-class Latina parents. Neither her mother nor Samantha appear to want or need public assistance, and there is no explicit broader familial or cultural acceptance of adolescent pregnancy as normal portrayed in the episode. In this segment, as in much of the series, teen pregnancy appears to be a problem solely because it is a "hard" (in Samantha's words) consequence of early and irresponsible sex, and its purported cyclical nature remains tied to parents' ineffectiveness at regulating their children's sexuality.

Many of these discussions likewise emphasize how the teen mother in question did not heed her parents' sound advice to avoid pregnancy. After talking with Felicia, whose mother had her as a teenager, about how she disappointed her mother by getting pregnant at sixteen, Dr. Drew addresses Alex, Felicia's boyfriend, saying, "You come from a broken family too."[38] Alex explains that his mother raised him and that he did not have a father growing up. In this way, Dr. Drew implicitly equates teen parenthood and growing up in a "broken family." Without elaborating on why he inquires about Felicia's mother's early pregnancy and Alex's family structure, Dr. Drew leaves the audience to refer back to his discussion with Brooke, one segment earlier, about the "heritage" of teen pregnancy in her family and how she ignored her mother's warnings about teen motherhood. The audience can thus assume that Felicia and Brooke (who appears to be white) became teen moms because of something inherent in their family structure, despite something explicit in their upbringing, and regardless of their race, class, or cultural context. Dr. Drew's references to cycles thus repurpose a large body of social science research and political discourse about poor racialized communities toward a color- and class-blind critique of "broken families" because they apparently (no matter how hard they try not to) propagate inappropriate sex. While the term *cycle* still deploys the stigma associated with denigrating images of poor people of color, its application to any kind of familial context that has begotten a pregnant teenager serves to distance the public image of teen pregnancy from its former social, economic, and political implications. The cycles that require breaking on *16 and Pregnant* threaten personal, familial futures first and foremost, affecting the national future perhaps only implicitly and secondarily.

CONCLUSION

The new discourse of teen pregnancy prevention forwarded by MTV and the National Campaign to Prevent Teen and Unplanned Pregnancy is a marked shift in terms of both representation and tactics. If the Personal Responsibility and Work Opportunity Reconciliation Act of 1996, which ushered in a new era of welfare, could be said to define the biopolitics of teen pregnancy in the 1990s and early twenty-first century, *16 and Pregnant* could likely be given that status for our current moment. The debates and political discourse leading to the passage of the act presented teen pregnancy as a structural issue and a personal issue. It was said to arise out of the conditions of poverty and the temptations of welfare, both of which were attributed the power to corrupt character and diminish personal responsibility. The only way to reduce poverty was to reduce teen pregnancy, which could be done with the "tough love" social engineering of welfare policy.

Although many of the regulatory measures of the act still affect the lives of teen parents on cash assistance, the most publicly apparent discourse around teen pregnancy undeniably emanates from and surrounds *16 and*

Pregnant and its spin-offs. As I have argued, the first two seasons of *16 and Pregnant* make very little of race, class, urban geography, the state of the economy, and the future of the nation in their depictions of what makes teen pregnancy occur and what makes it something to prevent. As these episodes appear to be primarily aimed at disciplining the sex lives of teenagers while generating profit, they present teen pregnancy as a product of personal behavior and a producer of personal drama and sacrifice. In doing so, they may help to debunk long-standing racist stereotypes surrounding adolescent pregnancy by portraying more white middle-class teen moms than poor teen moms of color, but this new biopolitics of teen pregnancy has many more implications.

Whereas 1990s teen pregnancy helped to usher in the severe regulation of welfare recipients and poor people at large through welfare reform, today's teen pregnancy operates in the service of promoting an apparently apolitical citizenship in which proper sex, reproduction, consumption, and recreation form the desired modes of participation in U.S. society. These episodes forward a multiculturalism that empties categories such as race and class of their connection to systems and hierarchies of power. While multiple policies and institutions differentially affect the choices of teens and teen parents—legislation and programs related to health insurance, abortion and contraception, sex education, welfare, immigration, and more—on the basis of race, class, gender, sexuality, and immigration status, this show is part of a broader trend of (a) portraying personal decision making as separate from social structures, (b) delinking social welfare and the formal state apparatus institutionally and in public consciousness, (c) channeling private funding and private industry into the business of cultivating a narrow definition of citizenship focused on intimate relationships, and (d) ignoring unequal access to resources and support for reproductive choices. While an older discourse of teen pregnancy forwarded racist and classist stereotypes and policies, it left open an opportunity for structural analysis (questions about the causes and consequences of poverty and racism) completely foreclosed in *16 and Pregnant.* The new biopolitical regime of teen pregnancy prevention, of which these texts are a part, coexists with and serves to completely obscure the more punitive work of welfare reform. As welfare reform pushes poor "noncompliant" families off the roles and into deeper poverty, materially enforcing their expendability, teen pregnancy prevention efforts ignore these families altogether. Rather than targeting the purportedly wayward teens of impoverished inner cities, these efforts focus on disciplining primarily white middle-class girls. In this way, they help to confirm and impose the disposability and invisibility of the nation's deeply impoverished.

Despite being significantly redefined, teen pregnancy remains in the public imagination a problem to be solved. Although some claim that the show is not effective in its teen pregnancy prevention efforts or may even be achieving the opposite, *16 and Pregnant* is at least in part a prevention strategy. As teen mom after teen mom is quoted as saying something similar to "I love my child. I don't regret my child, but I wish I had waited. I wish I hadn't gotten pregnant as a teenager, because I had to grow up so fast," it becomes clear that the goal is to prevent certain lives from beginning because those lives and the conditions they are thought to create are considered undesirable for individual bodies and, therefore, the social body. Even this explicit effort to dissuade teenagers in the audience from becoming parents "too early" is a somewhat confused and mixed set of messages. Often, their list of regrets form the narration to scenes of them loving their babies and surviving the experience relatively happily. There are other moments when the prevention message is disrupted entirely and teen pregnancy emerges as a valid choice. For example, in Christinna's episode, her husband, Isaiah, reasons that they will be fully able to realize all their life goals because when their child turns eighteen, they will be in their thirties with the rest of their lives in front of them, and they will not know what is "really important," he suggests, until they look into their child's eyes.[39] Nonetheless, Dr. Drew's urging to make "smart" sexual decisions provides the official message of the show and the backbone of the newest model of responsible adolescent citizenship. The proper adolescent citizen must be interested in the consumer practices and recreational activities defined by American popular culture, to which pro-creative sex and parenting are distinctly opposed.

NOTES

1. Piazza, "What Are the Most Dangerous Shows"; Jonsson, "A Force Behind the Lower Teen Birth Rate."

2. *16 and Pregnant*, seasons 1 and 2, 2009 and 2010.

3. Ouellette and Hay, *Better Living through Reality TV*, 12–14.

4. Abramovitz, *Regulating the Lives of Women*; Feldstein, *Motherhood in Black and White*; Gomez, *Misconceiving Mothers*; Hancock, *The Politics of Disgust*; Kerber, *No Constitutional Right to Be Ladies*; Kunzel, "White Neurosis, Black Pathology"; Luker, *Dubious Conceptions*; Michel, *Children's Interests/Mothers' Rights*; Roberts, *Killing the Black Body*; Solinger, *Wake Up Little Susie*.

5. Arai, *Teenage Pregnancy*, 4.

6. Luker (*Dubious Conceptions*, 84–86, 95–100) also points to the ways that teenage pregnancy had broad political appeal for tying concerns about African American reproduction and poverty to growing anxieties about increasing rates of out-of-wedlock births among whites. Conservative response to the freer sexual mores resulting from the social movements of the 1960s and 1970s combined with theories about the causes of poverty and welfare dependency to support the regulation of teen sexuality at large. However, the stigma of being an unwed mother applied primarily to those who were poor, unemployed, African American, and young.

7. Sparks, "Queens, Teens, and Model Mothers," 180; Neubeck and Cazenave, *Welfare Racism*.

8. Foucault, *The History of Sexuality* and *"Society Must Be Defended": Lectures*.

9. Wetzstein, "Congress Hopes to Cut Illegitimacy"; "Funders."

10. For example, the national campaign has provided witnesses at two of the three legislative hearings devoted exclusively to the issue of teen pregnancy between 1996 and 2010 (U.S.

Congress, "Teen Pregnancy Prevention" and "Preventing Teen Pregnancy"). The third included a witness who had served on a task force for the national campaign (U.S. Congress, "Social and Economic Costs," 9).

11. This is the language used by the national campaign to discuss its agenda before the House Subcommittee on Human Resources in 2001 (U.S. Congress, "Teen Pregnancy Prevention," 90). The MTV shows appear to be the most well-known endeavor of this sort to date.

12. Celebrity physician and addiction specialist Dr. Drew enjoys a large following resulting from his participation in the long-running radio series *Loveline*, in which he gives advice on sexual and relationship health. He is also known for *Celebrity Rehab with Dr. Drew* on VH1 and *Dr. Drew* on HLN (a CNN spin-off), as well as many other regular appearances on popular shows. He generally provides what is billed as expert opinion about a variety of personal issues.

13. For example, Republican senator Phil Gramm is quoted as saying, "It is a 'national policy of suicide,' . . . to continue the system under which a 16 year old can escape her mother by simply having a child and setting up an independent household with taxpayers' money" (Havemann and Dewar, "Dole Courts").

14. Teenage pregnancy rates have fallen, then risen, then fallen again in the years since welfare reform, with no determined correlation to welfare reform (U.S. Congress, "Teen Pregnancy Prevention," 5; Hao and Cherlin, "Welfare Reform and Teenage Pregnancy"; Acs and Koball, "TANF and the Status"; Duffy and Levin-Epstein, "Add It Up"). Also, whether welfare reform has alleviated or exacerbated poverty in its various forms has not clearly been determined (Danziger, "The Decline of Cash Welfare").

15. *16 and Pregnant*, season 2, "Unseen Moments Special."

16. *16 and Pregnant*, season 2, "Unseen Moments Special." Similarly, Ebony says that pregnancy is "getting in the way" of things, such as prom (*16 and Pregnant*, season 1, episode 4).

17. Amber's boyfriend buys a PlayStation and then later agrees to take it back to the store (*16 and Pregnant*, season 1, episode 3). Felicia's boyfriend buys expensive shoes just when she cannot afford the new stroller her baby needs (*16 and Pregnant*, season 2, episode 12). Christinna's husband buys new speakers for his car instead of things for the baby (*16 and Pregnant*, season 2, episode 16).

18. *16 and Pregnant*, season 1, episode 2; *16 and Pregnant*, season 2, episodes 1, 8, 9, 11.

19. For example, at the end of her episode, Kailyn says that the hardest thing about being a teen mom is "the fact that you have to give up your youth, your social life—it's nonexistent" (*16 and Pregnant*, season 2, episode 10). Also, many of them discuss the stares, gossip, and loss of friends as a result of being a pregnant and mothering teenager (*16 and Pregnant*, season 1, episode 2; *16 and Pregnant*, season 2, episode 11, "Life after Labor," April 20, 2010).

20. *16 and Pregnant*, season 2, episode 17.

21. *16 and Pregnant*, season 2, episode 17.

22. Scholars trace the emergence and popularization of theories of cultural pathology to describe "black family structure," "single motherhood," and "long-term dependency" (O'Connor, *Poverty Knowledge*; Katz, "The Urban 'Underclass'"; Neubeck and Cazenave, *Welfare Racism*, 152–54). All of these came to be increasingly associated with and attributed to teenage pregnancy in the 1980s and 1990s (Luker, *Dubious Conceptions*, 81–108; Pillow, *Unfit Subjects*, 37–39).

23. *16 and Pregnant*, season 2, episode 17.

24. *16 and Pregnant*, season 2, episode 17.

25. Pillow, *Unfit Subjects*, 1.

26. *16 and Pregnant*, season 2, episode 17.

27. For further discussion of neoliberal multiculturalism, see Duggan, *The Twilight of Equality*, 43–66; Chow, *The Protestant Ethnic*, 128–34.

28. Arai, *Teenage Pregnancy*, 115–16; Sylvester, *Second-Chance Homes*; Hudley, "Issues of Race," 115.

29. Skolfield, "Draft Talking Points."

30. *16 and Pregnant*, season 1, episode 6.

31. *16 and Pregnant*, season 1, episode 6.

32. Laura Briggs (*Somebody's Children*, 223, 235) discusses adoption as an ideal neoliberal solution to the increased poverty resulting from the state's abandonment of poor and working-class families. As she points out, poverty is assumed to be reason enough to separate a child from his or her birth parents, and the equation of what is "best" for a child within adoption debates is often assumed to be wealthy or middle-class parents.

33. *16 and Pregnant*, season 1, "Life after Labor."

34. *16 and Pregnant*, season 1, episode 6.

35. Although the first two seasons include a significant amount of focus on curtailed options for consumption and education—things that could be considered related to a life of poverty— evidence of serious financial hardship, real concern for survival, or dependence on social welfare rarely appears. Instead, as noted, financial concerns revolve mostly around sacrifices of luxury, recreation, and independence from parents.

36. Interestingly, Lori and Ashley—the other two pregnant teens in seasons 1 and 2 who choose adoption for their babies—are both products of teen mothers as well. Lori's birth mother could be said to have preempted Lori's potential poverty by giving her up for adoption, and Lori does the same for her baby (*16 and Pregnant*, season 2, episode 5). Ashley's mother appears to have escaped the fate of poverty that teen moms have been said to inflict on themselves and their children and has also managed to help Ashley foreclose that possibility for her daughter (*16 and Pregnant*, season 2, episode 19). In this way, the discourse that linked generational poverty, welfare dependence, and teen pregnancy so tightly is even further unraveled.

37. *16 and Pregnant*, season 2, "Life after Labor," April 20, 2010.

38. *16 and Pregnant*, season 2, "Life after Labor," December 28, 2009.

39. *16 and Pregnant*, season 2, episode 16.

Chapter Seven

Sensationalizing the Sentimental

National Culture and Futurity

Melanie Anne Stewart

Everywhere I go, I meet people who represent the best of America. They're hopeful, hardworking, determined, and proud. These Americans are quiet heroes. They raise strong families, run our factories, and grow our food. They coach Little League and soccer. They serve on the PTA; they're volunteers, help our neighbors; and they dream big dreams. The vision, the values, the character, and the can-do spirit that you find in our small towns have made America great. This is the America known for thriving farms and factories, for prosperous towns and cities, great colleges and universities, for solid communities and churches, all of them born out of American optimism, nourished and sustained by hard work and a belief that the American future is one of the limitless possibilities and that opportunity is an American birthright. There was a time not so long ago when each of us could walk a little taller and stand a little straighter because we had a gift that no one else in the world shared: we are Americans. We knew it without question, and so did the world. Those days are coming back. That's our destiny. . . . America's greatest days are yet ahead.—Mitt Romney, "The Best of America"

This futurist ode appeared in a video advertisement for 2012 presidential candidate Mitt Romney.[1] In the video, Romney's words are accompanied by a montage. Iconic footage from U.S. history is interspersed with sentimental familial imagery—a group of children reading, a young boy playing basketball, a girl staring into the distance. Romney's combination of historical national greatness, family values, and the potential of a prosperous national future plays to a sentimental national culture fixated on family values and children as the markers of futurity.[2] The Romney advertisement illustrates how specific familial ideologies, values, and morals are cemented to ideas of proper personhood and citizenship and thus embedded in ideas of national futurity. Romney's sentimental propaganda illuminates my discussion, which illustrates the paradoxes inherent in the MTV shows *16 and Pregnant, Teen Mom*, and *Teen Mom 2*.

Since airing in 2009, *16 and Pregnant* and its subsequent spin-offs *Teen Mom* and *Teen Mom 2* have documented the lives of pregnant teenagers. According to MTV, the aim of *16 and Pregnant* is to provide educational entertainment, focusing on "a 5–7 month period in the life of a teenager as she navigates the bumpy terrain of adolescence, growing pains, rebellion, and coming of age; all while dealing with being pregnant."[3] The show's successors, *Teen Mom* and *Teen Mom 2*, each follow four of the teenagers featured in seasons 1 and 2 of *16 and Pregnant*, respectively, to document their experience with their "new responsibility of being a mother."[4] With the shows, MTV claims to provide a responsible form of social programming, demonstrating the difficult reality of mothering as a teen, which would subsequently caution teens about the reality of teenage pregnancy, and promoting the use of birth control or complete abstinence. The shows are affiliated with the National Campaign to Prevent Teen and Unplanned Pregnancy, which offers free DVDs of *16 and Pregnant* along with a discussion guide for use in classrooms and other educational spaces. While the supposed educational premise of the shows is admirable in their publicly intended aims, this chapter argues that the mode of delivery, combined with the use of extratextual sources, forever thwarts the show's social aims. This chapter draws on examples across all seasons of *16 and Pregnant, Teen Mom*, and *Teen Mom 2* and engages with extratextual sources, including social media sites, tabloid articles, and their accompanying commentary sections. Through close textual analysis of the shows and their extratextual resources, I argue that the show's situation within two conflicting national cultures—the sentimental national culture, concerned with children, family, and futurity; and the sensational national culture, concerned with celebrity, money, and self-image—consistently thwarts its intended aim of preventing teen pregnancy.

I begin with a description of two competing national cultures at work within the contemporary United States: the sentimental and the sensational. First, drawing on the work of queer theorists Lauren Berlant and Lee Edelman, I describe how the image of the Child has become synonymous with notions of hope and national futurity. To illustrate this claim, I draw on key themes circulating throughout the mass public spheres and demonstrate how the family values of a sentimental national culture have become unquestionable in contemporary U.S. life. Second, I describe the central components of what I term the "sensational" national culture, whose obsession with celebrity, scandal, and social gains appears out of sync with the sentimental national culture. I demonstrate how the role of "celebrity" functions in contemporary life as the epitome of social success, and I argue that the combined power of reality TV and social media is frequently utilized to propel ordinary citizens to infamy. Finally, I discuss how the *Teen Mom* shows' appeal to both these opposing cultures, thus creating a paradox that will thwart the shows intended social aims.

SENSATIONALIZING THE SENTIMENTAL OR SENTIMENTALIZING THE SENSATIONAL? NATIONAL CULTURE IN THE CONTEMPORARY UNITED STATES

Political propaganda, such as the Romney advertisement, poignantly illustrates how images of a sentimental national culture obsessed with family values circulate unquestioned throughout the political and public spheres. As the Romney advertisement suggests, within the sentimental culture of the contemporary United States, the nation's value and futurity are imagined not for its preexisting, laboring citizens but for its future citizens—the toddler learning to read, the boy playing basketball, the girl that "dreams big dreams." Romney's description of America's "quiet heroes"—those citizens who are "hopeful, hardworking, determined, and proud" and who use these attributes to the benefit of the national future—highlights how the political public sphere has become an intimate public sphere in which sociocultural membership is imagined through personal acts and morals, particularly when these acts stem from or are directed toward familial ideologies.[5] As Berlant poignantly describes, "in the process of collapsing the political and the personal into a world of public intimacy, a nation made for adult citizens has been replaced by one imagined for fetuses and children."[6]

While I reference the Romney advertisement here, it is important to note that the political use of familial imagery to tug on the sentimental heartstrings of voters is by no means unique to the Romney campaign. The image of the Child has appeared with increasing prevalence in political and public spheres as the marker of hope and futurity.[7] In his excellent analysis, Edelman notes how "politics . . . remains, at its core, conservative insofar as it works to *affirm* a structure, to *authenticate* social order, which it then intends to transmit to the future in the form of its inner Child. That Child remains the perpetual horizon of every acknowledged politics, the fantasmatic beneficiary of every political intervention."[8] The use of the Child as the beneficiary of political interventions has become a particularly useful tool within the political sphere. In recent decades, issues previously considered private concerns—pornography, abortion, reproduction, marriage, and family—are now circulated en masse as key components in political debates about what "America" stands for.[9] While these concerns all have a familial undertone, their primary concern is with the protection of children. The image of the Child is invoked on both sides as key to debates on economic and social issues, as in policy suggestions and campaign propaganda: pornography will corrupt the minds of children and thus must be eradicated;[10] legislation allowing same-sex marriage must either be crushed in the name of protecting our children from the immorality of homosexuality or forcefully endorsed to allow for a future in which all citizens are afforded the same rights and benefits.[11] These double-binded debates are endless; however, these two examples poignantly demonstrate the manner in which the image of the Child is used as an alibi for almost all ideologies within the political and public spheres.

The use of the Child as the marker of futurity in the political sphere is just one facet of the sentimental national culture to which *16 and Pregnant, Teen Mom*, and *Teen Mom 2* appeal. A clear political device, the use of the Child in politics is effective only because of the mass social consensus that an appeal on behalf of children is impossible to refuse.[12] This notion is in no small part due to the circulation of the Child within all spheres of contemporary life as synonymous with hope, national future, innocence, and purity, and this association is consistently capitalized on. For example, a cursory glance at contemporary advertisements sees marketers using the image of the Child to sell everything from laundry detergent to water, cars, and financial services.[13] Additionally, in the past three decades, mothers and motherhood have had an increasing level of media attention that continues to this day. As Susan Douglas and Meredith Michaels note, "mothers and motherhood came under unprecedented media surveillance in the 1980s and beyond. And since the media traffic in extremes, in anomalies—the rich, the deviant, the exemplary, the criminal, the gorgeous—they emphasize fear and dread on the one hand and promote impossible ideals on the other."[14] Both of these extremes are demonstrated in *16 and Pregnant, Teen Mom*, and *Teen Mom 2*.

For example, Maci Bookout of *Teen Mom* is represented as exemplary of successful teenage mothers. Maci lives on her own, goes to college, supports herself and her son, and manages to successfully coparent him despite a strained relationship with the child's father. Contrasted against Maci is the criminal Amber Portwood (*Teen Mom*), whose deviant behavior led to her incarceration for up to five years. The use of extremes within the media reinforces the notion that we need to protect the children from the deviant and criminal mothers to which they are born. Additionally, the other extreme markets and depicts an extreme and perfect form of mothering to which all women are expected to aspire. The media, as the political and public spheres' product and tool, define what constitutes caring for and protecting our children, which prevailing heteronormative ideals mandate.

A persistent feature within the media is what Douglas and Michaels term the "new momism." The new momism is a consistent feature of the sentimental culture, insisting that "no woman is truly complete or fulfilled unless she has kids, that women remain the best primary caretakers of children, and that to be a remotely decent mother, a woman has to devote her entire physical, psychological, emotional, and intellectual being, 24/7, to her children."[15] The new momism is represented in Romney's advertisement, in which the "best" American citizens raise strong families, coach Little League and soccer, and serve on the PTA. However, several concerning issues exist when political and social propaganda centers on familial imagery.

First, they are in effect marketing the lifestyles for which they strive, appealing to the prevailing logic that the future must be both productive and reproductive, thus redefining women in relation to their reproductive potential. And MTV's series on teenage mothers only reaffirms this. The shows want to make teens wait until they are older and financially secure before becoming mothers. But that they will become mothers is unquestionable. At the end of each episode of *16 and Pregnant*, each teen laments that she wished she had "waited" to have children, rather than wishing she had never had children. The futures of these teens were unquestionably reproductive.

Second, they fail to account for the socioeconomic conditions that befall a large proportion of America's citizens. It is never widely acknowledged within the public sphere that the weight of these futuristic expectations bears down unequally on U.S. citizens. For the socioeconomic underclasses, the sentimental national culture posits the fantasmatic idea that if you work hard, remain optimistic, and are a good person, America and the dream it promises will ensure that all other aspects fall into place per the "American birthright." These fantasmatic notions are frequently cited in the personal narratives of *16 and Pregnant*, *Teen Mom*, and *Teen Mom 2*. For example, at the end of Amber Portwood's *16 and Pregnant* episode (season 1, episode 3), Amber is seen questioning her future with the sentimental logic illustrated throughout the political and public spheres: "Will Gary and I actually get married? Will we have more kids? Will we ever be able to make ends meet or buy our own home? Or am I just too young to handle all of this? It's hard to tell. As long as there is a happy family behind her she should be a good person when she gets older, ya know? I think we're doing pretty good so far, so we'll see how the future turns out." Amber's sentimental visioning of her future is rooted in the political and social promises made to her, however out of sync with the reality of her individual situation. She believes that if she works hard and her family is grounded in love, then she can live the familial good life of the American dream marketed throughout the political and public spheres. For Amber, who has no high school diploma, no formal qualifications, and little financial and familial security, her pregnancy seems to afford her a promising future that is tied to the image of the Child.

The sentimental national culture's central claim is clear: if we want a national future, we need to not only protect the children but also create them. The new momism and the media, combined with the futurist odes of political propaganda and prevailing notions that children secure our national future, create what Edelman terms "reproductive futurism." For Edelman, the image of the Child has become so central to discourse surrounding the future that to imagine a future that is not in some sense tied to the image of the Child and to reproduction is no longer possible: "The Child . . . marks the fetishistic fixation of heteronormativity: an erotically charged investment in the rigid sameness of identity that is central to the compulsory narrative of reproductive futurism."[16] In exalting the Child and embedding it within narratives of national futurity, contemporary sentimental culture markets reproduction as compulsory in discourses on what will count as proper personhood. Edelman notes that within contemporary culture, "if . . . there is *no baby* and, in consequence, *no future*, then the blame must fall on the fatal lure of sterile, narcissistic enjoyments understood as inherently destructive of meaning and therefore as responsible for the undoing of social organization, collective reality, and, inevitably, life itself."[17] While it is clear that the political and public spheres market reproduction, children, and family values as the epitome of the American good life, the desire for a specific, acceptable family formation is never widely acknowledged. Through the mediation of mass media and the public sphere, the desired child of the sentimental national culture is largely white, middle class, and born to heterosexual married parents who have jobs and homes and are generally financially secure, even though such a desire is out of sync with the reality of the contemporary United States.[18]

In *Teen Mom* and *Teen Mom 2*, MTV continues to follow participants who both exemplify and oppose this epitome of American good life. For example, Leah Messer of *Teen Mom 2* is, at the time of filming, either engaged or married to the father of her twin daughters, lives in her own home, has a job as a dental assistant, and owns her own car. In addition to this, Leah and her husband manage to finance extensive and costly medical care for one of their twin daughters, Ali, who suffers significant development issues. In contrast to the doting, sentimental narrative of Leah is *Teen Mom 2* cast member Jenelle Evans, whose narrative seldom includes her son, Jace, who remains under the primary care of Jenelle's mother. Throughout *Teen Mom 2*, as Leah rejoices as Aleeah manages to take her first steps, Jenelle's narrative sees her run away with stolen credit cards and be involved in domestic violence, drug abuse, arrests, and court appearances. Jenelle appears incapable of resisting the "fatal lure of sterile, narcissistic enjoyments," raising the question why MTV, with the educational premise of documenting the trials of teenage motherhood, continues to air her life when it no longer includes any such motherhood-related trials. The popularity of the *Teen Mom* franchise, at least in part, answers this question. Jenelle provides dramatic flair and controversy to a series, which otherwise would revolve around the more mundane theme of broken-down relationships and custody negotiations. In a sensational consumer culture preoccupied with the dramatic rather than the ordinary, MTV plays to an audience whose desire for controversy far outweighs any desire for sexual health education or visions of domestic bliss.

Appearing in parallel to the sentimental national culture I have described is what I term the "sensational" national culture, a culture obsessed with celebrity, financial gains, sex, social networking, material possessions, and image. This sensational national culture centers on overtly public people who are granted greater presence and a wider scope of agency than those who make up the rest of the population.[19] While some of these powerful individuals are of course politicians, the majority are imbued with a sense of power through their labeling as "celebrity." P. David Marshall argues that "the celebrity structures meaning, crystallizes ideological positions, and works to provide a sense and coherence to a culture. Celebrity status operates at the very center of the culture as it resonates with conceptions of individuality that are the ideological ground of Western culture."[20] This individualizing culture is illustrated poignantly in the narratives of *16 and Pregnant*, *Teen Mom*, and *Teen Mom 2*, with each episode framed around the teenage mother's perceived success or failure. The shows present teen pregnancy as an individualistic experience, and the teens are represented as either successful in reconfiguring their identities around their newfound motherhood or as failures when they fall victim to the "fatal lure of sterile, narcissistic enjoyments" as the reality of their new role as mother becomes overwhelming (see Murphy, this volume).

The driving force of contemporary sensational national culture is the media and technology's centrality to everyday life. Within sensational national culture, there is a strong connection between more traditional forms of media, such as television, film, and magazines, and newer forms of media, typically dubbed "social media," such as Twitter, Facebook, and a variety of online discussion spaces. The combination of traditional media genres and social media serves to fuel a national culture obsessed with celebrity, image, and public displays of humiliation and controversy. Seemingly at the sensational national culture's epicenter is reality TV. While MTV is quick to define *16 and Pregnant*, *Teen Mom*, and *Teen Mom 2* as "docu-series," in contemporary visual culture the genre is indivisible from the reality TV genre. Although recent decades have seen a proliferation of television shows under the rubric of reality TV, academics have noted how the genre has no single, discernible, or defining feature. The increasing array of academic scholarship on the genre has produced discussions on the hybridity of its form, its representation of identity, and its obsession with both image and celebrity. However, one of the most prolific areas of research has been the relationship between reality TV and documentary.[21] Early scholars of the reality TV genre defined it "as a televisual form that blurs traditional distinctions between information and entertainment, documentary and drama, [and] public and private discourses."[22] It is easy to see MTV's *16 and Pregnant*,

Teen Mom, and *Teen Mom 2*, with their aim of educational entertainment, reflected in this description. However, the relationship between reality TV and documentary is a tenuous one, with reality TV frequently being considered a lighter, less intellectual form of documentary. This association has led to the mass cultural impression of reality TV as "trash TV" with little social or political value. [23]

The linking between social media and reality TV is exceptionally strong, with many reality TV participants using social media spaces to mediate their representation, garner support, and generate publicity. The dramatic increase in technological advances in the past few decades has led to an increased prevalence of smartphones, tablets, and laptops at the fingertips of today's youth and has aided in the intersection of reality TV and numerous other extratelevisual devices. These extratelevisual devices are a prominent feature within sensational culture and include online discussion spaces, tabloid magazines, fan sites, blogs, and unofficial and official websites of reality TV's subjects. Of particular interest to this discussion is the prevalence of comment sections on news and media reports, which allow readers to post and debate their opinions on a subject or topic with a wider audience.

The intersection of extratelevisual discourses and reality TV is particularly prevalent in the plethora of reality shows produced by MTV and so aids in propelling the shows' subjects to celebrity. In 2009, the same year the network aired its first seasons of *16 and Pregnant* and *Teen Mom*, MTV launched the first season of its successful show *Jersey Shore*, which serves as an illuminating example of the power of reality TV and social media. The antics of the show's subjects, on *Jersey Shore* and off, saw them plastered on gossip sites and in tabloid magazines, propelling them to notoriety and making them into celebrities. As Misha Kavka notes, the show itself has become a cultural industry, with its own set of linguistic devices and terms. For example, Kavka argues that the *Jersey Shore* acronym GTL—gym, tanning, and laundry—"has literally become a term of cultural currency, meaning not only that it circulates broadly in culture but also that it functions as an exchangeable token, something that can be traded in for celebrity." The cast members heavily utilized the power of social media tools such as Twitter to aid their transition from unknowns to celebrities and with all the financial and social rewards that accompany such a label. Whereas previously the label "celebrity" was reserved for those with a discernible skill—acting, athletics, music, activism—the *Jersey Shore* cast is a poignant example of reality TV's capacity to turn "ordinary" people, without any such discernible skills or aspirations, into celebrities. The entire cast has capitalized on their participation in the show, with seven of the original eight receiving their own endorsement deals or entertainment projects. [24] As I write this chapter, *Jersey Shore* cast member Michael "The Situation" Sorrentino is a contestant on

Celebrity Big Brother UK, cementing his transition from the ordinary to celebrity.

It is difficult not to see the connection between the actions of the *Jersey Shore* and *Teen Mom* casts. If the educational message of *Teen Mom* is safe sexual practices, then the message from *Jersey Shore* is that acting out, particularly when under the influence of alcohol and drugs, is not only fun and entertaining but financially and socially rewarding. The reality show participants who successfully manage to use social media both to mediate their representation and for self-promotion get the most desirable of all careers in our sensational national culture—that of celebrity—and the show's educational premise does not negate the desire for such a label. In the following section, I draw on several *Teen Mom* and *Teen Mom 2* cast members to discuss how the young women are configured as mothers in the MTV shows and, paradoxically, as celebrities in the cultural texts of a sensational national culture fueled on scandal.

BAD MOTHERS, GOOD REALITY STARS: *16 AND PREGNANT* AND *TEEN MOM*

In August 2010, Farrah Abraham and Maci Bookout of *Teen Mom* appeared on the cover of celebrity tabloid magazine *Us Weekly*, illustrating their transition from ordinary teenage mothers into one of the public commodities commonly referred to as "celebrity." The teens, photographed with their children, appear visually flawless in their presentation. Out of sync with this image of perfection is the paradoxical headline reading "Inside Their Struggles." Caryn Murphy's chapter in this volume poignantly notes that the *Us Weekly* cover initiated an array of media coverage for the teenage mothers featured on *Teen Mom*. Subsequently, the teenage mothers joined other celebrity teen parents, such as Bristol Palin and Jamie Lynn Spears, on a plethora of magazine covers, all of which contain feature stories about the trials of teen motherhood, which are "ultimately presented as triumphs over adversity." Presenting teenage mothers as triumphant even in the face of such adversity marks *Teen Mom* as speaking to a sentimental national culture concerned with hard work, the protection of children, and family values. The shows present teen pregnancy as an individualistic experience, and the teens are represented either as successful in reconfiguring their identities around their newfound motherhood, as with Maci and Leah, or as failures when the reality of their new role as mother becomes overwhelming, as with Jenelle or Amber. However, *Teen Mom* and *Teen Mom 2* fail to acknowledge the political and social implications that result from individualizing the experience of teenage motherhood. In presenting the young mothers' triumphs or failings as individual experiences, the show fails to accurately represent the socioeconomic issues that so heavily affect the majority of pregnant teens and, indeed, mothers in general.

Although the sentimental national culture permeates the contemporary mass public sphere with family values and imagery, teenage pregnancy is no longer perceived as a social problem but rather an individual failing. Previously considered a victim of social circumstances, the teen mother has transitioned to a pathological subject concerned with her own narcissistic pleasures. [25] In individualizing the narratives of the cast, MTV serves only to compound this issue. The change in public opinion is represented poignantly in the story of *Teen Mom* cast member Amber. Earlier in this discussion, I note the hopes and dreams that Amber iterates at the end of her first MTV show in 2009. However, three years later Amber's future, at least for the next 2.5 to 5 years, holds nothing but jail. [26] Amber's journey on the reality TV show has been among the most tumultuous, which only *Teen Mom 2* cast member Jenelle rivals, and includes domestic abuse charges, drug abuse and subsequent drug arrests, and court-ordered rehab programs.

Most recently, Amber has come under fierce scrutiny after she opted to endure a five-year jail sentence rather than attend a drug rehabilitation program. The audience commentaries to news reports of Amber's private indiscretions represent the pathologized subjectivity of teen mothers. One responder to CNN's report of Amber's jail time says "heartbreaking my *** [*sic*]. Do the crime, pay the piper. Teens shouldn't be moms and this is a direct result of liberalism and the mentality 'if it feels good, do it.'" Another poster, identifying as "response2cnn," questions, "You mean that lack of judgment that results in getting pregnant as a teen might also result in committing crimes that leads to years in jail? Who would have thought it?" Other commentators are more concerned with wider social issues, such as jail sentences for personal drug use, the cost of prison time on taxpayers, and the disparity between Amber's sentence and those with more financial means and/or social prominence. [27] As expected, many other comments express concern for the future of Amber's daughter (Leah), with one responder exalting, "I feel so sorry for her little girl. One day she is going to find out the true reason she does not see her mom. I'm sure her father tries to keep the truth from her now because she is so young, but she will learn it when she gets older." [28] Interestingly, the range of comments seen on a report from CNN, typically considered a high-status news corporation, is paralleled in lower-status tabloid reports with a different demographic, such as *Perez Hilton*, *TMZ*, and *The Hollywood Gossip*. Tabloid websites such as these are products of a sensational national culture that cannot get enough of celebrity scandal. In a biting comment to *The Hollywood Gossip* report of Amber's decision, "Chip" berates the teenage mother:

I mean I enjoy the show because I love watching train wrecks unravel and self-implode on TV. That's why we all watch it and she is the worst kind of person; selfish and STUPID! I don't mean like "man, you are stupid!" I mean can't get a GED hasn't yet grasped 5th grade English. The saddest reality is that Gary is a waste of space too but a far superior option for Leah than bet [*sic*] fat dumb worthless ass! Fact! Hooray reality TV and the trash it produces![29]

Chip's comment here is interesting, and the use of the word "produces" is particularly poignant. In the on- and off-screen narrative of Amber's life, what remains open for debate is whether Amber's demise is a result of her lack of judgment, as one of the commentators suggests; the fatal lures of sterile, narcissistic enjoyments that Edelman describes; or her participation in the sensational national culture's commodification. Did MTV "produce" in Amber a "good" reality star at the expense of her mothering role? While there is no definitive answer to this question, it is fair to say that Amber's participation in the show had a negative impact on both her life and the life of her daughter, and unlike the majority of the population, Amber's daughter Leah will be able to watch an MTV-edited version of her formative years.

Comments such as Chip's illustrate the central paradox of *16 and Pregnant*, *Teen Mom*, and *Teen Mom 2*: their situation within the genre of reality TV and the sensational national culture that accompanies it consistently thwart any wider social aspirations. According to Chip, "all" the people that watch *Teen Mom* tune in to see "train wrecks," to see people and their lives imploding in front of them. In a sentimental culture that exalts the child, Amber is an example of a "bad" mother, while, paradoxically, to a sensational culture that praises celebrity and controversy, Amber is the epitome of a "good" reality star. The episode "Lashing Out" (season 2, episode 10), which sees Amber punching her child's father (Gary Shirley) in the face, saw a spike in the show's ratings, which continued through the season's end, rising from between 2.5 and 3.5 million viewers at the beginning of the season to 4.0 and 5.6 million viewers in the final three episodes.[30] Months before it aired, details of the domestic violence between Amber and Gary circulated heavily on tabloid gossip sites, detailing that MTV captured the whole event. The publicity that such sites generate can be said to have contributed to the spike in the ratings. Amber's story truly illustrates one of the show's central issues. As the user Chip suggests to us, the consumers of reality TV watch because they want to see "train wrecks"; they want controversy; and through Amber and Jenelle, MTV provides that controversy, translating it into media publicity and increased ratings for the network. In this sense, its situation within the sensationalist genre of reality TV, which praises its Snookis and Ambers, and reviles the boring life of domesticity, thwarts the educational premise of *16 and Pregnant*, *Teen Mom*, and *Teen Mom 2*.

The legal battles of Amber and, subsequently, Jenelle, not only called into question the duty of care that MTV provided but also served to demystify the network's representation of the trials of teen motherhood. While MTV claims that it illustrates the real-life trials of teen motherhood, notably absent from the series is specific information on the social welfare that the young women receive, if any, and their parents' financial contribution. The shows go to great lengths to represent the young women as victims of financial hardship, yet such hardship is represented through a need for diapers or formula rather than the more costly health care, pre- and postnatal care, hospital fees, and so on. In this sense, the shows dangerously misrepresent the financial burden of child rearing. The teens are represented as needing to work, in addition to schooling and child rearing, when in reality the women are paid a hefty fee for their participation in the show. Original reports circulating in 2010 revealed that the *Teen Mom* cast earned "$60,000 to $65,000 per season."[31] However, due to Amber's legal woes, the *Teen Mom* participant was forced to make her salary public knowledge, admitting that she earns $140,000 per six-month contract, which equates to $280,000 per year.[32] While it is not clear if Amber receives a premium for her notoriety, the financial rewards afforded the young women, who, like the *Jersey Shore* cast, lack any discernible or deserving talents, serve to contradict MTVs claims that they represent the "reality" of teen pregnancy. Even though Amber's financial rewards are now public knowledge, MTV continues to perpetuate the notion that the girls are subject to financial hardship. In the penultimate episode of the original *Teen Mom* series, Amber argues with Gary over day care costs, claiming she that cannot afford the $400-a-month fee, yet she earns a whopping $23,000 a month. Since the show began airing in 2009, three teenagers featured—Maci Bookout, Farrah Abraham, and Jenelle Evans—had breast augmentations, a surgery not financially available to the majority of young mothers yet one that speaks of an image-obsessed sensational national culture. One of the perceived strengths of *16 and Pregnant*, *Teen Mom*, and *Teen Mom 2* was that the youthful audience demographic to which they appeal is of similar age, similar socioeconomic conditions, and similar life experiences as the cast members. The high financial and social rewards bestowed on these teenagers not only serve to make a mockery of the show's aims but also market pregnancy as financially and socially rewarding, however out of line with reality these rewards may be.

In the wake of each major legal or social battle one participant encounters, the show comes under increasing scrutiny. For example, ranging across comments on tabloid reports of Amber's indiscretions is the role of MTV and celebrity physician Dr. Drew Pinsky in the demise of the cast members. One frequently cited concern in online tabloid report's comment sections is the lack of a duty of care that MTV and the show's producers provided. Of primary concern is the failure of producers and crew members to intervene in the domestic violence of both Amber and Jenelle. One particularly harrowing scene from *Teen Mom 2* sees current boyfriend Kiefer verbally and physically abuse Jenelle as the MTV cameras film from a distance. Another scene sees Jenelle viciously attacking another teenage girl as Kiefer cheers her on from the sidelines. It is difficult to believe the socially responsible message of the show as the adult producers idly stand by while two young girls fight, concerned more with their controversial footage than the well-being of the show's participants. And *Teen Mom* and *Teen Mom 2* are not the first time that MTV has come under such scrutiny. When a *Jersey Shore* episode saw a man punch cast member Snooki in the face, MTV received intense criticism for airing the scene and ultimately opted to follow the show with a domestic violence awareness message. It is difficult to consider *Teen Mom* and *Teen Mom 2* as socially responsible programming for the prevention of teenage pregnancy when they air scenes that speak directly to a national culture obsessed with train wrecks and scandals.

Kim Kardashian, herself a product and beneficiary of the celebrity-obsessed sensational national culture, blamed the MTV network for increasing teen pregnancies following a report claiming that ninety girls at a Memphis high school had given birth in the past twelve months. The Kardashian slams MTV for making "teen pregnancy seem cool in the eyes of young girls" and, with an allusion to the power of reality TV and the sensational national culture, notes that "these kids from these shows are all over the news, even on the covers of magazines, and have become almost like celebrities, but girls, these are not people you should idolize!"[33] Kim Kardashian fails to see the hypocrisy of her statement, seeming to offer herself as someone who could be idolized in their place. While teenage mothers' celebrity status may be unwarranted, Kardashian fails to acknowledge not only that she herself is an example of what a person can become through effectively utilizing reality TV and social media but that the highly publicized, celebrity lifestyle she consistently touts and represents serves to further position the celebrity identity as the ultimate career in the contemporary United States. Interestingly, it was the two most publicly controversial cast members, Amber and Jenelle, who lashed back at the Kardashian, highlighting the hypocrisy of her statement: "Last time I checked, Kim Kardashian had a sex tape floating around on the internet and I'm pretty sure she made a lot of money off it. She made a sex tape when she was younger and she wants to bash the girls on *Teen Mom*? If you read the articles about the show, they do nothing but talk about how the show reveals how hard it is for all of us. It doesn't glamorize anything! It shows the heartache we've all gone through." However, paradoxically, Amber continues, "We may be 'celebrities' because our face is out there, but it's only because we've done some bad things. That's not glamorous."[34] Amber fails to note that the financial and social rewards of celebrity are inherently glamorous to a sensational culture obsessed with financial gains and social prominence.

Unlike other public figures who gain power, notoriety, and financial rewards through artistic talents or educational, political, or athletic promise, the world of reality TV promises a young audience the dream of such power, notoriety, and financial rewards with seemingly little to no effort and, as is the case with *Teen Mom*, often without completing a high school education. Although Amber claims that the *Teen Mom* cast members are celebrities only because of their "bad" actions, some young mothers are attempting to utilize the media for self-promotion in the same manner that saw the *Jersey Shore* cast members cement themselves as celebrities. For example, as the original *Teen Mom* aired its final season, Farrah Abraham released a memoir entitled *My Teenage Dream Ended*, which, although greeted with mixed reviews, was ultimately featured on the *New York Times* bestseller list.[35] In addition to her foray into writing, Farrah has recently attempted to forge a career as a singer, with the teen mother having released two singles thus far.[36] Additionally, Farrah has utilized the power of social media to up her tabloid presence and, thus, celebrity status, starting "Twitter wars" with Kardashian family members as well as actress Demi Lovato. The specifics of these Twitter arguments are detailed on celebrity tabloid sites, increasing Farrah's visibility to the sensational national culture.[37] While Amber maintains that the teen moms' celebrity is a mere by-product of their participation, Farrah, Jenelle, and other *Teen Mom* and *Teen Mom 2* cast members are actively pursuing further media attention for self-promotion to cement themselves as permanent celebrity figures within a sensational national culture.

CONCLUSION

With *16 and Pregnant*, *Teen Mom*, and *Teen Mom 2*, MTV speaks directly to a sentimental national culture concerned with family values and the protection of children and a sensational national culture obsessed with celebrity, money, and scandal. The educational premise of the show represents the sentimental culture's desire to procure a particular type of American good life, consisting of financially and socially stable parents of an appropriate age, to secure the national future. In seeking to prevent teenagers from becoming mothers, the show positions teenage mothers as inadequate in comparison to the mothers featured in the mass public sphere and thus reinforces the sentimental mythology of heteronormative family values. However, the shows also serve to contrast the abilities of the teenage mothers they represent. Using the mandates of good motherhood that circulate through the mass public spheres of the sentimental national culture, MTV represents some of its young mothers as success stories, for example, Maci and Leah, and others as failures, for example, Jenelle and Amber. By continuing to document the narratives of Amber and Jenelle long after the trials they encountered no longer revolved around motherhood, MTV plays to a sensational national culture that relishes scandal and controversy. Amber and Jenelle are paraded as examples of bad mothers for the sentimental culture to criticize, falling victim to the sterile lures and narcissistic pleasures that Edelman describes, yet their consistent presence on celebrity gossip sites and in tabloid magazines labels them as good reality stars and, ultimately, celebrities.

The mass-mediated images of the sentimental national culture market a family-orientated lifestyle that offers the promise of the American good life and futurity imagined through the Child. In an economic climate where youth unemployment is rapidly rising, the issue of teen pregnancy could be less about lack of judgment or education and more about securing a future.[38] In a society that exalts the Child, attempting to transition from the identity of the Child to the identity of the hardworking adult is difficult when employment opportunities are scarce. As the future of some young women appears uncertain in this regard and mass-mediated messages consistently market the Child as the bearer of futurity, it is possible that teen pregnancy is more about securing a future through reproduction rather than inadequate sex education. While it is impossible to discern whether or not this claim is factual, what is certain is that the financial and social rewards offered to the participants in the MTV shows, regardless of how they perform their role of mother, are universally appealing. In addition to this, the episodes are laden with sentimental imagery of the children learning to walk, going to day care, and having birthday parties. The trials of teen motherhood that MTV claims to represent are essentially inaccurate representations of financial circumstances, arguments regarding coparenting responsibilities, and relationship strife. The major trials appear in the stories of Amber and Jenelle and relate to activities not specific to teen motherhood, such as domestic violence or drug abuse. Therefore, the combination of the sentimental and the sensational serves not to educate teens on the dangers of teen pregnancy but rather to market them as financially, socially, and emotionally rewarding. In a society obsessed with celebrity, sex, and money, the combination of teen motherhood, financial rewards, and infamy thwarts the educational premise of the shows.

NOTES

1. Romney, "The Best of America."
2. Edelman, *No Future.*
3. Baretto and Gatti, "MTV Press."
4. Baretto and Gatti, "Network Greenlights."
5. Berlant, *The Queen of America,* 5.
6. Berlant, *The Queen of America,* 1.

7. See Edelman, *No Future*; Berlant, *The Queen of America* and *The Female Complaint*.

8. Edelman, *No Future*, 2–3.

9. Berlant, *The Queen of America*, 1.

10. Jilani, "Three Leading GOP."

11. For example, the American Family Association launched a campaign targeted at the Home Depot for supporting gay pride events, claiming it was "deliberately exposing small children to lascivious displays of sexual conduct by homosexuals and cross-dressers, which are a common occurrence at these events. "

12. Edelman, *No Future*, 2.

13. For example, Evian Water simulated a large collection of babies roller-skating and performing tricks to a hip-hop backing track, reminding us that "naturally pure and mineral balanced water supports your body's youth." During the 2012 Super Bowl, an E*Trade Financial Services advertisement showed a toddler telling his father to go and discuss his financial future with the company, implying that if he does so, he can give his children "everything" in the future.

14. Douglas and Michaels, *The Mommy Myth*.

15. Douglas and Michaels, *The Mommy Myth*.

16. Edelman, *No Future*, 21.

17. Edelman, *No Future*, 13.

18. O'Reilly, *21st Century Motherhood*, 7.

19. Marshall, *Celebrity and Power*, ix.

20. Marshall, *Celebrity and Power*, x.

21. See Murray and Ouellette, *Reality TV* ; Kavka, *Reality TV*; Hill, *Restyling Factual TV*.

22. Kavka, *Reality TV*, 3.

23. Kavka, *Reality TV*, 1–12.

24. Kavka, *Reality TV*, 182.

25. Tyler, "Pramface Girls," 211.

26. "Amber Portwood Chooses Prison."

27. Frequently cited is the actress Lindsay Lohan, whose felony drug charges parallel Amber's; however, Lohan's sentencing of 90 days represents a clear disparity in comparison to the five years handed down to Amber.

28. Duke, *"Teen Mom* Amber Portwood."

29. "Amber Portwood Chooses Prison."

30. Gorman, "Tuesday Cable Ratings."

31. "Teen Mom Stars Earn More Than $60,000 a Season!"

32. "So True? So False?"

33. Kardashian, "To All Young Girls Out There."

34. Finn and Rhames, "Kim Kardashian."

35. Durham, "'My Teenage Dream Ended.'"

36. "Farrah Abraham."

37. Schreffler, "Twits-War!"

38. "Employment and Unemployment."

Chapter Eight

Pathological Motherhood, Parental Relationships, Expert Counseling, and Heteronormativity

A Framework of Anxiety and Reassurance through MTV's Teen Mom

Martina Thomas

In Western societies, the powerful and elite dictate what is deemed normal. These authority figures include individuals in government, education, media, and health care. In labeling what is viewed as normal, authority figures also present what is abnormal or pathological. Concerns regarding acceptable behavior, partnership, and ethnicity are some of the mandates that authorities dictate to the masses.[1] These requirements of cultural norms are further reified in other areas of life. One of the most influential institutions in popular culture is media—specifically, reality television.

In June 2009, the show *16 and Pregnant* aired on America's MTV network. The show was so successful that MTV created a spin-off to follow four of the original six cast members. *Teen Mom* subsequently aired in December 2009 and has recently commenced its fourth and final season. On the MTV show website, the following statement describes *Teen Mom*: "In *16 and Pregnant*, they were moms-to-be. Now, follow Farrah, Maci, Amber, and Catelynn as they face the challenges of motherhood. Each episode interweaves these stories revealing the wide variety of challenges young mothers can face: marriage, relationships, family support, adoption, finances, graduating high school, starting college, getting a job, and the daunting and exciting step of moving out to create their own families."[2]

In this chapter, a critical analysis of *Teen Mom* explains how the display of pathological motherhood, as well as difficult relationships with the parents of the teen mothers, create anxiety for these cast members. However, to alleviate some of the uncomfortable pressure on these emerging mothers, counseling experts are used to create a sense of reassurance for them. Using the concept of heteronormativity as a framework, I argue that the show's constructed representations of the "challenges of motherhood" and the editing of the show create a display of constant immaturity and sense of dependency for these young mothers. While they may want to be independent, these teen moms are constantly infantilized and reminded that they do not and can never fit the heteronormative ideal.

In this chapter, I provide further evidence of this argument through a discussion of the following: (1) transitions between commercial airtimes to convey producers' creation of pathology through the use of juvenile cartoon caricatures; (2) specific plot narratives of cast members to amplify how pathological motherhood and difficult relationships with family members create anxiety; and (3) the use of counseling experts in cast member narratives, along with the use of Dr. Drew on the reunion show, to help these women find reassurance in their lives.

THEORETICAL BASIS FOR ANALYSIS

Foucault notes that individuals in authority, through dictating normativity, seek not only to protect citizens but also to mold desirable characteristics of these citizens through their authoritative actions.[3] In doing so, these officials create the need to separate those who are desirable from those who are deviant. Part of this surveillance is linked to a person's sexuality; sexual preference is ultimately attached to ideology surrounding marriage and kinship ties.

This formation of the desirable citizen is further reiterated by Judith Butler when she states, "Variations on kinship that depart from normative, dyadic heterosexually based family forms secured through the marriage vow are figured not only as dangerous for the child, but perilous to the putative natural and cultural laws said to sustain human intelligibility."[4] As Butler notes, to be not only successful but also *safe* in a kinship organization, a child must have one mother and one father to sustain the normal and natural state of the family. When an individual steps out of these established norms, one becomes pathological and is seen as threatening to "human intelligibility." Single mothers are therefore considered harmful to their children because they are not part of a dictated union.

To understand the relationship between heterosexuality and motherhood, a historical analysis of motherhood is helpful. The "cult of true womanhood" or the "cult of domesticity" dictated how white upper-class women in England and the United States during the nineteenth century should properly act.[5] One of the key components to what was required of a true woman was that she provided a home for her children and husband and cared for their needs.

Over time, the requirements of motherhood dictated by the government shifted on the basis of the needs of the country. For example, as World War II progressed, women in the United States joined the workforce while husbands were away from their families. Yet, as mothers became employed workers, mother-blame theories soon became popular, and mothers were oftentimes blamed for their children's lack of care.[6] This was due to their inability to fulfill the roles of the "good mother" as they pursued employment in their husband's absence.

In addition to mother-blaming theories, the Moynihan report,[7] inspired by Oscar Lewis's[8] culture-of-poverty theory, pathologized black families in the United States for lack of a nuclear family structure. Despite the progression that women made in attaining equality with men, the "cult of true womanhood" abides in Western ideology and disallows for variation of motherhood for many women. Good motherhood and all that is attached to it (middle to upper class, white, married, heterosexual, mature, older in age, unemployed in the labor market, child care provider, and/or self-sacrificing) are still opposed to bad motherhood and all that is attached to it (lower class, black, single, immature, younger in age, employed in the labor market, and/or uneducated).

In *Teen Mom*, some of the elements of bad motherhood and lack of heteronormativity are emphasized and essentially create a sense of anxiety for cast members and viewers alike. MTV producers exploit this pathology of teenage motherhood through the use of transitions between commercials and narratives that caricature and infantilize cast members in their roles as mothers. In addition, some of the teen moms reveal problematic relationships they have with their own parents—negative interactions that these cast members worry will mirror their own relationships with their children in the future. Because of constant repetition of bad mothering practices and dysfunctional relationships that are put on display for viewers, these mothers seek counseling in an effort to determine how they can achieve more appropriate heteronormative ideals. These teen moms appear to experience temporary reassurance through counseling, but anxiety ensues when the teen mothers fail to meet heteronormative expectations—a vicious cycle that has been met with sometimes dire consequences. This evidence is presented in greater detail in the following sections of this chapter.

TRANSITIONS

Throughout the *Teen Mom* series, producers emphasize the uncomfortable juxtaposition of being a mother and being a young teenager, as evidenced by their use of transitions. Here, I use the term "transitions" to refer to the visual changes used to introduce the show when it begins, as well as visual changes used to signal shifting between cast member storylines or to signal a commercial break. All of these transitions are similar in appearance throughout the show and add to the visual continuity of *Teen Mom*. These transitions have stayed consistent throughout the series, despite the changes experienced in cast members' lives, as the girls go from teenagers without children to teenagers who become mothers.

At the outset of the show, producers use a scrapbook with the colorful title "TEEN MOM" on the front, along with caricatured doodles of a blue safety pin, a red heart with an attached white banner, a pacifier with a green grip ring, and a rubber duck with an orange beak. This scrapbook is outlined with a pink quilt; a red, white, and blue pom-pom; and a white baby bottle.

In this introduction, the producers are setting the stage for discomfort in their audience. Should viewers see these young women as immature teenagers not fit to be mothers? Are these mothers choosing between motherhood with a white baby bottle on one side of the bed and their teenage years with a red, white, and blue pom-pom on the other side? The narratives that producers highlight through the editing process justify the use of these satirized and childish transitions found on *Teen Mom*, as some of the mothers are deemed unfit and immature, while others do not regret their position as mothers but would have chosen motherhood at a later time in life.

In addition, at the beginning of each segment, the scrapbook opens with an image of one of the teens along with a doodle that a high school teenager would scribble in her notebooks during school. The aesthetic offered during these transitions presented by producers reifies the cast members' inexperience and minimizes their positions as teenage mothers. These transitions occur before and after every narrative for each cast member, as well as before and after each commercial break, and they are offered as a reminder to viewers that no matter how mature these mothers may seem, their youthfulness and age hinder their ability to parent properly.

For example, cast member Farrah, who finished an associate's degree in culinary arts and has moved to Florida to pursue a bachelor's degree during the series, decides that she wants to become a more responsible single mother to daughter Sophia. In the second season, she decides to move out of her parents' home to gain independence. In the fifth episode of the second season of *Teen Mom*, Farrah decides to sell her car online to buy a better vehicle.[9] However, in her attempt to be more responsible, she is cheated out of her money through an online scam. This is an especially vulnerable time for

Farrah. MTV viewers see her discussing the ordeal with her friend, while she is crying. Ironically, MTV flanks her disturbing storyline with the usual infantile transitions that are a hallmark of the series. In the beginning of the storyline, MTV producers present her name "FARRAH" in capital, bold, green letters and quickly transition to another teen mom's storyline, with the similar block name in bold, green letters.

Catelynn, another teen mom, made the difficult decision to place her daughter Carly for adoption so that she could finish high school and attend college. In the second season, Catelynn and her boyfriend Tyler, who is the biological father of Carly, celebrate their daughter's first birthday.[10] In the beginning of the episode, Catelynn's name is presented as block letters, although this time the lettering is in purple. In this episode, Catelynn and Tyler meet with the social worker at the adoption agency to discuss how they have been doing. During the conversation, Catelynn and Tyler reveal that their parents are not supportive of their decision to place Carly for adoption. Catelynn cries and talks about the hurt she experiences because of the lack of support from her mother. The segment closes with the sound of a camera shutter taking a picture of Catelynn crying, the photo being placed inside the *Teen Mom* scrapbook, and the scrapbook closing for a commercial break. In spite of the difficult issues that these teen moms go through, these transitions convey a sense of immaturity to viewers of the show.

Throughout the series, there is no effort to change these transitions, despite the maturity that these mothers have displayed in making important decisions. For instance, during the finale episode of season 3, Farrah is getting ready to celebrate her daughter's second birthday.[11] This is the first story of the episode. The *Teen Mom* scrapbook flips opens with a photograph outlined with a white border, taped in the white pages of the scrapbook. The photograph is of cast member Farrah leaving her home with presents in her hands, along with a cartoon image of a white cupcake with a green number "2" lighted candle on the bottom-right corner of the scrapbook page. This photograph transitions from a still photograph to video of Farrah walking down her front porch stairs. The name "Farrah" appears in the left-hand corner in large, green, block capital letters, outlined in black. Here again, Farrah's position as a mother throughout the series is viewed as infantile and therefore pathological.

The producers do not alter these transitions to highlight the evolution that these girls have experienced as a result of being parents. They limit these transitions to images of juvenile cartoons, reinforcing that these mothers are pathological because of their age. They also imply that the better alternative to being a single teenage mother is to be an older married mother.

CAST MEMBER NARRATIVES

In addition to the transitions provided by MTV, cast member narratives demonstrate a pattern of anxiety and reassurance. Here, I describe the narratives of each mother as portrayed on the show and the events and situations they experience that are typically associated with characteristics of bad motherhood. In addition, I describe interactions between the teen mothers and their families, as well as a synopsis of any counseling they have experienced to address the challenges in their lives that are stressed during the series.

The first cast member, Farrah, is a single mother of two-year-old daughter Sophia. In the second season of *Teen Mom*, viewers of the show discovered that the father of her child was killed in a car accident. Since revealing this tragic end of her boyfriend's life to viewers, Farrah has been learning to cope with this loss by attending counseling. This counseling has been used to help her not only grieve and deal with her depression but also work on her relationship with her mother, who physically assaulted Farrah, both on and off camera. Her mother eventually is charged with domestic assault and ordered to complete community service hours, which is documented for viewers on the second season.[12]

MTV producers have highlighted the tumultuous relationship between Farrah and her parents throughout the series, with very little focus on the support and love she receives from them. For instance, early in the first season, Farrah begins dating as a single mother, although her parents voice strong disapproval.[13] Farrah desires to achieve heteronormativity by finding a partner that can ultimately help raise her daughter. By the fifth episode, Farrah recognizes her parents' wisdom and shifts her focus to single parenthood, as she notes that guys her age are not ready for committing to a mother with a child.[14] Through these experiences, Farrah feels anxiety because of her parents' disapproval and because she is a single parent. While she aims to be a good mother and follow the advice of her parents, by the seventh episode of the first season, Farrah's relationship with her parents has deteriorated greatly, and she ultimately decides to move out of their home. Shortly after, her mother assaults her, which contributes to the "pathological motherhood" narrative that is conveyed in the show. Season 2 centers on how Farrah and her mother attempt to repair their relationship.

By the taping of the third-season finale, the relationship between Farrah and her mother is greatly improved, due in part to the counseling they attend together and separately.[15] During this episode, Farrah is trying to decide on whether to further her education in Florida and let her parents take care of Sophia while she is away from home. In an effort to motivate Farrah to allow Sophia to stay with her parents, Farrah's mother states, "You have to work on yourself so you can be happy for baby." Here, Farrah's mother is noting that the sadness and anger she experiences over the loss of Sophia's father will hurt her daughter and ultimately make her a bad mother. However, Farrah does not mask the anxiety over a potential decision that would require leaving her daughter behind. Allowing her daughter to stay with her parents is what constitutes bad mothering in Farrah's mind as she attempts to make this decision.

In Farrah's narrative, she has a strained relationship with her parents, which causes anxiety. While the relationship with her parents eventually improves, this cast member continually doubts her decisions for herself and her daughter, as her parents constantly remind her of why her decisions are wrong. Counseling seems to help provide reassurance that Farrah is making the right decisions, but that confidence in her parenting skills does not last long when she is confronted with her parents' opinions of her decision-making skills.

This anxiety and reassurance are highlighted as Farrah and her parents attend a counseling session in the tenth episode of the third season. [16] During counseling, Farrah admits that she would rather have Sophia live in Florida when she attends school, while Farrah's mother disagrees and states, "The concern I have is for Sophia. . . . I don't think it is wise at this moment. . . . I don't know why a person would want to go out and self-actualize and do all the things they want to do in life, but harm somebody in the process. . . . I believe Sophia will be harmed." The counselor later replies, "Farrah is the parent and she makes the call on her. She is not asking for approval." The support she receives from her counselor in that moment helps reassure Farrah that her decision is what is best for her daughter.

In comparison, Catelynn is a teenage mother who placed her daughter Carly for adoption with a heterosexual white Christian couple. Throughout the series, she and her boyfriend Tyler have remained together. There is a complexity in their relationship, however, that lends to an abnormal, non-heteronormative narrative. Catelynn's mother and Tyler's father are married, which makes this couple stepsiblings. Tyler's father is a drug addict who is regularly absent and in jail. Catelynn's mother struggles with alcoholism, which contributes to her angry outbursts captured for viewers. Her mother appears emotional and angry during several episodes because of this addiction to alcohol and because of the difficulties associated with her husband's regular absence, such as being a single parent to Catelynn's younger brother. Similar to Farrah's mother and her display of violence, Catelynn's mother presents a narrative of pathological motherhood through her addiction and anger.

The reiteration of the family dynamics shows a poor relationship in Catelynn and her mother's exchange. For example, in the sixth episode of the second season, Catelynn's mother is upset because her husband is in a court-ordered drug rehabilitation program. [17] In an effort to support her through this rough time, Catelynn asks her mother, "What do you need from me?" She responds, "I need help!" She then proceeds to state that Catelynn is lazy because she has not helped with chores around their home. Eventually, Catelynn gets up and cleans for her mother. Despite her desire to help her mother feel better, it is clear that Catelynn cannot assist her, which creates anxiety in this situation. In the following episode, Catelynn goes shopping for a prom dress with her mother.[18] Her mother is aggressive in her negative opinion of all the dresses that Catelynn likes. Later in the episode, Catelynn confides to her friend about her mother's difficult attitude: "She hates me because of me giving up Carly for adoption." Again, MTV producers highlight the dysfunction associated with Catelynn's life, particularly her relationship with her mother, as a cautionary tale to young viewers.

Eventually, Catelynn and her mother go to counseling together in an effort to improve their relationship. In the fourth episode of season 3, while at a counseling session together, Catelynn's mother admits that she does not have a good relationship with her daughter but would like to improve it.[19] She notes, "Ever since she gave the baby up, we haven't been close. . . . It wasn't that I was disappointed in her or mad at her because of it. I just felt like I was an outsider looking in. And I would find something out here and there and it wasn't from her." Catelynn then states that she does not confide in her mother because of her angry responses, which are highlighted by MTV producers throughout the series. The counselor asks Catelynn if she thinks her mother is "unpredictable," to which she responds affirmatively. This upsets Catelynn's mother and makes her cry. Eventually, her mother tells the counselor that she is proud of her daughter for making the difficult decision to place Carly for adoption, which is a welcome surprise to Catelynn. Through this counseling, this teen mother gains the assurance needed that she can have a better relationship with her mother and that she made the right decision to place her child for adoption, especially since she experiences constant anxiety over her family issues.

In Catelynn and Tyler's experience, friends, teachers, and social worker all agree that this couple made the right decision to choose adoption for their daughter. Despite the disapproval they experience for this decision from their family members, both Catelynn and Tyler constantly comment on how difficult their lives would have been if their daughter lived in the unstable environment that MTV producers capture for viewers. This narrative highlights that Carly's life could have resulted in disaster if these teens decided to keep their daughter in the toxic environment that obviously creates anxiety in their own lives.

As a cast member on *Teen Mom*, Amber has been personified as a dysfunctional mother with the most problems. This teen mom has a daughter, Leah, with her on-again, off-again boyfriend Gary. Gary and Amber attempt to achieve heteronormative ideals, as they consistently state that they want to stay together as a family for the sake of Leah. Despite this, their relationship has serious problems. For example, in season 2, Amber physically abuses Gary after he comments that she is a bad mother to Leah. [20] Because of this physical assault, Amber is legally mandated to take anger management and counseling to deal with her anger, depression, and anxiety. Like fellow cast members Farrah and Catelynn, Amber has a volatile relationship with her mother, who she notes is essentially absent in her life. In 2011, Amber attempted suicide. She was ordered to a residential counseling facility to work on her problems, which is captured for viewers on *Teen Mom*'s fourth season. [21] Nevertheless, Amber continues to struggle and has recently decided to go to jail for a five-year sentence instead of attending mandated court counseling for substance abuse. [22]

This narrative is the most disturbing in comparison to the other cast members. Amber displays violence and anger—characteristics that she states are a result of her anxiety disorder. In spite of this, she is in court-mandated counseling regularly, which is used to assure this cast member that her life is valuable and that her daughter needs her. Amber's narrative reflects the harsh reality of her anxiety surrounding motherhood and her difficult relationship with her daughter's father.

MTV producers fail to highlight Amber's attempt to improve her life, unless in a negative context. For example, in the second episode of the first season, Amber's aspirations to obtain her GED are presented. [23] In the midst of achieving her goal, though, Amber has to deal with Gary's negative attitude. She acknowledges this by stating, "Gary doesn't care that I want to get my GED. But I am doing it for Leah." Very rarely does the show stress how much Amber studied for the GED test in seasons 1 and 2. However, when Amber's attempt at her GED goals is revealed for viewers, there is a great deal of anxiety presented in the form of Amber's doubt that she can achieve her goals, based chiefly on the dysfunctional relationship she has with Gary. MTV focuses on Amber's inability to reach the heteronormative ideal of family life that she aspires to provide for Leah. Unfortunately, Amber does not receive much reassurance about her mothering during her tenure on the series.

Finally, cast member Maci and her narrative focus on the complexity of coparenting her son Bentley with her ex-boyfriend Ryan, whom she describes as selfish and immature. Throughout the series, these coparents have attended counseling to better their relationship. While counseling did not give Maci and Ryan the confidence to continue a romantic relationship, it did give them the assurance that they could successfully coparent. They are able to use the tools they receive in counseling to create the best possible situation for their son. While Maci has challenges with her ex-boyfriend throughout the series, her focus is on the well-being of Bentley. She, unlike the other cast members, has a great deal of support from her parents, which is occasionally depicted to viewers.

During the third season, Maci is living with her current boyfriend Kyle, who appears to be a positive role model in Bentley's life. Yet, there is a lot of tension in their relationship. In the third-season finale, this couple is having a conversation about Maci's desire to get married.[24] Kyle states that he is not sure if he wants to make that type of commitment. Maci then replies that she is "a thirty-year-old in a nineteen-year-old body" and that she cannot wait forever for Kyle to make a decision regarding marriage. Maci concludes her segment by crying and saying that she thinks she "screwed a lot of things up" when she got pregnant with her son Bentley. Similar to Amber's aspirations of achieving the ideal nuclear family for Leah, Maci's anxiety stems from her inability to establish a legal union with her boyfriend Kyle—a concern that very few nineteen-year-old American girls have to think about, unless in the context of young motherhood. In this case, MTV producers create this site of pathological motherhood in Maci's desire to be married.

Maci is by far one of the most stable and mature parents on the show. Her major problem is with her ex-boyfriend Ryan, who does not appear to sacrifice as much as Maci does for the sake of Bentley. Despite this, the cast member's desire to marry and therefore pressure her boyfriend to make a long-term commitment imposes heteronormative ideals. Conversely, Kyle remains cautious and does not want to commit to Maci for the rest of his life—at least not right now. Rather than respect him, Maci comes off as desperate for a union, which is abnormal in a society that places a great deal of importance on a college education as a young adult. This seems to be the balancing act that this teen mom faces as she struggles with her anxiety to find what is most important to her during the third season of *Teen Mom*—family or finishing college.

REUNION SHOWS AND DR. DREW

As noted earlier, *Teen Mom* utilizes counseling experts throughout the show to help these young ladies with the hardships associated with teen motherhood. These counselors are especially highlighted in the show during Farrah's and Catelynn's narratives, where cameras invade the normally confidential counseling sessions. More recently, the fourth season shared Amber's visit to a residential facility in California as well as the counseling sessions that she experienced while there.

In addition to the counselors used on the show, Dr. Drew hosts the reunion specials at the end of each season. As a famous white American male medical doctor, his expertise is drawn on during the season finale as he quotes statistical data on teen pregnancy. For example, on the third-season reunion, upon the return from each commercial break or prior to interviewing one of the teen moms, he consistently notes that there is a pattern of teen pregnancy in the United States.[25] He states, "If you are a teen parent, then there is a good chance that your child will be a teen parent." He then asks the cast members, "What will you do to prevent this?" His approach to pathologizing teen pregnancy shows how much these teen moms rely on his expert status, considering that his view of teenage pregnancy is inconsistent with statistical data from the Centers for Disease Control and Prevention, which notes a 37 percent *decrease* in the national teen birth rate from 1991 to 2009.[26]

Dr. Drew's expertise does not go unnoticed by the cast members. For example, on the season 3 reunion show, Maci states that since Dr. Drew is present and can serve as mediator, she would like to address communication problems she is having with her ex-boyfriend Ryan.[27] She notes that he has a "switch," where, one minute, they get along and the next, he calls her negative names. Ryan notes that Maci pushes his buttons and that he cannot hear her after reaching a certain point during arguments. Dr. Drew then advises these coparents that during these types of situations when communication is difficult, they should agree to discuss the problem at a later date. Maci and Ryan both agree that that is good advice and tell Dr. Drew that they intend to follow his instructions.

Here, the use of Dr. Drew as a counseling expert helping these single teen mothers adds to the rhetoric of pathology often associated with lack of heteronormative ideals. Because they are teen moms, these cast members need help and advice about the proper way to deal with their issues to gain reassurance as mothers. Season after season, they are reminded of this need for expertise on parenting as Dr. Drew takes center stage on reunion shows. This expert even alludes to the fact that he stays in contact with cast members off camera to give them advice and help. This continual guidance and direction are often a reminder that perhaps, if these teen moms had waited to have their children, pursued their education, and gotten married first, they would not need Dr. Drew's help now.

CONCLUSION

This chapter highlights how the constructed representation of MTV's *Teen Mom* creates both anxiety and reassurance for cast members. This constructed representation of the "challenges of motherhood" emphasized how the edited juvenile transitions and difficult relationships with parents establish a sense of anxiety in cast members and viewers alike. Through the use of caricatured editing transitions, MTV producers further pathologize the "challenges of motherhood" for these cast members. Viewers understand the difficulties but learn that these issues are oftentimes self-imposed and made worse through the decisions of these cast members. It serves as a warning to viewers that they too can end up in these problematic and pathological positions. The discomfort and anxiety are extended to viewers to make them think twice about potential decisions that can have negative altering effects on their lives.

In terms of difficult parental relationships, Farrah's mother undermines her decisions regarding Sophia, while Catelynn's mother finds it difficult to accept her decision to place Carly up for adoption. In these narratives, Farrah has to contend with violence from her mother, and Catelynn has to contend with anger and "unpredictability" from her mother. Amber notes that her mother has been absent, while Maci's parents are generally supportive, although very rarely is that support captured for viewers.

In response to the "challenges of motherhood," counselors featured throughout the series, as well as Dr. Drew, help alleviate anxiety surrounding their problems. While they find reassurance, viewers note that the respite from their anxiety is short-lived, as these women are oftentimes reminded that they do not fit heteronormative ideals. MTV producers emphasize the negative aspects of these cast members' lives in hopes that viewers notice that the mothers are unable to function without the help of counselors. Unfortunately, help-seeking behaviors in the United States remain largely stigmatized in the mainstream. Therefore, the use of counselors in addition to the rhetoric of pathological teenage motherhood does well to further reinforce risks associated with early teenage sexual behavior.

What is lacking in this popular reality television show is appreciation for the complexity of these teenagers' lives as mothers. Their support systems are rarely acknowledged. When they are, the display can be perceived as deviant, as in the case of Farrah's and Catelynn's complicated relationships with their mothers. These displays of support are also in the form of counselors who serve not only as help in difficult times but as individuals who remind these teens of why they are displaying pathological mothering practices in the first place.

In presenting each narrative as abnormal, these mothers are stereotyped as problematic, infantile, and absent of heteronormativity. In this case, lack of heteronormativity in Farrah's narrative is due to the absence of a committed relationship and violence with her own mother, who does not set a good example of mothering. In Catelynn's narrative, the reminder of her inability to take care of her biological child, whom she places for adoption, along with her abnormal family situation lends to this inability to achieve heteronormativity. In Amber's case, the inability to keep a "nuclear family" intact and the display of violence in her home are what stop her from achieving heteronormativity. Finally, Maci's narrative includes hardships with the father of her child, along with a new boyfriend who does not want to marry her—realities that restrict her from realizing heteronormativity.

Despite these presentations, a savvy viewer of this television program should understand that while these teen moms may endure hardships, their realities on this show are mediated. This edited construction of their "lived experience" on display for viewers is really only a small portion of their lives. Support systems are not revealed; presentation and achievement of goals are largely absent; and acknowledgment of maturity in motherhood displayed by cast members' decisions is virtually nonexistent. MTV producers present *Teen Mom* as a show based on "constructed reality" that cannot be relied on as an accurate representation of cast members' lives. However, MTV producers displaying cast members in this pathological way have enabled the network to generate a "successful" show that draws in numerous viewers.

NOTES

1. Rubin, "Thinking Sex."
2. "About *Teen Mom* (Season 3)."
3. Foucault, *Discipline and Punish.*
4. Butler, "Is Kinship Always Already Heterosexual?" 16.
5. Welter, "The Cult of True Womanhood."
6. Bowlby, *Child Care and the Growth of Love.*
7. Moynihan, *The Negro Family.*
8. Lewis, *La Vida.*
9. "Secrets and Lies," *Teen Mom*, season 2, August 16, 2010.
10. "The Next Step," *Teen Mom*, season 4, August 1, 2012.
11. "Pros and Cons," *Teen Mom*, season 3, September 20, 2011.
12. Salomone, "Debra Danielson."
13. "How Many Chances?" *Teen Mom*, season 1, December 14, 2009.
14. "A Little Help," *Teen Mom*, season 1, December 29, 2009.
15. "Pros and Cons."
16. "Stay with Me," *Teen Mom*, season 3, September 6, 2011.
17. "Trial and Error," *Teen Mom*, season 2, August 31, 2010.
18. "Senior Prom," *Teen Mom*, season 2, September 7, 2010.
19. "Spring Break," *Teen Mom*, season 2, August 10, 2010.
20. "Lashing Out," *Teen Mom*, season 2, September 28, 2010.
21. Chang and Behrendt, "*Teen Mom* Star."
22. Everett, "*Teen Mom* Star."
23. "How Many Chances?"
24. "Pros and Cons."
25. "Finale Special: Check Up with Dr. Drew—Part 1," *Teen Mom*, season 3, September 27, 2011.
26. "About Teen Pregnancy."
27. "Finale Special: Check Up with Dr. Drew—Part 2," *Teen Mom*, season 3, October 4, 2011.

Part III

Making Room for Daddy: Images of Teen Fatherhood

Chapter Nine

16 and Pregnant, Masculinity, and Teen Fatherhood

Reconciling or Reinforcing Stereotypes?

Jennifer Beggs Weber and Enid Schatz

Just as much of the academic work on teen pregnancy and parenthood focuses on young women and largely ignores their male partners, the narratives on *16 and Pregnant* are from the teen mothers' points of view. Teen fathers on the show have a narrowly defined script of possibilities, one limited by tropes of masculinity. In almost all episodes, the fathers are portrayed as irresponsible, immature, and unwilling or unable to "step up." While these representations may be meant to discourage teen pregnancy among girls by reminding viewers that "sex won't make him yours and a baby won't make him stay";[1] they go further, reinforcing a dominant cultural norm that fathers, particularly teen fathers, are not going to provide for their children nor even "be there."[2]

Whereas girls are taught to be mothers from a very early age with clearer definitions of how to be a "good mother" (e.g., providing basic care and nurturance), how to be a "good father" (outside of being a "breadwinner") remains vague.[3] While there are limited examples of how to be a "good dad" on *16 and Pregnant*, the show makes it clear that young men's lack of preparation and their inclination toward "boys behaving badly" make it nearly impossible for them to "step up." When given the opportunity to speak for themselves, however, young fathers highlight their desire to "be there" for their children, even if they cannot provide financially for them.[4] In this chapter, we focus on tensions between what it means to be a "good dad" and "being a man" as presented in the first two seasons of *16 and Pregnant* and through interviews with twenty-six teen fathers from a small Midwest city.

PARENTING ON REALITY TV

Although MTV's *16 and Pregnant* is sometimes labeled a "docu-series," perhaps to make it more aligned with documentary—read "real"—portrayals than with "reality TV," Slocum defines shows of this type as reality soaps.[5] Their primary feature is that "they find compelling storylines in hundreds of hours of videotaped life and, through careful writing and editing, shape the real-life subjects into reality-show characters."[6] He goes on to frame these shows as moving beyond documentaries, as they are not just a form of observation but also a form of storytelling—creating a story from the available footage. Douglas's reading of reality TV similarly highlights its crafted nature with calculated casting, out-of-sequence editing, and the majority of footage shot ending up on the cutting-room floor.[7] Thus, it is not always clear how representative the crafted story is of the lives of those on-screen. The story created is both "real and unreal."[8]

The appeal of reality TV is that it provides a lens into others' lives with the aim of making us connect with them, feel superior to them, or figure out how to live our own lives better.[9] While *16 and Pregnant* purports to be about teen pregnancy, the main theme of the show is instead the relationship between the teen parents.[10] A primary message, aside from teen motherhood being challenging, is that she will be a *single* teen mother—teen fathers are likely to be peripheral at best or leave altogether.[11] Thus, one of the aims of the show is to connect with teenage girls and provide them with a warning suggesting that they avoid this predicament by living their lives better.

In addition, reality TV helps to shape and reinforce ideas about gender roles and values.[12] By bolstering certain identities and cultural norms, reality TV helps to mold gender role expectations.[13] Parenthood is a way of performing gender;[14] *16 and Pregnant* exploits this performance to show how intricately connected femininity and motherhood are,[15] while simultaneously highlighting the tension between young men's masculinity and fatherhood. In the case of fatherhood on *16 and Pregnant*, the editing creates a particular image and story of what teen fatherhood looks like in the United States, which further supports the overall agenda of the show warning young women from becoming teen mothers because their partners are not likely to "step up" or stick around.[16]

Thus, it is not surprising that on the show, the teen mother is shown completing the majority of caregiving,[17] whereas young men are repeatedly shown more concerned with sports, stereo and videogame equipment, and their cars rather than with caring for and supporting (financially or emotionally) their partners and children. Males' focusing on material objects rather than relationships fits with tropes of masculinity, especially in boyhood, that are associated with space, freedom, exploration, trouble (good and bad), adventure, and independence,[18] as well as being separate from family life.[19]

Fatherhood, which denotes the need to be responsible, contribute financially, et cetera, then clashes with general expectations of young masculinity in ways that motherhood and femininity do not.[20] This conflict or, at the very least, liminality influences the ways in which teen fathers navigate both fatherhood and masculinity but also the ways in which the labels and definitions of "good" and "bad" dads are constructed on the show and in reality.

TEEN FATHERHOOD IN THE UNITED STATES

Teen fathers in the United States are reported to be more often African American or Latino,[21] more often from lower socioeconomic backgrounds,[22] and more likely to take part in deviant and delinquent behaviors, such as gang membership and drug use.[23] As the "fact sheet" connected to *16 and Pregnant* reminds readers, "8 out of 10 guys don't marry the teen mothers of their babies and most couples don't stay together at all."[24] So not only are teen fathers at risk for poverty and delinquency, but it is also unlikely that they will marry their child's mother. This does not mean that young fathers are fully absent from their partners' and children's lives; however, it does contribute to the overarching stereotype that fathers are generally bad boys. And conventional wisdom dictates that bad boys make bad fathers.[25]

A primary feature of being a good father in the United States is defined as having the ability to financially support children.[26] Thus, for many young men, becoming a father is incentive to finish their education, find employment, or discontinue delinquent behaviors.[27] Because many of these men had absent or abusive fathers, often the young fathers in these studies express a desire to parent differently than their fathers parented them.[28] The structural realities of limited economic opportunities mean that even good intentions do not necessarily lead to young men's ability to fulfill these aims.[29]

"Good fathers" should also be "loving, affectionate, involved, nurturing and consistent in the raising of [their] children."[30] For many teens, the birth of a child interrupts the process of transforming "immaturity, habits and attitudes of childhood into responsible adult behaviors."[31] Thus, it is not surprising that young fathers struggle with issues related to responsibility and maturity and that it becomes easy to stereotype them as uninvolved and irresponsible.[32]

For obvious reasons, financially supporting a family is challenging for the types of men who often become teen fathers. In addition to limitations stemming from age and education, these teen fathers often live in neighborhoods with limited (legitimate/legal) economic opportunities and high rates of incarceration.[33] Although middle-class white heterosexual men may be able to integrate caregiving into the provider role, as a form of "nurturing" or being "responsible" while remaining masculine,[34] these attributes are less likely to be viewed as a possible route to masculinity and good fatherhood among lower-income men and men of color.[35] Thus, men who are likely to become young fathers need to find other routes to becoming "good fathers."

In work by José Rubén Parra-Cardona and colleagues, being a good father according to teen Mexican fathers involved moving beyond the deviant behavior of their past—for example, recovering from addiction and stopping gang and other illegal activity—and "demonstrating a commitment to their children by remaining actively involved in their lives."[36] As in a number of other studies, being involved in the life of one's child's largely came in the form of "being there" and, when possible, providing material and emotional support.[37] Parra-Cardona et al. found that their respondents tapped into positive notions of masculinity that connected to responsibility; "being a man" was synonymous with "taking care of your responsibilities."[38] While the young men in Parra-Cardona's study did struggle with the idea of becoming fathers, for the most part, in their view they were making an effort to be committed fathers. This sort of effort, though, is either downplayed or altogether lacking on *16 and Pregnant*. Instead, teen fathers are generally portrayed as absent, selfishly choosing themselves rather than "being there" for their partners and children.

DATA AND METHOD

We are both avid viewers of *16 and Pregnant* and *Teen Mom* and have used these shows as a teaching tool and as researchers. We have watched most episodes multiple times and evaluated many of the themes related to race, class, and gender. We also have examined the episode summaries, episode guides, blogs, and other products created by MTV and the National Campaign to Prevent Teen and Unplanned Pregnancy that are related to the show, to understand how they view and present ideas related to fatherhood. We watched all the episodes from seasons 1 and 2 of *16 and Pregnant* and selected four young men as case studies—one "bad father" and one "good father" from each season. The "bad" fathers typify most of the portrayals of young men on the show; we selected two young men who highlight clashes between masculinity and fatherhood in multiple ways. The two "good" fathers were among the very few that provide exceptions to the rule suggested by MTV that teen fathers are "bad fathers." By being "good" in ways unattainable for the majority, these two young fathers show the limited script of possibilities for most young men.

To understand the portrayal of fathers, we re-viewed the episodes used as case studies, taking notes on the themes and actions presented that related to masculinity and fatherhood and where the two either complemented or came into conflict with one another. These included the relationship (or lack thereof) between the teen parents, caregiving practices of the father, "stepping up," affinity for "male" activities (sports, cars, etc.), notions of responsibility (e.g., financial contributions), and what it means to "be a man." We transcribe some of the language used by others about the young men, as well as their own words that describe their feelings and actions. Our analysis shows how MTV crafts a particular image of teen fathers, which highlights the tension between being a "good father" and the natural tendencies of young men to be irresponsible, immature, and focused more on their stuff (trucks, video games, other women) than on generating and maintaining a positive relationship with the teen mother or child.

We complement the analysis of fathers on *16 and Pregnant* with in-depth interviews with twenty-six teen fathers from "Greenlawn," a relatively diverse Midwest city with a population of about eighty-five thousand.[39] In 2009, the teen birth rates for Greenlawn and the surrounding area were even higher than state and national averages (e.g., 31.6 per 1,000 for women fifteen to seventeen years old, compared to 19.7 for the state and 19.3 nationally).[40]

As part of a larger study on teen fatherhood, the lead author conducted in-depth interviews with twenty-six young men in 2010. Interviews lasted one to two hours and were recorded, transcribed, and accompanied by field notes made immediately following the interview. Each of the men received a $20 gift card to a local discount store in exchange for his time. The Institutional Review Board at the University of Missouri approved the study.

Due to the difficulties of locating teen fathers, since they are not as identifiable as teen mothers, the respondents in this study were part of a convenience sample.[41] They were contacted through snowball sampling and gatekeepers (teachers, principals, and other members of the community) who offered access into several different networks of teen fathers. The sample was primarily working-class but included individuals from the middle or upper-middle classes and some whose families would be classified as living below the poverty line. Fifteen men identified as white, eleven as black or biracial. They were sixteen to twenty-one years old at the time of the interview, but all had fathered their children while still teenagers (nineteen or younger). Importantly, all of the men claim paternity; they identify as fathers, openly claiming and/or parenting their children.

The interviews followed a conversational structure, influenced by an interview guide and the individual respondent's interests. At some point in the interview, each respondent was asked, "What does it mean to be a good dad?" It is their responses to this particular question and the ways that fatherhood and masculinity are linked that we analyze in this chapter. There is no stratification of the sample in the analysis, since men of different classes and race used similar ways of talking about what it meant to be a "good father."

ANALYSIS

The majority of the episodes of *16 and Pregnant* focus on relational issues
between the teen moms and their babies' fathers,[42] yet the show's portrayal
of teen fathers is limited in scope. Teen fathers, in general, are frequently
stereotyped as absent, selfish, and uninvolved;[43] the teen fathers on *16 and
Pregnant* are similarly typecast into one of two categories: "good dads" or
"bad dads," with the majority of fathers falling into the latter group.

The adjectives used to describe the teen fathers in MTV.com's episode
summaries are almost always disapproving. The descriptors include *unfaith-
ful, irresponsible, immature, inconsistent,* and *video game playing.*[44] *Video
game playing* signals the link in the eyes of MTV between "bad" fatherhood
and a stereotypical expression of young men's masculinity. The images presented on the show are of teen fathers who live up to these negative descriptors and who show their masculinity not through being providers but through
their interest in sports, their cars, video games, and other women.

The dominant message of the show is that teen moms will also be single
moms—the father will be absent at worst, peripheral at best. But even if he is
there, she will do the majority of the work.[45] Of course, the show is positioned from the mother's perspective, her voice narrating the strategically
chosen displays of various events and discussions. And although the father's
voice is heard throughout, his perspective is rarely given more than scant
attention. The reality that child care often falls on the shoulders of women
should perhaps go without saying, but the stories that MTV tells about the
role of teen fathers is overwhelmingly negative.

Teen Moms Are Single Moms

> Adam promised to step up now that Aubrey's here. But it seems he's stepping
> out instead. (Chelsea, season 2, episode 4)[46]

Chelsea's comment succinctly summarizes teen fathers' portrayal on *16 and
Pregnant*. Many of the fathers are present, even if only sparsely, during the
scenes when the focal character is pregnant, sporting promises of commitment to their new family. But a predictable pattern usually follows—eventually, they will fight and he will leave. The young man is unwilling to take on
the selfless burden of having and caring for a child. Adam, for example,
repeatedly promises Chelsea throughout her pregnancy that he will "be
there" for the long haul, but Adam's unreliability is reinforced by Chelsea's
recurring unanswered calls and texts. And while Adam is there before and
during the birth, the baby's complications require an extended stay at the
hospital. When the day arrives for Chelsea to take the baby home, Adam is

unreachable. Having stayed up the night before working on his car, he sleeps through her phone calls, subsequently missing the baby's homecoming.

Maci and Ryan's (season 1, episode 1)[47] story follows a similar path. Ryan, too, makes many promises in the beginning: he proposes marriage; he and Maci move into their own apartment; he has the baby's name tattooed in large script on his right side. But as with Adam, after the baby is born, his role as a father moves from generally peripheral to largely absent. Maci's voice-over complains that Ryan "gets a lot of quality time in with his friends" while taking on little to no responsibility in the care of their son.

In season 2, the same script continues: teen pregnancy plays out differently for teen mothers and teen fathers. In Kailyn and Jo's episode (season 2, episode 10),[48] unlike the other two couples highlighted, Jo's parents mediate Jo and Kailyn's relationship. Their admonishments that he "step up" and "be a man about it" are a constant thread throughout the episode. Jo insists that he is "trying to help her out, so she's not a single mother." Despite being reprimanded by his parents for the selfishness that his comment represents, Jo's statement speaks to larger issues at play—particularly the assumption that teen mothers will also be single mothers.

The repeated representations of unreliable and absent teen fathers suggest to viewers that teen moms will have to shoulder the responsibility of a new baby without the fathers' help. This theme is reinforced in various situations—not just those of abandonment or fickleness. For example, during Maci's pregnancy, Ryan works second shift as a diesel mechanic while Maci is in school during the day; their schedules leave little time for them to be together. Consequently, Maci's description of their situation during her pregnancy includes claims of loneliness stemming from Ryan's absence. Jo and Kailyn also struggle to find time to spend together, balancing her school and his third-shift work schedule. Arguments ensue throughout the episode about his not being around. The general absence of their partners contributes to the idea that (teen) fathers are only peripherally important. Whether he is working or he leaves altogether—either way, he will not be around.

While it could be argued that these displays of young fathers working show "responsible masculinity," because their absence is due to their acting as providers, the choices they make about how to spend their money often contradict that image. In most of the shows where young men have access to money—whether money they earn or money they receive from parents—they often are shown spending that money on tattoos, their cars, stereo or video game equipment, or generally on themselves, rather than selflessly providing for their partners and children. Thus, even when young men are shown as capable of being providers, their access to money is often used to show their tendency toward irresponsible choices that reinforce the theme that the teen mother will have to manage on her own.

Bad Boys Make Bad Dads

> When I told Josh I was keeping the baby, he broke up with me. (Nikkole,
> season 2, episode 2)[49]

Teen mothers are expected to grow up, take their lives and their babies' lives seriously, and think about the future (e.g., school, self-sufficiency). Fathers, however, are most often portrayed as not having to take the responsibility seriously. This gendered distinction stems from the combination of two cultural assumptions. First, the feminization of birth control has resulted in the supposition that women are responsible for birth control and pregnancy prevention. Hence, the consequences that result from failing to manage birth control effectively become primarily theirs.[50] Second, as suggested by Michael Kimmel's work on young men, the stage of adolescence is becoming longer and longer for many men, and this stage is wrought with learning and maintaining gendered roles and expectations. However, the historical markers that traditionally signified masculinity (e.g., family, steady job) have come to denote adulthood for men and women. The consequence, according to Kimmel, is a general confusion of what it means to be a man, specifically an adult man.[51] These points—combined with cultural expectations that link masculinity to freedom, space, independence, and toughness—result in a script that sets young masculinity against fatherhood.[52]

A frequent theme on the show is the mothers' wishing aloud that the fathers would/had to grow up too. For example, when Adam steps out of the picture, going three weeks without seeing his daughter, Chelsea says, "The reality is he's just not ready for this. He's not ready to grow up and take responsibility. He's not ready to get a job and be . . . a little family." But Adam's absence is nothing new. The on-again/off-again status of their relationship did not just begin with their daughter's birth. Even before she was born, scenes repeatedly portray Adam's ordering Chelsea around, being emotionally manipulative and generally selfish. The same is true for Ryan. The classic scene where Ryan orders a pregnant Maci to get out of the truck and check for a flat tire proves illustrative. And then there's Josh and Nikkole—a relationship plagued by control and verbal abuse—that which the aforementioned quote adeptly demonstrates.

In addition to having poor relationship skills, teen fathers on the show are portrayed as being more interested in sports, cars, and video games than their partners and children. Ryan is shown repeatedly spending time and money on his dirt bikes. In season 1, episode 3, Gary gets reprimanded by Amber for buying video-gaming equipment when he is supposed to be saving for diapers.[53] Similarly, in season 2, episode 16, Christinna questions Isaiah's priorities when he uses some of his paycheck to buy expensive stereo equipment for his car.[54] These images of new fathers as more interested in *things* than their families reinforce stereotypes of masculinity as a selfish endeavor that can be accomplished only through "bad behavior."[55]

.The importance of these examples rests in the message they send about who teen fathers are. The majority of teen fathers on *16 and Pregnant* are portrayed not just as bad dads but as bad guys in general. Rarely are teen fathers portrayed as good guys making bad choices in their struggle to make sense of new fatherhood. Importantly, this "bad boys make bad dads" script further stereotypes teen fathers as generally bad characters, as men who will callously abandon the mother and her baby.

Good Dads: The Exception Proves the Rule

> I did not have to sell that truck. I did not have to work two jobs. I did not have to move out. I did not have to buy her everything. I didn't have to do none of it, but I did it because I wanted it to work. (Corey, season 2, episode 8)[56]

According to MTV, when it comes to teen fathers, the "good ones" are few and far between. Typically, each season presents only one or two fathers as being "good dads." Here we present two well-known "good dads" as examples: Tyler (season 1, episode 6)[57] and Corey (season 2, episode 8).[58] When these fathers are set alongside the myriad of irresponsible absent dads portrayed in the other episodes, their existence serves only to reinforce the idea that most teen fathers are bad fathers.

When the question "Who are the 'good dads' on *16 and Pregnant*?" was posited to students in our class on teen pregnancy and parenthood, which uses the show as a platform for raising topics of discussion, nearly all one hundred of them unequivocally answered that Tyler and Corey were "good dads." Tyler's and Corey's stories provide some direction in terms of what it means to be a father; however, the fact that their situations are somewhat extraordinary, relative to the majority of other fathers on the show, serves only to inadvertently reinforce negative stereotypes.

Corey is slightly older than Leah, and having already graduated from high school and gained full-time employment, Corey's location is also different from the majority of the other teen fathers portrayed on the show. His position, however, is used to strategically portray what a "good" teen father looks like: he works; he provides; he makes sacrifices; but most important—he's "there." Having gotten pregnant after only one month of dating, Corey and Leah decide to stick it out, to make it work, but as the quote neatly demonstrates, there is a distinct difference between the expectations of teen mothers and teen fathers. While teen mothers are expected to make sacrifices, to "grow up," fathers don't have to. Especially given the brevity of their relationship prior to getting pregnant, Corey's commitment to and sacrifices for Leah and their twins become even more powerful. Despite the obviousness of Corey's love for his daughters, he too is rarely around, largely because he's working two jobs. In this episode, his absence is presented as sacrifice rather than callous abandonment.

Corey fulfills the culturally defined primary roles of all fathers, working *and* providing, but importantly, his ability to do so compared to many of the other fathers on the show has much to do with his age and social position. These tasks are much harder to accomplish by young men who have not finished high school. His access to a livable wage may increase his inclination to use that money to support his family, whereas, as discussed earlier, the small amounts of cash that other young fathers have is often shown being spent for seemingly frivolous items in place of supporting their families.

Tyler is also admired as one of the select few "good dads." His love for his unborn child, as demonstrated by the letter he writes to her (read through his tears of simultaneous joy and sadness), serves as the primary example of his commitment to Catelynn, to his daughter, and to being a "good dad." The catch, however, is that Tyler does not actually *father*. The act of placing their daughter for adoption exempts Tyler from needing to financially, physically, emotionally, or socially parent his child. So, in contrast to the teen fathers in other episodes, he does not face the day-to-day struggle of balancing self, child, parenting, work, relationships, and the like—the topics that seemingly characterize many of the other episodes.

The stories of Tyler and Corey serve as exceptions. Teen fathers are not expected to be "good dads," so on the rare occasion when they are, their success is to be highlighted. Taken together, their stories also serve to reinforce the stereotype that most teen fathers are unreliable and immature. But, more than just stereotypes, these assumptions serve as a powerful backdrop to the story that MTV tells about teen fathers, providing two important points: first, being a good dad (or a bad dad, for that matter) is framed as a choice—one that teen mothers do not have; second, being a "good dad" is about being there—or being strong enough to admit that you cannot be there.

This last point serves as the only seemingly similar characteristic between Corey and Tyler. Both of them are "there"—for the pregnancy, for the birth, and for the hard decisions that come afterward. They are there when Leah and Catelynn, respectively, become stressed or depressed, playing the classic role of the hero, saying "everything will be okay." Also, Corey and Tyler cry in their respective episodes. Although this may seem trite, these displays signify that they are emotionally present and supportive in a way that is not stereotypically "masculine," particularly for young men. Their commitment to their partners is portrayed as exceptional and therefore somehow super-masculine. However, Tyler and Corey are atypical—in their situations, in their reactions, in the ways in which they participate (or do not participate) in the parenting of their children—further reinforcing the general rule that teen fathers are generally selfish, absent, and uncaring. It is also of note that both

Tyler and Corey are able to become "good" fathers in the eyes of viewers because of the continuation of their stories on *Teen Mom* and *Teen Mom 2*. While not all of the fathers whose stories are seen on these extensions of *16 and Pregnant* are positive, for both Tyler and Corey, their portrayals as "good dads" are literally "seen" through their extended stories.

Fathering in Greenlawn

> I mean, a good dad is there when you need him . . . when you want him to be. I mean, he'll basically do anything for ya. (Josh, twenty, with two sons)

The limited script of possibilities that MTV offers its viewers mirrors the views of other teen fathers. In response to questions about what it means to be a dad, Joel's (nineteen, with one daughter) answer was common: "That's hard . . . because I'm still learning myself." Similarly, Tre, a sixteen-year-old with a baby on the way, said, "I just . . . I don't really know what to do." The uncertainty expressed by young fathers attempting to verbalize what it meant to be a (good) dad speaks to the absence of larger discourses that tell men how to father, particularly for young men for whom being a breadwinner is difficult due to economic conditions and socioeconomic status.

Much of the research on teen fathers relies on the central tenet that fatherhood and masculinity, generally, are based in large part on being a financial provider.[59] According to a number of studies, teen dads identified their inability to provide financially as a barrier to being a good father.[60] This issue becomes especially problematic given the limited job availability for young fathers, stemming from factors such as age, lower educational attainment, and decreased skill sets. Fourteen of the twenty-six fathers in this study reported being employed. However, of these fourteen, ten worked at part-time minimum-wage jobs, so the amount and stability of their contributions were typically low. As William Marsiglio states in his work, "Since many disadvantaged fathers feel inadequate about their ability to fulfill the breadwinner role, they often dissociate themselves from it in order to minimize their sense of inadequacy."[61]

In place of seeing their role solely as a provider, the young men from Greenlawn highlighted something they could do: "be there." For these adolescent fathers, "being there" was the equivalent of being a "good dad." For example, Daniel, eighteen with a six-month-old and another baby on the way, explained that "just being there makes me a good dad." Similarly, Tre, who admitted that he did not "really know what to do," went on to say that being a dad is about "just being there with your child, just being there for his life."

For many of the young men, the idea of "being there" was about more than just physical presence, however. Similar to the stories of Corey and

Tyler, the narratives of the young men interviewed speak to tensions among expectations of fatherhood, masculinity, and breadwinning, particularly for men with limited opportunities. For instance, Paul, eighteen, with a daughter, said the following about being a good dad: "[He] makes the money to spend on her . . . but it's not just spending money on your kid. You gotta be there for 'em." Quinton, sixteen with a newborn daughter, offered a similar response about being a "good dad":

> To be there for it, to support it, to love it, and to know that material things doesn't matter, that your child would rather for you to be there than to have all . . . all [types] of material things to remember you by because those material things . . . sooner or later, they gonna go away. The clothes, the shoes, sooner or later she's gonna grow out of it . . . so I feel that to be a good father is just . . . try to give your all and to always be around and to try to love it unconditionally.

Hence, the theme of "being there" is an attempt to negotiate the expectations of fatherhood in the face of the limited job availability for young fathers, stemming from factors such as age, lower educational attainment, and decreased skill sets.

DISCUSSION

Teen fathers face significant challenges to provide (e.g., school, minimum wage jobs), so "being there" becomes a way for them to define good fatherhood in achievable terms. What is different about fathering and mothering, both in Greenlawn and on *16 and Pregnant*, is that while dads have a choice of whether or not to "be there," mothers do not. Although abortion and adoption are available choices, for teen mothers on *16 and Pregnant* and adolescent girls faced with pregnancy more generally, keeping the baby is largely presented and viewed, not as a choice, but as a nondecision. Subsequently, "being there" for young mothers is an expectation, something that is supposed to come naturally and therefore is not rewarded (although it is punished when not fulfilled). Yet, fathers who make the choice to "be there" are rewarded, like Corey and Tyler. Framing teen fathers' participation as a "choice," not something that is constrained and often determined by structural realities, allows MTV to create a simple dichotomy between "good dads" and "bad dads." By showing young men as making a choice to spend their money or time irresponsibly, it reinforces the idea that teen mothers are destined to struggle alone. However, as viewers, we have to remember that this is a simplified and crafted version of the realities these young men and women face.

One of the main differences between what we know about the young men from Greenlawn and the young men portrayed on *16 and Pregnant* is their point of view about what it means to be a "good dad." The young fathers from Greenlawn are given the opportunity to express their intention to "be there" for their children. Even when MTV allows the young fathers' voices to be heard, these segments are chosen to fit the overall limited script of possibilities outlined by the show. Perhaps, if asked, the fathers on the show would also express their intent to "be there" for their children and the wish to be able to help and provide in some way.

The popular press often asks if *16 and Pregnant* and *Teen Mom* glamorize or show the challenging reality of teen pregnancy and parenthood.[62] The data thus far show that teens view the messages largely as a warning, that teen motherhood is difficult.[63] We know less about how the limited script of masculinity and fatherhood presented on the show is affecting young men's ideas about parenting. Is it "good" to show teen fathers as "bad fathers," or does it simply reinforce a pessimistic view of the roles that young men can and do play in the lives of their partners and children?

Either way, we need to problematize the seemingly simple portrayal of teen fathers as selfish and uncaring. Although this stereotyping fits neatly within the messages that MTV seems to be sending—that teen pregnancy is always and everywhere a social problem, specifically one that unequally burdens teen mothers more than men—it fails to consider the contradictions among masculinity, femininity, parenting, and youth, which teen mothers and teen fathers must both negotiate.

NOTES

1. National Campaign to Prevent Teen and Unplanned Pregnancy, *"16 and Pregnant*: Important Things."
2. Furstenberg, "Good Dads–Bad Dads"; Luker, *Dubious Conceptions*; Hernendez, *Fatherwork in the Crossfire.*
3. Thorne, *Gender Play*; White, "About Fathers."
4. Lemay et al., "A Qualitative Study"; Parra-Cardona, Wampler, and Sharp, "'Wanting to Be a Good Father'"; White, "About Fathers."
5. Slocum, "The Real History of Reality TV."
6. Slocum, "The Real History of Reality TV," para. 3.
7. Douglas, *The Rise of Enlightened Sexism.*
8. Smith, "Critiquing Reality-Based Televisual Black Fatherhood."
9. Douglas, *The Rise of Enlightened Sexism*; Slocum, "The Real History of Reality TV."
10. Peters and Aubrey, "MTV's Docu-series Delivers."
11. National Campaign to Prevent Teen and Unplanned Pregnancy, *"16 and Pregnant*: Important Things."
12. Dowd, "'Telling It Like It Is'"; Douglas, *The Rise of Enlightened Sexism*; Pozner, *Reality Bites Back.*
13. Dowd, "'Telling It Like It Is.'"
14. Walzer, *Thinking about the Baby.*
15. Murphy, "Teen Momism on MTV."

16. Murphy, "Teen Momism on MTV"; National Campaign to Prevent Teen and Unplanned Pregnancy, "Evaluating the Impact."

17. Murphy, "Teen Momism on MTV"; Peters and Aubrey, "MTV's Docu-series Delivers."

18. Thorne, *Gender Play*.

19. White, "About Fathers."

20. Hays, *The Cultural Contradictions of Motherhood*; Walzer, *Thinking about the Baby*.

21. Martin et al., *Births*.

22. Bunting and McAuley, "Research Review"; Klein, "Adolescent Pregnancy."

23. Thornberry, Smith, and Howard, "Risk Factors for Teenage Fatherhood."

24. National Campaign to Prevent Teen and Unplanned Pregnancy, *"16 and Pregnant*: Important Things."

25. Kiselica, *When Boys Become Parents*; Luker, *Dubious Conceptions*; Paschal, *Voices of African-American Teen Fathers*; Weber, "Becoming Teen Fathers."

26. Furstenberg, "Good Dads–Bad Dads"; Roy, "You Can't Eat Love," 253.

27. Lemay et al., "A Qualitative Study"; Parra-Cardona, Wampler, and Sharp, "'Wanting to be a Good Father.'"

28. Lemay et al., "A Qualitative Study"; White, "About Fathers."

29. Roy and Dyson, "Making Daddies into Fathers."

30. Morman and Floyd, "Good Fathering," 117.

31. Thompson and Walker, "Satisfaction with Parenting," 678.

32. Hernendez, *Fatherwork in the Crossfire*.

33. Thornberry, Smith, and Howard, "Risk Factors for Teenage Fatherhood."

34. Connell, *Masculinities*; Townsend, *Package Deal*.

35. Roy and Dyson, "Making Daddies into Fathers."

36. Parra-Cardona, Wampler, and Sharp, "'Wanting to Be a Good Father,'" 379.

37. Roy, "You Can't Eat Love"; Roy and Dyson, "Making Daddies into Fathers"; White, "About Fathers."

38. Parra-Cardona, Wampler, and Sharp, "'Wanting to Be a Good Father,'" 380.

39. Weber, "Becoming Teen Fathers."

40. Martin et al., *Births*.

41. Lemay et al., "A Qualitative Study"; Thompson and Walker, "Satisfaction with Parenting."

42. Peters and Aubrey, "MTV's Docu-series Delivers."

43. Kiselica, *When Boys Become Parents*; Luker, *Dubious Conceptions*; Paschal, *Voices of African-American Teen Fathers*.

44. For example, see "MTV's *16 and Pregnant* Season 1," http://www.mtv.com/shows/16_and_pregnant/season_1/episode.jhtml?episodeID=153833#moreinfo.

45. Murphy, "Teen Momism on MTV."

46. "Chelsea," *16 and Pregnant*, season 2, March 9, 2010.

47. "Maci," *16 and Pregnant*, season 1, June 11, 2009.

48. "Kailyn," *16 and Pregnant*, season 2, April 20, 2010.

49. "Nikkole," *16 and Pregnant*, season 2, February 23, 2010.

50. Luker, *Dubious Conceptions*; Weber, "Becoming Teen Fathers."

51. Kimmel, *Guyland*.

52. Kimmel, *Guyland*; Thorne, *Gender Play*.

53. "Amber," *16 and Pregnant*, season 1, June 25, 2009.

54. "Christinna," *16 and Pregnant*, season 2, November 30, 2010.

55. Kimmel, *Guyland*.

56. "Leah," *16 and Pregnant*, season 2, April 6, 2010.

57. "Catelynn," *16 and Pregnant*, season 1, July 16, 2009.

58. "Leah," *16 and Pregnant*, season 2.

59. Furstenberg, "Good Dads–Bad Dads"; Roy, "You Can't Eat Love."

60. Allen and Doherty, "The Responsibilities of Fatherhood"; Dallas and Chen, "Experiences of African American."

61. Marsiglio, *Fatherhood*, 330.

62. Danielle625, "Teens Want Fame"; Hoffman, "MTV's *Teen Mom*."

63. National Campaign to Prevent Teen and Unplanned Pregnancy, "Evaluating the Impact."

Chapter Ten

Teenage Fathers

The Disruption and Promotion of the
Heterosexual Imaginary

Andrea M. McClanahan

From 2009 to 2010, the birthrate among teenage girls in the United States dropped 9 percent. In a nineteen-year period (1991–2010), the birthrate among teenage girls dropped 44 percent.[1] Despite the decline in teen births, the coverage of pregnant teenage girls has increased through a variety of reality television shows, including *Teen Mom* and *16 and Pregnant*. McCarthy explains, "Reality television [serves] as a place where popular culture and social science [overlap] via a realist ideal in which social norms, mechanisms of conformity, ritualized scripts, and modes of interaction [are] put on display."[2] Reality television, especially shows aired on MTV aimed at teenagers and young adults, provides a playground of representations for how individuals are to act in various situations. Furthermore, these television shows are narratives that can be seen as "an iconic social representation of moral action, an expression and preparation. . . . Narrative enables us to understand the actions of others and endow them with meaning, because it is through narratives that we live and understand our own existence."[3]

In approaching the television shows *Teen Mom* and *16 and Pregnant*, I embrace the idea that gender is a performance.[4] I also view fathering as a performance because what is considered "good" or "bad" fathering behavior is socially constructed in the same way our beliefs about what it means to be a man or woman are constructed. Many studies have unveiled representations of fatherhood in texts, including religious narratives,[5] sitcoms,[6] and reality programming,[7] but few have looked at the construction of teenage fathers.[8] In the case of teenage fathers—where representations are scarce—the media images work to show young men how to be fathers and perform fatherhood. For instance, a search on Amazon.com for "self-help books for teenage mothers" yielded over one hundred books, such as *Surviving Teen Pregnancy: Your Choices, Dreams, and Decisions*,[9] *Your Pregnancy and Newborn Journey: A Guide for Pregnant Teens*,[10] *Teen Moms: The Pain and the Promise*,[11] and *Dear Diary, I'm Pregnant: Teenagers Talk about Their Pregnancy*.[12] While several of the titles suggest that the books could apply to both mothers and fathers, the descriptions of the books and the visual images on the cover, which often include female faces or bodies, clearly show that the books are geared toward teenage mothers. In a similar search on Amazon.com for "self-help books for teenage fathers," the results were far fewer: two. The books *Teen Dads: Rights, Responsibilities, and Joys*[13] and *Teenage Fathers*[14] appear to be the only books available exclusively for young men facing a life-changing situation. The lack of literature available to young men about fathering makes it necessary to evaluate the images of teenage fathers being shown on television—especially on MTV, where the key audience is young adults. Mia Consalvo argues that media representations of young men are important to dissect, "as they may show gender as a process being worked out—rehearsed, refined, and modified."[15] Furrow explains, "The social influences that have shaped the role of fathering can be identified within the cultural narratives that record the beliefs and values of a given era."[16]

In this chapter, I interrogate the representations of teen fathers in various episodes of *16 and Pregnant* and *Teen Mom* to uncover how the heterosexual imaginary is supported and disrupted. I argue that the construction of teenage fathers on these television series argues against the heterosexual imaginary— or the belief that, to achieve a sense of well-being in life, one must be involved in a heterosexual romantic relationship.[17] Ingraham asserts,

> Through the use of the heterosexual imaginary, we hold the institution of heterosexuality as timeless, devoid of historical variation and as "just the way it is" while creating social practices that reinforce the illusion that as long as this is "the way it is" all will be right in the world. Romancing—creating an illusory—heterosexuality is central to the heterosexual imaginary.[18]

The heterosexual imaginary is an important concept in understanding the potential underlying causes of teenage pregnancy. The idea that young women get pregnant on purpose to keep their boyfriends is a pervasive one. In the *Teen Mom* episode "Teen Dads," Dr. Drew points out that "eight out of ten dads do not marry the mothers of their children,"[19] making sure that young women realize that getting pregnant is not a viable means to maintain their romantic relationships. Despite the statistics proving that the majority of teenage pregnancy situations do not end in "happily ever after," the young women portrayed in *16 and Pregnant* and *Teen Mom*, at least in the beginning of their journeys, largely expect their relationships with the babies' fathers to work out. This hope in the "happily ever after" demonstrates collusion with the heterosexual imaginary. Taking the heterosexual imaginary a step further—into what is expected of a heterosexual relationship—after being involved in a romantic heterosexual relationship, the couple is supposed to reproduce. The production of a nuclear family—with a mother, father, and biological child—feeds into the performance of heterosexuality and the fulfillment of the heterosexual imaginary.

In the remainder of the chapter, I focus on (a) analyzing *16 and Pregnant* and *Teen Mom* for areas where the heterosexual imaginary is supported, (b) uncovering the key constructions of teenage fathers in *16 and Pregnant* and *Teen Mom* to demonstrate where the heterosexual imaginary is called into question, and (c) discussing how the disruptions of the heterosexual imaginary through the construction of teenage fathers can be seen as a deterrent for teenage pregnancy. I accomplish these goals through a textual analysis of various episodes of *Teen Mom* and *16 and Pregnant*. While my primary focus is on the individuals included in the first season of *16 and Pregnant* and the first incarnation of *Teen Mom*—Maci and Ryan, Amber and Gary, Catelynn and Tyler, and Farrah—I include some of the story lines from other seasons as males speak about their experiences of being a teen father.

EVIDENCE OF HETEROSEXUAL IMAGINARY

For a thorough analysis of *16 and Pregnant* and *Teen Mom*, an understanding of how the heterosexual imaginary is supported through the texts is necessary. Specifically, the portrayals of teen moms and their romantic relationships or how the teen moms construct their romantic relationships in the television series often falls into the hegemonic notion of the heterosexual imaginary. The heterosexual imaginary relies on the concept of hegemony, "the active engagement of individuals with the ideology of the dominant sectors of society and therefore active cooperation in their own domination."[20] When we support the dominant ideology of romance and relationships, we are abiding by the hegemonic notion of the heterosexual imaginary.

In a cursory evaluation of *Teen Mom* and *16 and Pregnant*, the presence of the heterosexual imaginary appears to be healthy and pervasive. The idea that the teenage mothers will remain romantically paired with their babies' fathers is shown through the focus on the teen moms' relationships with those fathers and in the multiple instances of engagements and, in one case, a wedding. The young women focus on their relationships with the babies' fathers in terms of wanting it to work out and hoping that their romantic partner will mature when the child arrives.

The dream of success of the romantic relationship with the teen couples is shown most prominently in episodes of *16 and Pregnant*. The first young woman to whom audiences are introduced in the series is Maci. Maci is involved with the baby's father, Ryan, and they are having a son, Bentley. Through the course of the *Teen Mom* series, the audience views the demise of Maci and Ryan's relationship. However, in Ryan and Maci's episode of *16 and Pregnant*, the belief that the couple will stay together is prominent. Maci explains, "My boyfriend Ryan started chasing me when I was a sophomore. I wasn't into him at first because he rides four wheelers which to me are not cool. But eventually he swept me off my feet. He even put a ring on my finger."[21] After the explanation of her relationship to the audience, we are immediately shown Maci shopping for her wedding dress, with friends helping her create the image of the "white wedding" by encouraging her to try on dresses. The idea of a wedding as the ultimate goal reinforces the heterosexual imaginary.[22] Maci makes various statements to reinforce her desire to make her relationship work. She says, "I feel like I want to make him [Ryan] happy. If he is happy going out then I'll take the responsibility for Bentley."[23] This desire to make her romantic partner happy—even at the expense of her own happiness—demonstrates her collusion with the heterosexual imaginary. Maci believes that if she can keep Ryan happy by taking responsibility for Bentley, she and Ryan will have a more successful relationship. By the end of Maci's episode of *16 and Pregnant*, the audience is certain that Maci and Ryan's relationship is over.

In *Teen Mom* season 1, the audience gets to view the relationship between Maci and Ryan again—as the two resume their relationship in hopes of making it work for Bentley. In the first episode of *Teen Mom*, Maci is planning her wedding to Ryan.[24] In the second episode, Maci breaks up with Ryan, saying when she leaves their apartment, "I feel like I've got a hundred pounds lifted off my back."[25] However, shortly after their second breakup, Maci has a change of heart and returns to Ryan in hopes of making it work,[26] including going to therapy with Ryan to fix their relationship.[27] The struggles of trying to make the relationship work—even though it is obvious to the audience that they should give up—demonstrates the power of the heterosexual imaginary.

Maci is not the only young mom convinced that she can make it work with her baby's father. Amber, her daughter Leah, and Leah's father, Gary, live together. In Amber and Gary's episode of *16 and Pregnant*, Amber is unwavering in her commitment to her relationship, romanticizing the fact that she is "with the guy I lost my virginity to."[28] While the couple obviously has problems related to financial decisions and anger issues—from both Amber and Gary—they are fulfilling the romantic fantasy of a nuclear family. During Amber's *16 and Pregnant* episode, Gary proposes saying, "I want to be there for both of you guys." Amber responds by saying, "I'm the happiest girl in the world."[29]

Amber and Gary's engagement is short-lived during the first season of *Teen Mom*. However, in season 2, the two are shown as restarting their relationship. Amber states, "I want to get married. I want to be engaged to him again."[30] Amber gives Gary a silver key to her heart to celebrate Valentine's Day. Gary presents Amber with a teddy bear, flowers, and bracelet exclaiming, "I just didn't think we were going to get back together."[31] By the end of the episode "Valentine's Day," Gary takes a ring off Amber's hand and gives it back to her claiming that it is a "promise" that they will be together. Amber's desire to get married—to be in a committed romantic relationship with her baby's father regardless of how bad the relationship may be—demonstrates the pervasiveness of the heterosexual imaginary.

The stories of Maci and Amber are just two of the many stories that follow the same pattern of being together, getting engaged, breaking up, getting back together, and breaking up again. At this point, among the young parents featured on both *16 and Pregnant* and *Teen Mom* or *Teen Mom 2*, there has been only one couple who had a child and then married each other—Leah and Corey. The audience watches as the two plan their wedding, and despite Leah and Corey's reservations about actually getting married, they have a camouflage-themed wedding at the end of season 1 of *Teen Mom 2*.[32] However, their relationship does not last, and they are speaking of divorce by the end of season 2.[33] The majority of the couples demonstrate a strong desire to make their relationships work. They have bought into the idea that they will be better off together than alone—especially since there is a child involved.

On the surface, *16 and Pregnant* and *Teen Mom* appear to be promoting the heterosexual imaginary—showing the couples as working to stay together at any cost to be fulfilled. Additionally, the depictions of the necessity for a lifetime commitment through an engagement or marriage because of having a child intensify the belief in the need for a nuclear family, thus truly fulfilling what is expected in a heterosexual relationship.

However, as with most narratives, contradictions exist. Ben Agger argues, "Criticism *does* transform its object, opening it to new versions of itself by bringing to light its hidden assumptions and inconsistencies—deconstruction's aporias."[34] Simply, aporias are contradictions that exist within a text: "Aporias are interpretively crucial because they can explore some of the internal pressures bursting forth from within the texts but carefully suppressed in the interest of surface appearances."[35] The "surface appearance" of *16 and Pregnant* and *Teen Mom* is that a romantic relationship with the father of the teenage mother's child is of the utmost importance. Upon a closer reading of the two television series, it becomes evident that the idea of the heterosexual imaginary is problematized throughout the various narratives. I argue *16 and Pregnant* and *Teen Mom* disrupt the heterosexual imaginary through the representations of teen fathers.

As mentioned before, dissecting the images of teen fathers is imperative because there are few media representations where people see the lives of teenage fathers. Unfortunately, the images shown throughout *16 and Pregnant* and *Teen Mom* of teen fathers are largely negative—especially when they are paired with the mothers of their children. These images directly contradict the belief that a heterosexual relationship is the path to a happy life. Furthermore, the belief that having a nuclear family—mother, father, biological child (or children)—should be the ultimate goal in life is problematized through the representations of the fathers in *16 and Pregnant* and *Teen Mom*.

REPRESENTATIONS OF TEEN DADS

After various episodes of *16 and Pregnant* and *Teen Mom* were analyzed through the lens of the heterosexual imaginary, three key areas in relation to teenage fathers emerged: dad as dunce, donor dad, and fantasy father.

Dad as Dunce

The majority of the fathers on the show are portrayed as fathers who are immature and foolish. Typically, fathers who appear in this manner are seen as deadbeat dads because they fail "to live up to [their] parental responsibilities."[36] Jay argues that the portrayal of the fathers on *Teen Mom* helps to deracialize deadbeat dads in the media[37] because the majority of the young men on the shows are white. However, this does not make the portrayal of the teen dads as uninvolved or immature—regardless of their race—any less stigmatizing or influencing to young men who may watch the shows. Furthermore, I prefer not to classify the portrayals of young fathers who fall into the arena of immature and foolish as deadbeat fathers because the issue is complicated by their age and inability to obtain employment that produces significant income to support their family. The portrayal is also problematic because of their maturity level—most of the young men on the show are between the ages of sixteen and eighteen. The only older father is Ryan— father of Bentley. However, he still acts immature and foolish when it comes to being a caregiver of his son. Because of these distinctions, I am classifying this theme as "dad as dunce"—to accurately describe them as being shown to the audience as foolish, immature, irresponsible, and unsupportive (of both the mother and the child).

The teen mothers play a role in constructing the fathers as dunces through their conversations with the cameras and their friends and family members. In a study on representations of young men in *Seventeen* magazine, Lock and

Harp found that young girls influence the construction of masculinity—promoting a view of young men as "mean, foolish, and perverted."[38] Certainly, the young women on *Teen Mom* and *16 and Pregnant* influence the view of young fathers as dunces through comments they make about the behaviors of their babies' fathers. Additionally, in a study of representations of young men in teen magazines, Prusank found that "the incompetence of boys/men in the arena of personal relationships is held up in contrast to the assumed 'natural' competence of girls/women in this arena where the assumption is that problems are most likely to be detected and resolved by the female."[39] The representations of teen fathers on the show often reflect that they are simply incompetent when it comes to understanding the needs of their child and their child's mother.

The representations of the fathers as incompetent are where many of the problems between the teenage parents originate and where relationships begin to fall apart. Ryan and Gary are the two key representations of dad as dunce, as they demonstrate similar behaviors showing them as uninvolved parents. Both Ryan and Gary choose to spend time doing things other than parenting or spending time with their significant others. Additionally, both fathers actively ignore their children in various scenes in *16 and Pregnant* and *Teen Mom* showing they are not engaged fathers.

Ryan, father of Bentley, seems to have problems committing to spending time with his son and being a supportive partner to Maci, his child's mother. It is important to note that Ryan is twenty years old when he becomes a father, older than the other teen fathers in the series. However, his older age does not appear to make him a more responsible father. In Maci's episode of *16 and Pregnant*, Ryan and Maci argue about Ryan staying out all night. Maci questions him about what time he gets off from the night shift and why one night he comes home at five in the morning and other nights at seven in the morning. His response is simply "Maci, you're acting stupid as hell."[40] While someone could read his response to Maci as verbally abusive, I believe his statement reflects his unwillingness to accept wrongdoing and the possibility that he is not being a good father. The lack of involvement in his child's life and in the mother's life continues as Maci tells her friends, "I'm really hoping Ryan will take his turn tonight, but it is always my turn." She encourages him to hold Bentley when he is crying, but Ryan just ignores the crying. Ryan's father even confronts his son, saying, "I feel like you and Bentley need a little more time together. It is going to be October and he is going to be one. I told you that when it's gone, it's gone forever. You can't go back. And you don't want to miss not one thing. Not crawling, not talking, nothing."[41]

Ryan remains disengaged from his son throughout the first few seasons of *Teen Mom*. In "How Many Chances?" Maci confronts Ryan, stating, "You walk in the door and don't even acknowledge that Bentley is here. You don't.

You didn't at all. I don't care if you leave me here but you are leaving him here too. You're ignoring him. I can find somebody else to be with but he can't find another dad. . . . You'd have to get your relationship right with him [Bentley] before I'll even want to try to be with you. So until you figure out how to be a dad, a real dad."[42] Shortly after the confrontation, Maci leaves Ryan for the second time as a result of his actions as a bad dad.

Maci and Ryan's relationship remains tumultuous through the course of the series of *Teen Mom*, with several situations where Maci confronts Ryan about his actions even when Bentley is with him. In the episode "Places You'll Go," Maci is seen asking Bentley such questions as "Who feeds you? Who plays with you? Who changes your diaper?" Bentley's two-year-old response is "Mimi."[43] Maci then questions Ryan's commitment to his son when in his care—claiming that he is not taking care of Bentley but rather that his mother is taking on sole responsibility for their son. Maci even threatens, "Keep acting like an idiot and you're not going to have him."[44] Other instances of Ryan being a dunce are showcased when Maci makes statements about his ability as a parent, saying, "Sometimes it feels like I'm taking care of two babies."[45] Ryan's actions and Maci's statements clearly work to construct Ryan as a dunce. Ryan even argues with the representations of him as a father in the season 2 "Finale Special: Check-Up with Dr. Drew" by stating, "It is the way TV made me look."[46] Ryan's inability to comprehend his actions as having an effect on his son and Maci shows that he is disconnected from what it means to be a father—demonstrating that he is unaware of acting like a dunce when it comes to being an involved father.

Gary, Amber's significant other and Leah's father, is also portrayed as a dunce. Amber introduces Gary to the viewers by stating, "Gary spends his spare time playing video games."[47] This statement alerts the audience to be ready for some duncelike behavior from her romantic partner. Gary is immature. Gary admits early on, "We took most of the precautions" to prevent pregnancy—except wearing a condom because Amber argues, "You [Gary] don't like condoms."[48] Later on in the introductory episode of Amber's story, Gary admits to purchasing a $500 video console using money that should have been saved for their newborn. When Amber confronts Gary, saying that they could have used that money for food, he responds, "There's ramen noodles and celery."[49] Gary is shown ignoring his daughter when she cries, and he makes statements to Amber like "All you do is stay home and take care of the little one, which is what I would rather do."[50] He demonstrates that he does not understand the time and skills required to be an effective parent, dismissing all that Amber does to take care of Leah as being easy.

Gary has problems navigating what it means to be a good father and falls quickly into being a dunce—one that does not pay much attention to his daughter or his significant other. Furthermore, he dismisses the work that

Amber does to care for Leah implying that taking care of a baby is easy while what he does at work is difficult. Throughout the series, the audience sees Gary grow as a father but not necessarily out of the dunce category. At the end of the *Teen Mom* series, Gary does obtain full custody of Leah. However, by the end of the series, Amber has had multiple problems with the law for her anger issues and drug use—going through rehab and finally being imprisoned for five years. By default, Gary has to learn to become a better dad. Unfortunately, the audience does not get to witness the potential transformation.

In season 4 of *16 and Pregnant*, we are introduced to another dad as dunce, Devoin. While there is some airtime for Devoin in the episode, the majority of it works to construct him as a dunce through conversations that Briana, the mother, has with her family and friends. The episode featuring Briana created such a controversy over Devoin's lack of support that an article appeared in the *Huffington Post* questioning, "Is Devoin the worst new dad in the history of the show [*16 and Pregnant*]?"[51] The audience learns early on that Devoin has been absent from Briana's life for the majority of the pregnancy, even though he promised her much more. Briana's friend remarks, "He promised you when he found out you were pregnant that he would care for you and support you and now he isn't doing anything." Briana replies, "He like glamorized the whole situation. He was like, yeah Briana, we're going to do this together. I have a job. I'm going to take care of her. We are going to be like a family."[52]

The conversations revolving around Devoin construct him as a dunce because he is not willing to be a part of his child's or the mother's life even though he promised to be a good parent when Briana found out she was pregnant. In the few times that the audience does see Devoin, he does not say much. He argues with Briana about what having a child is doing to him, stating, "You know how stressed out this is? I'm forced to get a job!" Briana quickly responds, "I'm forced to be a mother." After Briana gives birth to her daughter, Nova, Devoin leaves to play basketball with his friends. Briana cries to her mother and says, "I really was expecting more out of Devoin. . . . I don't want to be sad anymore. It's like I really can't enjoy being a mother anymore because this is not what I wanted. I'm pretty sure he doesn't worry about Nova the way I do. He doesn't love Nova enough to stop what he's doing. I don't know what to do anymore."[53]

I include the story of Briana and Devoin in my analysis because they present an interesting story line. Briana's sister becomes pregnant at the same time and chooses abortion because she knows that she cannot rely on her baby's father. Briana mentions several times that she chose to keep her child and not have an abortion because of the promises that Devoin made to her when she first found out she was pregnant. These promises fed into her belief in the "happily ever after" or the heterosexual imaginary. She believed that she would have her child and her romantic partner and they would be happy. Unfortunately, it did not take her long to realize that Devoin was a bad dad and that he was not going to live up to his promises of supporting her and their child. At one point, Briana admits to her sister, "If I could go back and make the decision you made, I would do it."[54] Briana is a cautionary tale to young couples facing pregnancy—to young women who believe that they will live in happy romantic relationships with their babies and their babies' fathers and to the young fathers who are faced with deciding whether they should be fathers or not.

Donor Dad

While the majority of couples selected for *16 and Pregnant* and *Teen Mom* have custody of their children, there are two instances where the couples have chosen another option—abortion or adoption. In the two cases where the couples choose abortion or adoption, the teen fathers seem to have significant input in the decisions and vocalize their reluctance to raise a child at this point in their lives. William Marsiglio refers to this as *paternity-free manhood*: the idea that "men may be reluctant to assert their preference [to not have a child] if they are in love with a partner who forcefully asserts her desire to give birth to their child."[55] This preference to not have a child—or consider alternatives to parenting, such as abortion or adoption—is not something that is regularly discussed by men or shown in the media. Luckily, the two young men portrayed in *Teen Mom* and *16 and Pregnant* who vocalized their support of choosing abortion or adoption were involved with women who were open to discussions of not having the child or not being the primary caregiver.

Because the studies on paternity-free manhood have focused more on individuals who are past their teenage years, I prefer not to use the term to classify this theme within *16 and Pregnant* and *Teen Mom*, instead using the phrase "donor dad." Utilization of this phrase is not meant to imply that the fathers had no involvement in the decisions regarding raising their children or choosing another option; rather, the phrase is used to represent young men who have elected to not raise their children—either through choosing from the beginning of the pregnancy not to be the paternal caregiver or by assisting their significant other with the decision to end the pregnancy. While one could argue that Devoin may fit into the category of donor dad, I prefer to place him in the previous category of dad as dunce because he encouraged his partner to keep their child and promised to be an involved parent. His transition to not wanting to be the primary caregiver happened after the decision to have and raise the child was finalized.

Before delving into the two key instances of donor dads depicted in the television series, it is important to understand that there is an instance of one young father admitting that he did not want to be a parent but wanted, instead, to choose another option—either abortion or adoption. When Jo and Kailyn, parents to Isaac, begin arguing in front of his parents, they ask, "Did you consider other options?" Jo responds, "She didn't like the idea of adoption." Kailyn questions Jo, "Did you want to look into adoption more and didn't say anything?' He responds, "Maybe I did." When his parents confront him later about his being unsupportive of Kailyn, he simply says that "it was her decision" to have the baby.[56] This exchange between Jo and Kailyn is a clear example of paternity-free fatherhood—he was reluctant to present his real feelings about becoming a father because he did not want to hurt her. His inability to voice his preferences leads to a tough situation where he and Kailyn are trying to coparent while not being involved in a romantic relationship.

One of the key representations of donor dad in *16 and Pregnant* is through the special episode "No Easy Decision."[57] This episode focuses on Markai and James, who were already featured in an episode of *16 and Pregnant* during the second season where audiences witnessed Markai and James become parents to Za'karia while arguing about their relationship because of James's infidelity.[58] The two return to film a special episode because Markai becomes pregnant again shortly after giving birth to her daughter.

"No Easy Decision" focuses on the couple's decision to end Markai's second pregnancy. James is open about his feelings of not wanting to be a second-time father. The episode starts off with him saying, "Let's not jump into this. Let's think about what is best for all of us. Not just me, not just you, not just Za'karia but all of us." He vocally struggles with his feelings about ending the pregnancy, explaining to Markai that he does not want to be an absent father. He states, "I think abortion is the best option for our family." While he was supportive of her first pregnancy and, in many ways, embraced fatherhood with their daughter Za'karia, he makes it clear that he is unwilling to parent another child. He concedes that the decision will affect Markai more than him, especially after the procedure.

While there have been four seasons of *16 and Pregnant*, four seasons of *Teen Mom*, and two seasons of *Teen Mom 2* as of this writing, this is the only episode—which is half the time of the regular episodes—where the option of abortion is addressed. One positive aspect of the episode is that it shows young men who are faced with the possibility of being fathers that it is okay for them to voice their opinions about what they think is best for their life. James handles the situation well until the end of the episode, where he says to Markai, "I told you not to even think of that thing as a baby."[59] In this one statement, James reminds Markai and the audience that he does not understand the struggles that a woman faces when making the decision to have an abortion. He treats Markai's pregnancy as a problem to be taken care of—not a potential child. He does not understand Markai's emotional feelings connected to her pregnancy and reprimands her when she verbalizes her belief that this "problem" is their child. This angers James because to him, he is just a donor dad in regard to this pregnancy.

Markai and James appear happy in "No Easy Decision" despite their rocky relationship in her episode of *16 and Pregnant*. Yet, they choose not to engage in parenthood for a second time. They disrupt the image of the perfect family who would embrace the possibility of another child and would see it as fulfilling their lives even more. Markai and James are more realistic about their ability to parent two young children and remain involved parents. This recognition of their limitations provides an alternative to the heterosexual imaginary—recognizing that not everything associated with the "ideal" heterosexual relationship is positive.

The final instance of donor dad is shown by Tyler. Tyler is Catelynn's boyfriend and Carly's biological father. Tyler and Catelynn are an interesting couple in a few respects. First, the couple has been romantically involved since seventh grade. Second, Catelynn's mother married Tyler's father after Catelynn and Tyler began dating. Third, while they have had minor episodes contemplating whether they should be together, they have stayed together as a romantic couple through all four seasons of *Teen Mom*—the only couple to do so. Finally, they are the only couple followed throughout *Teen Mom* to choose to place their child for adoption as soon as she was born.

Tyler and Catelynn are extremely realistic about their ability to raise a child as teenage parents—recognizing fairly early, despite resistance from their family members, that they would not be able to provide for their daughter in the ways they deem acceptable. Tyler admits to viewers that he was raised by a deadbeat father, Butch, and does not want to be like him. We find out at the end of *Teen Mom* season 4 that Butch told Tyler that he loved his cocaine more than Tyler.[60] Butch argues with Tyler over his decision to place his daughter for adoption, saying, "I couldn't do it. I would find some way. . . . I think about it like this. Here's my son, sixteen or seventeen years old. He has this baby, and he gives it away. Just gives the kid away to some great family, which are great people, and, uh, he didn't man up. You didn't man up. You wasn't the cowboy I thought you were."[61] Butch's behaviors play a key role in Tyler's doubting his abilities to effectively parent his daughter. Tyler states, "Me not having a dad in my life was a huge thing in my choosing adoption." Tyler follows this statement by addressing Butch even though he is not in the room. "You asshole. If you were around, I probably would have decided to parent her."[62] The discussions and depictions of Butch throughout the series show the impact that a deadbeat dad can have on a child. Butch had a child and then did not make his child a priority. Instead, he spent twenty years of his life in and out of jail for various crimes.

Having a deadbeat father makes Tyler more realistic about how being a teenage father will affect his life and the life of his daughter. Tyler admits, "I think keeping the baby would totally ruin us. I don't think our lives are very stable to raise a child. . . . We don't have a job. We aren't graduated."[63] The couple selects to have an open adoption, where they are able to choose the parents for their daughter, receive updates about her as she grows older, and visit her occasionally. As the couple prepares to give their child over to the new parents, Tyler writes a letter to his daughter:

> First off, I want to tell you I love you so much. Words can never explain the love a father has for his daughter. When your mom and I found out she was pregnant with you we didn't know what we were going to do. We were so young and inexperienced in life yet. After thinking and thinking, we came to the decision that adoption was the best option for you. The thought of what kind of dad I wanted to be and what you deserve in life just didn't mix. I think about you every day. You are everything to me. I don't want you to ever ever think that I didn't want you. I will always love you. You are in my thoughts every day. Love, your daddy.[64]

Once Catelynn gives birth to Carly, the audience sees Tyler and Catelynn crying, with Tyler repeating, "We can do this. We can do this. She is going to have such a good life. She is going to be so happy."[65]

While Butch claims that Tyler did not "man up," Tyler made a decision that was mature and responsible. He recognized the possibility that he would be like his father, and he did not want the same fate for his daughter. Furthermore, the decision for Tyler and Catelynn to place their daughter for adoption may have been the decision that saved their relationship. The other couples on the show who decide to parent their children are not successful in building a "happy home," with a biological father, a biological mother, and a child. While Tyler and Catelynn reject the next step in fulfilling the heterosexual imaginary—embracing parenthood—their relationship with each other is supportive and, from what is shown in the television series, successful. I believe that Tyler and Catelynn represent the most productive disruption to the heterosexual imaginary throughout *16 and Pregnant* and *Teen Mom*. Even though they have elements of a "happily ever after" story, their ending did not come from raising a child together.

Fantasy Father

The final portrayal of teenage fathers in *16 and Pregnant* and *Teen Mom* is that of the fantasy father. While there is only one clear instance of this portrayal, I feel that it is important to discuss because it does work to disrupt the heterosexual imaginary. Derek, the father of Farrah's daughter, Sophia, is never shown in the series because he died in a car accident two months before his daughter's birth. His death is not discussed in her episode of *16 and Pregnant* or in the first season of *Teen Mom*. When Farrah does discuss

Derek in *16 and Pregnant*, she does not have positive things to say about him. She explains to her friends, "I haven't told the baby's father that I'm pregnant. I broke up with him because he's way too jealous and immature."[66] The audience is able to see Farrah arguing with Derek over the phone about her decision to go out and his incessant questioning of her ("What guys are going to be included in that, Farrah?"). Farrah finally says, "I quit talking to him altogether. I just don't want him in my life because he turned out to be a bigger and bigger problem. I thought he would change for the better because we were dating, but I guess it's like people change for the worse the longer you date them."[67]

By the time that Farrah reveals to the viewers that Derek died two months before Sophia's birth, her vision of Derek changed completely. She explains, "He would have been loving and supportive and taken care of both of us,"[68] and she makes these claims even though she and Sophia's father did not speak for four months before his death. We see her idealize Derek throughout the remaining seasons of *Teen Mom*. When she first reveals the death to the audience, she is speaking to her counselor. "He passed away. And, so, that happened. I'm upset about it every day. Sophia will not see her dad. That's sad. That really upsets me."[69] Throughout season 2 of *Teen Mom*, Farrah often reflects on how wonderful things would be if Derek were still alive. During the season 2 "Finale Special: Check-Up with Dr. Drew," Farrah is questioned about her views of Derek. She says, "I never pictured [Sophia] not having Derek there." Dr. Drew responds by saying, "It seems like you feel like you'll never find another Derek. . . . No one will ever match up to him. You'll never let anyone replace him." Finally, Dr. Drew questions Farrah's image of Derek: "Seems like you idealize him an awful lot. I heard your mom just briefly say things weren't as rosy as you painted them." Farrah responds, "I'm not painting the picture that is rosy. I know what the realistic situation was. . . . I wanted everything to be different."[70]

Farrah does not admit to creating an image of Derek as a fantasy father. In seasons 3 and 4, she continues to speak about how her life would be better if Derek were still alive because she is convinced that he would have been a great father. Farrah's belief that her life would be better if she were romantically paired with Sophia's father is clear in the episode "Without You." In it, Farrah and Sophia move from Iowa to Florida and stop by Derek's grave before leaving. Farrah speaks to Derek, "Well Derek . . . it is really sad to me that I never got to see you do the things you wanted to do when you grew up. . . . Derek, I wish we could have gotten married, and I wish we could have spent more time together but . . . it just really hurts that I'm a parent by myself because I never wanted to be that person."[71] Farrah's belief in what could have been with her ex-boyfriend is difficult to watch as a viewer. The series reminds the audience that Derek and Farrah were not even speaking during the four weeks leading up to his death. Farrah is not living the dream of the heterosexual imaginary—she only thinks that she could be if Derek had not been killed in a car accident.

In season 4 of *16 and Pregnant*, the audience is introduced to another young mother, Kristina, whose fiancé, Todd, drowned while swimming. Kristina was in the water at the time and was saved by a lifeguard, and in her episode, she is dealing with the grief of losing her fiancé. [72] I did not include Todd in the theme of fantasy father, because the storyline—not continued in *Teen Mom*—had little time to develop. Additionally, Kristina does not say much in terms of her images of Todd's ability to parent and instead focuses on her own grief and questioning why she survived and he did not. Kristina does not deal with Todd's death until the conclusion of the episode, where she begins to see a therapist. While I could predict that Kristina has images of Todd as a fantasy father—one who is involved and caring—there is little evidence to support this claim.

DISCUSSION

The key representations of teenage fathers as dunces, donor dads, or fantasy fathers serve to disrupt the belief that being in a heterosexual romantic relationship—especially one that fulfills the expectation of children—leads to a sense of well-being. All the representations of teen fathers described in the chapter argue against the heterosexual imaginary by showing young viewers the unexpected consequences of having a child as a young couple. The problematizing of the heterosexual imaginary in *16 and Pregnant* and *Teen Mom* works as a deterrent to teenage couples thinking about having a child.

First, the representation of dad as dunce shows young women that their expectations of their significant other maturing during their nine months of pregnancy are irrational. Ryan, Gary, and Devoin are clear examples of young men who continued to live their lives as if they did not have any additional responsibilities after their children were born. Ryan stayed out all night and did not help Maci with caring for Bentley. Gary spent money on toys instead of items such as formula and food. Devoin checked out of Briana's life before Nova was born, and while he returned for the birth, he left quickly afterward to play basketball with his friends and never returned. While Ryan and Maci and Gary and Amber tried to make their romantic partnerships work, they were unsuccessful. They realized that their relationships were not salvageable and not beneficial to their lives or the lives of their children. Young females are able to see that becoming pregnant to live "happily ever after" with their boyfriend is foolish. There are no "happily ever after" stories of the main couples featured in *Teen Mom* and *Teen Mom 2* who decide to raise their children together.

Second, the key images of donor dads call into question the necessity for moving a romantic relationship into a nuclear family—the expected next step for heterosexual relationships. Jo admits that even though Kailyn chose to have their child, he would have preferred considering adoption more seriously. James and Markai make the decision that it would be irresponsible and potentially damaging to their romantic relationship to have another child, thus choosing abortion. Tyler and Catelynn quickly realize that they are too young to be parents and cannot provide for a child when neither has a high school degree or a means of earning an income that would support their daughter. While James and Markai and Tyler and Catelynn remain together, they do so because they made the decision to either not have another child or not parent their child. The representation of donor dad shows teen couples that the best path to staying together is to not move their heterosexual romantic relationship into a family situation. As I state earlier in the chapter, I believe that the story of Catelynn and Tyler is one of the most pervasive when it comes to disrupting the view of the perfect family—mom, dad, and biological child—for teen couples. Teens see how having a child tears a relationship apart while viewing a couple who made the difficult decision to relinquish their parental rights to salvage their romantic relationship.

Third, Farrah's construction of Derek as a fantasy father disrupts the heterosexual imaginary in that the audience can see how she, somewhat foolishly, holds onto the idea that if Derek were alive, she, Derek, and Sophia would be a happy family. Farrah believes in the "happily ever after" possibility even though her relationship with Derek before his death points to a similar relationship pattern that the audience has viewed with Ryan and Maci and Gary and Amber.

The analysis of teenage fathers in this chapter would not be complete without mentioning that several of the fathers, including Ryan, Gary, and Jo, have started showing signs of wanting to be more involved in their children's lives by spending time with and providing for their children. The *Teen Mom* series ends with the audience seeing Ryan discussing with his family the possibility of his suing for joint custody of Bentley. Additionally, Gary is given full custody of Leah, but this is mainly due to Amber's enrollment in a rehabilitation program for anger and drug use and then her having to spend five years in jail. Gary has no choice but to become a better father to Leah. Jo wrote a song under the name N.I.C.K.b. called "Life of a Teen Father," about his struggles with being a teen dad who is no longer in a relationship with his child's mother. Jo wants to be involved in Isaac's life and pushes for a custody agreement to ensure that he is able to see his son. He sings, "Am I supposed to believe that / The feedback / When we agreed back / That when Isaac was born / We would weather the storm / Not let our family be torn apart / Till you threw a dart / Straight through my heart."[73] Through these lyrics, Jo makes it clear that he was hopeful when he and Kailyn decided to have their son that they would be able to stay together and raise Isaac as a family. The realization that having a child did not lead to "happily ever after" pushed him to fight for custody to be an involved father.

Even though the teen fathers have made some progress in becoming better fathers, they have only done so outside a romantic relationship with their child's mother. Therefore, while the images of teenage fathers being more involved is a positive step toward showing young men as responsible young fathers, the representation of the maturity of the teenage fathers still disrupts the heterosexual imaginary—showing only positive images of teen fathers when they are no longer in a romantic relationship with their child's mother.

While there is no definitive answer on whether MTV's series *16 and Pregnant* and *Teen Mom* truly serve as a deterrent to teenage pregnancy, the disruption of the heterosexual imaginary through the various representations of teen fathers calls into question the belief that young women should have children to remain with their boyfriend—assuming that having a child will lead to a "happily ever after" ending. The narratives in *16 and Pregnant* and *Teen Mom* show that having a child while still a teenager and choosing to raise that child has a detrimental effect on teenage relationships. Lisa Chudnofsky writes,

> While tabloids have often spun rumors about their personal relationships, and critics of the series used these magazine covers as an argument that the show glamorized teen pregnancy, the majority of feedback we've heard from MTV's dedicated viewership has been rather validating. You've [viewers] seen *Teen Mom* as it was meant to be: a deterrent. You've learned the necessity of having safe sex, or practicing abstinence, as you watched the painful sacrifices the cast members made ever since they found out they were having a child. You've breathed multiple sighs of relief that it didn't happen to you. [74]

By showing teenage fathers as dunces, donor dads, and fantasy fathers, *16 and Pregnant* and *Teen Mom* have painted a realistic image of what might happen if a viewer becomes pregnant as a teenager. Romance disappears when a child enters the picture—the realities of being a parent take over and relationships dissolve. To maintain the illusion of the heterosexual imaginary, teenagers need to be teenagers and not become parents.

NOTES

1. Muskal, "U.S. Teen Births Fall."
2. McCarthy, "Stanley Milgram," 22.
3. Brown, *Society as Text*, 165.
4. Butler, *Gender Trouble*.
5. Furrow, "The Ideal Father."
6. Cantor, "Prime-Time Fathers"; Miller, "Masculinity in Popular Sitcoms."

7. Fogel, "Reality Parenting 101"; Smith, "Critiquing Reality-Based Television."
8. Jay, "De-racializing."
9. Arthur, *Surviving Teen Pregnancy.*
10. Warren Lindsay and Brunelli, *Your Pregnancy and Newborn Journey.*
11. Lerman, *Teen Moms.*
12. Englander, *Dear Diary, I'm Pregnant.*
13. Warren Lindsay, *Teen Dads.*
14. Gravelle, *Teenage Fathers.*
15. Consalvo, "The Monsters Next Door," 28.
16. Furrow, "The Ideal Father," 17.
17. Ingraham, *White Weddings.*
18. Ingraham, *White Weddings*, 16.
19. "Teen Dads," *Teen Mom*, season 3.
20. Corcorran, "Television as Ideological Apparatus," 142.
21. "Maci," *16 and Pregnant*, season 1, June 11, 2009.
22. Ingraham, *White Weddings.*
23. "Maci."
24. "Looking for Love," *Teen Mom*, season 1, December 8, 2009.
25. "How Many Chances," *Teen Mom*, season 1, December 14, 2009.
26. "Moving On," *Teen Mom*, season 1, December 29, 2009.
27. "A Little Help," *Teen Mom*, season 1, January 5, 2010.
28. "Amber," *16 and Pregnant*, season 1, June 25, 2009.
29. "Amber."
30. "Valentine's Day," *Teen Mom*, season 2, August 2, 2010.
31. "Valentine's Day."
32. "Judgment Day," *Teen Mom 2*, season 1, March 29, 2011.
33. "Falling," *Teen Mom 2*, season 2, February 7, 2012.
34. Agger, *Cultural Studies*, 96.
35. Agger, *Cultural Studies*, 102.
36. Marks and Palkovitz, "American Fatherhood Types," 113.
37. Jay, "De-racializing."
38. Loke and Harp, "Evolving Themes," 1.
39. Prusank, "Masculinities in Teen Magazines," 168.
40. "Maci."
41. "Maci."
42. "How Many Chances."
43. "Places You'll Go," *Teen Mom*, season 3, June 19, 2012.
44. "Places You'll Go."
45. "Maci."
46. "Finale Special: Check-Up with Dr. Drew," *Teen Mom*, season 2, October 19, 2010.
47. "Amber."
48. "Amber."
49. "Amber."
50. "Amber."
51. "*16 and Pregnant*: Is Devoin?"
52. "Briana," *16 and Pregnant*, season 4, April 3, 2012.
53. "Briana."
54. "Briana."
55. Marsiglio, *Procreative Man*, 94.
56. "Kailyn," *16 and Pregnant*, season 2, April 20, 2010.
57. "No Easy Decision," *16 and Pregnant*, season 2, December 28, 2010.
58. "Markai," *16 and Pregnant*, season 2, November 16, 2010.
59. "Markai."
60. "Wake Up," *Teen Mom*, season 4, August 28, 2012.
61. "Catelynn," *16 and Pregnant*, season 1, July 16, 2009.
62. "Wake Up."

63. "Catelynn."
64. "Catelynn."
65. "Catelynn."
66. "Farrah," *16 and Pregnant*, season 1, June 18, 2009.
67. "Farrah."
68. "Exclusive: *Teen Mom*'s Farrah."
69. "Valentine's Day."
70. "Finale Special: Check-Up with Dr. Drew."
71. "Without You," *Teen Mom*, season 3, August 16, 2011.
72. "Kristina," *16 and Pregnant*, season 4, May 29, 2012.
73. "Life of a Teen Father."
74. Chudnofsky, "Fond Farewell."

Chapter Eleven

What's a Baby Daddy to Do?

Fathers on the Fringe in MTV's 16 and Pregnant

Laura Tropp

In a powerful scene from an episode of *16 and Pregnant*, new father Colin has just lost his job. He breaks down and cries, "Like before he was born, this was one of my biggest fears. I feel like I'm failing." He turns to his baby and says, "Your daddy's sorry, though. He's going to do whatever he can."[1] Bloggers and critics praised these words and the program, for showing a responsible father. The father's reaction and the program's emphasis on his financial role, though, offer a limited view of how to define fatherhood. Since its premiere, the program has received much attention and debate, particularly concerning how it may or may not discourage teen pregnancy. Rarely mentioned in the media is how the program presents the image of the teen father. Most of the episodes of *16 and Pregnant* have a father at the side of the expectant mother during the pregnancy, and often this relationship dominates the episode. The fathers are sometimes supportive but are also overwhelmed with their new responsibilities and challenged by complicated relationships with the mothers of their children and with extended family members. This chapter explores how the program represents ambivalent views of fatherhood: girlfriends and family members constrain the power of the men to be in their children's lives; the drama of television emphasizes dysfunctional fathers; and the program frames the primary role of fatherhood as serving, first and most important, an economic function.

THE CHANGING ROLES OF FATHERS

In 2006, the Urban Dictionary cited *baby daddy* as its "Urban Word of the Day," defining the phrase as "the father of your child, whom you did not marry, and with whom you are not currently involved."[2] This term, referred to at times on *16 and Pregnant*, offers a new perspective on defining fatherhood independent of the child's mother. Of course, it is not a new phenomenon for fathers to take primary care for their children on their own. During the seventeenth and eighteenth centuries, death of mothers during childbirth left fathers responsible for the care and well-being of their children. In the United States, the Puritans treated the overseeing of child care as an important role of the father.[3] In more modern times, fathers care for children as a result of changing family patterns, such as divorce. However, the term *baby daddy* and the corresponding term *baby mama* refer to an even more ambiguous, disconnected, and sometimes nonexistent relationship between mother and father. The program *16 and Pregnant*, featuring teen moms with unstable relationships with the fathers of their children, is an ideal program to examine how television represents the functions of fathers when relationships are precarious.

Throughout *16 and Pregnant*, the teen fathers are shown to desire a relationship with their children, but their engagement is influenced by problematic relationships with the mothers of their children and the extended families. Their interest in being involved fathers matches changing societal roles of father. In *The Daddy Shift*, Jeremy Adam Smith finds, "The bottom line is clear: during the past decade, the number of caregiving fathers has risen dramatically. Dads now spend more time with their children than at any time since researchers started collecting longitudinally comparable data."[4] Some studies illustrate that men who delay becoming fathers until their mid- to late thirties have higher participation in the lives of their children.[5] In contrast, studies on teenage fathers illustrate the opposite in terms of their involvement in the lives of their children.[6] Yet, despite evidence that teenage fathers may be less participatory fathers—a theme illustrated throughout *16 and Pregnant*—it is important to acknowledge that scholars disagree on what it means to be a participatory father.

Scholarly research on fatherhood and its place in family life offers differing frames for viewing fathers. Some literature focuses on social and gender constructions of men and women, leading to varying expectations of duties for fathers and mothers.[7] Other scholars have lamented the gap between current cultural expectations of the involved father and actual practices. Ralph LaRossa explores the difference between what he describes as the culture of fatherhood and the conduct of fatherhood: "The division of child care in America has not significantly changed, that—despite the beliefs that fathers are a lot more involved with their children—mothers remain, far and away, the primary child caregivers."[8] Today, fathers may feel guilty for what may be unrealistic popular perceptions of fatherly involvement. Still, other scholars in this area have focused on fatherhood and identity theory, exploring the role that being a father plays in the lives of men and, subsequently, the rest of the family.[9]

Another area of study regarding fatherhood considers gatekeeping, in which fathers' access to children is controlled by the mothers. Arlie Hothschild, in *The Second Shift*, explored how this gatekeeping often tasked mothers with additional household and child care burdens at home after working during the day.[10] Scholars have also explored how motherly gatekeeping can discourage fathers from actively caring for their children.[11]

In addition to research on the role of fathers, scholars study media representation of fathers. The work on television dads focuses mostly on situation comedies, finding that fathers are often portrayed as bumbling or serve to provide a laugh for the audience.[12] Most of these studies focus on fictional rather than reality television, which now dominates commercial television. This examination of *16 and Pregnant* explores how a program that purports to depict reality constructs and reflects societal ambiguity about definitions of fatherhood. While the program documents the lives of real people, producers exert a great deal of control over the design of the show, though much of this remains hidden to the viewer. Producers actively choose which families appear in the program, thereby skewing which fathers are represented. Still, the popularity of the program and the way it seems to portray "real" families means that it has the potential to influence young viewers on how to conceptualize fatherhood based on the fathers that actually are represented on the program.

THE BIRTH TRANSITION:
THE RISE AND FALL OF THE FATHERS

Most episodes of *16 and Pregnant* have a beautiful moment, often mimicking the music video style that first made MTV famous, where the teen fathers witness the birth and hold their babies for the first time. The scene depicts the imagined birth experience of two parents proud and enamored by their new baby. Unfortunately, this moment is often the best, and sometimes the last, time where the fathers are represented as having a true place in the family and a sense of involvement in the well-being of the baby. The idealized birth moment in these episodes is antithetical to the historical model of traditional fatherhood. In earlier times, ambiguity surrounded the responsibility of fathers before birth, and until the most recent thirty years, hospitals denied fathers access to birthing rooms.[13] In contrast, in *16 and Pregnant*, the birth experience often represents the time where teen fathers have the most recognition and acknowledgment of their role as dads. Scholars recognize the power of the moment of birth for the father. Richard Reed writes,

> Until the baby rests in the father's arms, its identity has been thoroughly enmeshed in that of its mother. But holding him for the first time, a father has the opportunity to realize that the baby is an independent entity, physically capable of surviving without his mother, and able to develop a direct paternal relationship. [14]

Today, most expectant fathers have distinct roles and expectations for pregnancy involvement. Fathers are typically present for the first pregnancy test and through some rituals, such as dad-to-be classes, designed specifically for them. *16 and Pregnant* provides a new twist on this involvement: the expectant fathers are sometimes actively involved before the birth and are usually present at the birth (even if not involved before it), and then their involvement deteriorates or disappears postbirth.

Despite the fact that many people still perceive teen pregnancy as a shameful affair, it is no longer portrayed on *16 and Pregnant* as a private one. Most of the pregnant teens and expectant dads engage in the public rituals associated with pregnancy and expectant parenthood. The dads-to-be join the teen moms at doctor appointments, shop for furniture, participate in baby showers, and are present for the birth. Even in the case of Josh and Nikkole, despite his apparent embarrassment during an internal prenatal exam, he still remains there to support his girlfriend. [15] The teen fathers are expected to also display a certain amount of excitement about their baby, and the program highlights when the fathers deviate from this role. In an episode with Jamie and boyfriend Ryan, Jamie is talking with her friends about his lack of bonding with the baby during the pregnancy. Her friend reassures her by telling her that "a mother becomes a mother when she gets pregnant; a father becomes a father when he sees the baby." [16] This comment reflects Reed's notions of identity provided in the birth moments as well as the different expectations of gender roles assigned to mothers and fathers. Here, it is assumed that mothers-to-be will display natural, biological urges to mother, while fathers are presumed to wait until the baby is present to bond. Despite this, the pregnant women on the show still hope for optimal fatherly involvement in the pregnancy. Pregnant Brianna informs viewers about her boyfriend Devoin's lack of involvement, but she keeps texting him, determined to make him a part of the experience. [17] Both Devoin and Ryan do end up at the births of their children (though Ryan is five hours late and hungover), but that ends up being for both fathers the only real involvement with the baby.

In various episodes throughout all seasons of the program, a key moment of contention postbirth appears in the discussion of the birth certificate for the baby. Chelsea and Adam are in a rocky relationship, but after the birth, he asks for his name on the birth certificate. [18] While Devoin shows up to watch Briana deliver baby Nova, he becomes upset when she will not put his name on the birth certificate. In a previous conversation, she told him that she was going to name the baby Nova and asks him if he thought he should have had a say in that. When he says yes, she tells him her view on names: "If you want the last name, then you show me that you want the last name. I think the last name is more important than the first name. With the last name, you have rights. Without the last name, you have sh*t." [19] A similar naming discussion occurs with Sabrina and Iman. Sabrina's mother warns her not to put his name on the birth certificate unless he makes an effort to attend the birth and demonstrate his willingness to provide financially for the baby. [20] The birth certificate moment becomes one where fathers are first framed as being outside the process. They are not necessarily guaranteed to be named as the father officially, leaving the power and control to rest with the mother. While getting pregnant and carrying the baby earns the mother her right and power, the fathers need to prove themselves worthy of the title.

Even if the teens on the program are able to move past the birth certificate challenge, once the baby comes home from the hospital, the father's role continues to go downhill mainly because of his lack of interest in participating but, more often, because of the limits imposed on him by the mother of his baby and her extended family. Part of the issue with the transition is that there is not a dyad of a mother and a father taking home the new baby. Instead of being able to focus on being a couple with a baby, the family of the teen mom tends to be heavily involved, often because the teen mom still lives in her familial home. Blake, the father of Sarah's baby, sums it up best when talking about the involvement of her mother: "She ain't in this relationship. Why does she have to start in on me?" Unfortunately, though, the parents, typically just the mother of the daughter, are a part of the relationship. [21] The girls are legal minors, and they rely on the parents for financial, not to mention emotional, support. One mother wields this power strongly by telling her daughter Jordan that she has all the legal rights and can even control whether her daughter can have drugs during the labor. She uses this threat in an effort to control and restrict her daughter's relationship with the father of her baby, Tyler. [22]

The involvement of the parents of the teens (the grandparents of the baby) in this program shifts the relationship from a couple with a baby to a complicated power struggle. There is often confusion as to who has the power to make decisions or be involved, as illustrated with a conversation between Nikkole's mom and Josh while Nikkole is in labor in the hospital. Josh and Nikkole's mom start fighting, with his girlfriend's mother finally telling him, "It may be your baby, but this is my daughter. I trump you." [23] This comment illustrates a confusing dilemma where there are too many parental relationships within this family dynamic. Another common theme is the girls having to persuade their parents to let the fathers of their babies stay with them. Although Josh does not get along with Jennifer's parents, Jennifer convinces them to let him move in with her. Despite this, he leaves over a disagreement, which restricts his ability to see his twins.[24] In the case of Izabella, the family pressures the boyfriend by saying that he can move in with them only if he agrees to go to college, asserting their control over his life if he wants to be an involved father.[25] Cleondra and Mario cannot agree on where to live, with him saying that they should be together in his family's house: "Us three living there is just the easiest situation in every way. A family living in the same roof is normal." She responds, "I know it is normal, but with teen pregnancies, that's not always the way it works out. . . . I love that Mario wants us to live together as a family, but the thought of leaving home is making me nervous." Mario ends up frustrated that he has little say in where his daughter lives.[26] Even when the fathers do try to be involved in caring, the circumstances they face in terms of not being at the same location as the baby make it difficult. Zak, for example, does not live near Kianna and is only fifteen years old, so he has to rely on his mother for rides.[27]

A common theme among episodes within all seasons of the program is the loss of control experienced by these teen dads. In fact, all expectant dads lose control when their babies are born. They lose sleep, the attention of partners, and the ability to plan a day without considering the needs of a newborn. However, *16 and Pregnant* focuses less on these normal losses associated with fatherhood and instead on the lack of control over life decisions that teen parenthood creates for these fathers. The fathers are represented as selfish for refusing to sacrifice power and control over their girlfriends and their babies. Because of their less-than-full commitment to the mother of their child, other people's involvement in their relationship, and limited financial and emotional resources, the teen dads have great difficulty moving beyond the birth moment to any type of real participation in fatherhood.

EXPECTANT TEEN DADS AND THE DRAMA OF TELEVISION

The nature of television as a medium also influences how the program is shaped and how the audience perceives the fathers. Television favors drama, and reality television does not disappoint. Susan Murray has explored reality television as a mixed genre that borrows from documentary but incorporates other styles of television as well:

> Television networks can take a program that has somewhat liminal textual generic identifiers and sell it as either a documentary or reality program by packaging it in such a way as to appear either more educational/informative or more entertaining/sensational, or in some cases both.[28]

Viewers are given no information on how the couples who appear on the program are chosen, but one can assume that the couples that are chosen are meant to be interesting, with a story exciting enough to sustain an audience. Perhaps, more stable relationships or favorable father figures are ignored in favor of those that provide more drama. The show typically begins with the pregnant teen questioning the father's commitment, teases viewers with his involvement at the birth, and then shows a rapid decline postbirth. In fact, on the few episodes that do not follow this plotline, another drama exists in its place. In cases such as Farrah (where the father of her baby has died)[29] or Catelynn and Tyler (where both have decided to place their baby for adoption), the program focuses on other family conflicts.[30] In the episode with Kayla and Mike, Mike seems extremely supportive and committed as both a boyfriend and then an actual father throughout the episode. The show, however, rarely focuses on their relationship, choosing instead to focus on the more problematic relationship between Kayla and her mother.[31] In a typical couple depiction for the program, the start of an episode has Sabrina questioning Iman's commitment to her and their baby. He even misses the birth, and Sabrina contemplates ending the relationship. However, in a surprise twist, he shows up unexpectedly and stays to be a full-time father. The program ends up dwelling on how his visit resulted in drama between Kayla and her sister.[32]

In addition to the structure of the program, there is the message that the program producers want to send. The program walks a fine line between normalizing teen pregnancy and illustrating the problems with it. Each episode ends with a morality tale that the girls realize the mistake they made. The lack of fatherly involvement or unhappiness in their relationship typically ends up a part of this message.

The dissatisfaction within these relationships on the program fills each episode with a great deal of drama, something that television is ideal at depicting. David Thorburn writes about the structure of melodrama on television:

> The audience wants to be titillated but also wants to be confirmed in its moral sloth, the argument goes, and so the melodramatist sells stories in which crime and criminals are absorbed into paradigms of moral conflict, into allegories of good and evil, in which the good almost always win.[33]

In *16 and Pregnant*, crime may not exist, but heroes and villains remain. Since the program is told from the perspective of the teen mom, the fathers, inadvertently perhaps, star in the only major role left—the bad guy. Their circumstances, often including poverty, unemployment, and immature relationships with girlfriends, leave plenty of material for producers to sculpt this role. Whether it is Jennifer accusing Josh of kidnapping his sons, Jordan blaming Tyler for abandoning his daughter, or Jamie shutting Ryan out of a relationship with their daughter after he cheats on her, the fathers are often portrayed as the villains on the program.

MY BABY DADDY: TEEN MOMS AS GATEKEEPERS

The program, by framing the father figure in a negative way, then offers the teen mother to function as a gatekeeper for the child. In an episode of *16 and Pregnant*, Jordan is upset because her mother and her boyfriend Tyler cannot get along. When she finally brokers a truce, she says with relief, "I can't have my baby daddy and my mom not liking each other." Jordan's troubles illustrate a common theme of the program, which is the key role that the mother plays as a gatekeeper in the relationship between herself and the baby, her family, and the baby's father.[34] In writing about the changing role of fathers in our culture, Jeremy Adam Smith argues,

> By and large in our culture today, mothers are still the "gatekeepers"—that is, they control access to, and management of, children. Mothers can discourage fathers' involvement by holding them to unrealistically high or rigid standards, not giving them chances to learn from failures, redoing tasks, ridiculing efforts to help or participate, overseeing their child care in a critical, supervisory manner, and more.[35]

Illustrating the notion of gatekeeping described by Smith, the teen moms on the program serve as the intermediaries between the father and the baby. At times, the gatekeeping of the teen moms appears deliberate, but at other times the challenges that these teen moms have in managing their competing relationships and their different disappointments in their boyfriends are the cause.

16 and Pregnant sometimes represents gatekeeping as resulting from motherly instincts, connecting motherhood with what feminists might label an *essentialism*, where it is women who are naturally, rather than socially, meant to nurture their babies. A telling example is that of Cleondra and Mario, who bicker over where their baby should live. Cleondra's mother will not allow her to sleep over at Mario's house. Despite Mario's offers to take the baby to his home for a night, Cleondra thinks that a newborn should not be separated from its mother, a sentiment even Mario's mother agrees with. Eventually, Cleondra's mother agrees to allow her and the baby to spend the night at Mario's in what is designed to be a trap by both women to prove that Mario will not live up to his promises to help. Sure enough, Mario sleeps through the feedings and ends up proving of no help during the night. Of course, had Cleondra just allowed him to watch the baby by himself, he would have had no intermediary there between him and the baby.[36] Forced to caretake alone, perhaps Mario would have still slept through the night, but alternatively, he may have had no choice but to wake up and care for the infant. Mario and the viewers are not given the opportunity to find out how Mario could parent when faced with sole provider status, even if just for a night. The gatekeeping serves to reinforce the woman's maternal role and prevents her from gaining necessary help or providing Mario an opportunity, without interference, to develop his paternal role.

Scientists today are studying how fathers may have hormones activated during pregnancy and postbirth that encourage their involvement in fatherly roles. Some studies suggest that the testosterone hormone in a male drops after he becomes a parent and then continues to drop when he assumes increased parental roles.[37] *16 and Pregnant*, though, does not show most fathers on the program as even having an opportunity to nurture these fatherly instincts, while the mothers are presented as naturally possessing them. Most episodes conclude with the teen mother illustrating her growth into motherhood. The show, through its editing, offers us scenes of the mothers cuddling, dressing, feeding, and caring for their children. The show frames the teen mom's struggle as not about learning to be a mother but about dealing with the challenges of those around her, especially managing the relationship with the baby's father. By the end of each episode, the girls detail their struggles and sometimes express regret for the timing but not for becoming mothers. The program presents the experience of being a mother as a natural process that happens even despite the adversity facing these women. In contrast, the program presents the fatherly role as one with unclear expectations. The mothers on the program define who are good and bad fathers, based on varying standards. While some fathers fulfill these motherly expectations, more end up falling short and end up spending the remainder of the program less involved with their children. Motherhood is treated by the program as a biological function of women and fatherhood as a purely socially constructed one.

In addition to the motherly gatekeeping, the extended relatives limit the amount of involvement that the fathers can have in the lives of the baby. In one episode, parents of Kayla allow JR to stay overnight at her house once the baby is born, but the teens are not allowed to visit each other's rooms in the middle of the night. With JR restricted from her bedroom, Kayla must confront night duty herself.[38] The parents, while trying to protect her modesty, prevent their daughter from accessing any additional help during the nights, some of the hardest times in caring for a newborn. In another case, Jordan's mother will not allow the father of her baby, Tyler, to be in her house.[39] At the beginning of the episode, Tyler is angry, saying, "I'll fight her to the death. She is not going to keep my son away from me." Even when she relents and agrees to an open-door policy, Tyler admits that he does not feel comfortable in the home. Eventually, he ends up in a fight with Jordan's brothers, and by the end of the episode, it appears that he no longer will be a part of the baby's life.[40] Though Tyler and JR seem to want to be involved with their children, the gatekeeping done by the parental figures prevents them from being able to play a truly active role.

An extreme form of gatekeeping that appears within the program is the threat of loss of paternal rights. This rhetoric within the discussion is not necessarily rooted in actual law but in the teens' conceptions of what they think the law ought to be. Jennifer and Josh, who are parents of twins, have a confrontation while he is driving. Josh pulls over and lets her out of the car but drives away with the babies while she screams, "Josh, for your information, you are going to jail. That is called kidnapping." He pulls back over and drops the babies off and leaves. She still calls the police. "Say good-bye to your kids because you will never see them again."[41] He is taken away by the police, and we are told that he spent a night in jail. Another teen mom, Taylor, says about the father of her child, "If he can't take the right steps to become a better dad, then he can't be around Aubri." Her threat here indicates the control that the mothers appear to have, even when legal rights differ among states and with different domestic situations.[42] When Jamie is having a conversation with her parents (that is, her mother and her mother's boyfriend) about Ryan, the father of her child, and why he needs to be in her baby's life, she defends him: "But Ryan is still the father. He still has parental rights, so you do need to think about it." Her mother replies, "His name is not even on the birth certificate. He has zero rights." Later, when Jamie is with Ryan and he expresses his desire to spend time with the baby at his parent's house, she says, "I could have you arrested for kidnapping."[43]

At other times, the threats are not connected to the father's direct interactions with the child. For Nikkole and Josh, Nikkole becomes fed up with Josh when she sees him with another girl and reports him to the police for substance abuse.[44] Of course, this legal record now interferes with his paternal rights to his child. When Ryan cheats on Jamie, she responds by saying, "I don't want to keep Ryan away from his daughter, but that just might be what is best for now."[45] Through these legal threats, the program presents the mothers as having full control over not just the baby but the involvement that the father will be allowed to have in the baby's life.

16 and Pregnant, by showcasing dysfunctional fatherly relationships, illustrates the role that outside factors, such as the relationship with the mother, play in determining how a father will be involved with his child. The lack of control and responsibility seen by these fathers is contrasted with the amount of control and power given to the mothers. Certainly, there are some fathers represented as showing little interest in their babies, but more often, they simply have unstable relationships with the mothers. The fathers here are represented as not having a natural or definitive relationship with their babies but a precarious one that can be taken away at any time. Josh had been excited about having twins and wanting to marry Jennifer, but because of what he sees as too much interference by her parents, he ends up not visiting as often as he wanted, resulting in Jennifer taking control of the twins because of his lack of interest.[46] Tyler also had plans for Jordan to live with his family once the baby was born, but she moves back in with her mother. Feeling unwelcome in Jordan's mother's home, Tyler stops visiting, which results in Jordan's family declaring him a bad father.[47] These are just two examples of how motherly gatekeeping on the program results in a self-fulfilling prophecy where the fathers, because they know they do not have any real control, avoid bonding with their children.

"HE'S JUST THE SPERM DONOR": EXPECTATIONS OF FATHERHOOD

While postbirth the mothers engage in gatekeeping, prebirth there are various scenes throughout the program that illustrate the ambivalence of the teens trying to create an ideal family but wrestling with issues of control and what role the fathers should have. The program presents the teens' desires to create a family structure that few of them have ever experienced. A majority of the young men and women have had dysfunctional or nonexistent relationships with their fathers. The urge to create an idealized two-parent family structure is a consistent reason cited by the teens to explain their decision to keep their babies. In one episode, Nathan justifies his desire to be a dad: "I couldn't stand the idea of how my dad left. I wouldn't want to do that to her." His girlfriend Taylor concurs, "I was a huge daddy's girl, and he quit being there, and he would promise things, and it would break my heart when he wouldn't do it."[48] Disappointment in fatherly relationships is echoed in the conversation between Kianna and boyfriend Zak. Questioning him on whether he believes that it is realistic for them to raise their baby, he answers by focusing on his motivation for being a father: "I would be a better dad than my dad was. I have five memories that I can think of my dad off the top of my head. With my son, I want to be around for him. I want him to have lots of memories with me. Not just five."[49] Brian talks about how happy he is that the baby is being raised in his girlfriend Jordan's house because of its strong sense of family. It is an ironic sentiment because Jordan and her twin sister were abandoned by their parents, so their grandparents adopted them.[50] Valerie, another teen mom, explains that she was adopted: "I want [my daughter] to have something that wasn't possible for me. Her biological mom and dad in her life." When Alex is fighting with her mom about why she is still trying to keep contact with the baby's father, she explains herself: "I'm trying to prevent her from not having a father. That is my priority. My priority is that she has another parent, that she does have a dad because I barely had a dad and look how I am."[51]

The teens have finally reached a biological age where they can create a family, and although all admit to becoming pregnant accidentally, they want to make the best of the situation by creating an idealized experience of family for their children. Trying to attain this imagined perfect family is complicated because of their social and economic realities, the gatekeeping that the girls and their mothers engage in, and their lack of agreement on the definition of an ideal father.

The program presents the main purpose of fathers as serving as financial providers, a representation that conforms to the provider role identity attached to men that has been explored by scholars.[52] In one scene, Jenelle tries to explain to her parents how important it is to have her boyfriend Andrew in her life. She argues that Andrew can support her more than just financially, also "mentally." Her stepfather responds, "Mentally isn't going to put food on the table. . . . Mentally isn't going to buy the diapers." Later, after Jenelle finds out that Andrew has started drinking, her mother responds,

> He hasn't done anything for the baby, and I don't think he's capable. And I think that you better start putting him behind you, and, baby's father or not, like I told you, he's just the sperm donor, really, because you need to just think of yourself now and the baby. I just don't think he's the person for you.[53]

This scene illustrates a frequent refrain evident in the program—that if the man cannot provide financially for the baby, then he does not deserve a place in the baby's life. Often, this view is expressed not necessarily from the mother of the baby but from her parental figures. In an episode with Markai and James, he claims responsibility for his child, saying, "I'm gonna take care of mine," although her mother warns her, "You can't depend on baby daddy," since her children's father left them early on. Yet, later on, her mother says that she will not let him move in, and Markai worries, "If he doesn't find a place for us to live or a job, he's going to be looking in from the outside."[54] Similarly, with Sarah and Blake, Sarah's mother is angry at the lack of money that Blake is giving to Sarah. Eventually, after an argument with her mother, he leaves to go work on a shrimp boat.[55] The mothers of the daughters on the program, who typically have raised their children without the help of a father figure, often try to convince the girls that they do not need a man as well. Alex's mother tells her that she is better off simply breaking contact with her boyfriend Matthew.[56] Briana's mother tells her daughter, "Sometimes daddies are not willing to make it work."[57] Hope's mother warns her daughter, "I want you to expect nothing from this man because men suck."[58] Even Sabrina's mother advises her daughter that it may be best to forget about the baby's father, Iman, and have a fresh start, although Iman ends up becoming an extremely supportive boyfriend and father.[59] The mothers of the daughters serve here in the role of trying to subvert their daughters' attempts at forming an idealized family structure with what may appear to be an overreliance on an "imperfect" man.

This view of the father as solely a financial provider minimizes the other roles that fathers play in the lives of their children. In the case of Mike and Kayla, Mike is supportive of Kayla before she has her baby and after. He lives with them and assumes primary responsibility for his son after the birth. Kayla says, "Luckily, Mike is getting the hang of it and has been helping a lot." Later, Kayla's mother decides that Mike needs to start paying $300 rent, which is more than he can afford with his part-time job. The mother makes his remaining in her house conditional upon his paying rent, and he is forced to give up his primary caretaker role. Because Kayla must take on the full-time child care responsibilities, she can no longer remain in school.[60] Though the earlier arrangement worked better for the couple, the mother frames the economic value of the father as more important than the actual parenting one.

For some fathers shown on the program, their own belief in the importance of the financial role of the male figure prevents them from serving in any role. In the case of Justin and Ashley, he expresses to her regret that he cannot raise the child. He tells her, "If I had the money and all that, I would love to help take care of it, but I don't really want the baby growing up the way I did. I want it to have the things it needs." Justin acknowledges being the biological father of the child, but he also recognizes his inability to provide for this child. In his eyes, a key function of the father is financial support.[61] Matt, despite his lack of relationship with girlfriend Valerie, bonds with his baby and shows off his knowledge of parenting books. Eventually, much to the dismay of Valerie, he announces that he is moving two hundred miles away for a full-time job.[62] Colin serves in the military and emphasizes his need to return so that he can set up a stable home for Devon and the baby, even though it means time away from them.[63]

The program minimizes the potential importance that the father can play in the daily life of the child at the expense of focusing on only the financial provider role. The fathers on the program are deemed failures because of their inability to provide this sort of assistance. Ann Shola Orloff and Renee A. Monson have written about how "the capacity to father is based on labor market status."[64] Women can mother just by nature of their biology, but men are expected to father primarily by working to offer economic support to the mother and the child. This view, reinforced consistently on *16 and Pregnant*, constrains society's views of women and men. It neither allows men to have the potential to develop strong relationships with their children outside their role as economic provider, nor does it encourage women to see themselves as more than simply a biological, natural mother.

CONCLUSION

16 and Pregnant provides a view into the challenging world of parenting when the parents are teenagers themselves. The program also reflects societal confusion over how the role of fathers is constructed, and it prefers to emphasize the power that mothers have to control fatherly access to children. Since the episodes frame the mother as bearing the primary care of child raising, the program positions the motherly role as a natural one. It also represents women as having the power to make the decision, even legally, over whether the father should play a role in the life of the child. Finally, it represents financial support as the most vital role that a father should play, at the expense of nurturing or offering other emotional support. With the program's following being a young audience of teenagers still formulating beliefs about the role of fatherhood and motherhood, it is important to consider the meaning making that *16 and Pregnant* has the power to influence.

NOTES

1. "Devon," *16 and Pregnant*, season 4, May 22, 2012.
2. Urban Dictionary, http://www.urbandictionary.com/define.php?term=baby+daddy.
3. Thurer, *The Myths of Motherhood*, 167, 171.
4. Smith, *The Daddy Shift*, xi.
5. Heath, "The Impact of Delayed Fatherhood," 511.
6. Bunting and McAuley, "Research Review," 295.
7. Lamb, "The History of Research," 37.
8. LaRossa, "Fatherhood and Social Change," 457.
9. Tichenor et al., "The Importance of Fatherhood," 246.
10. Hochschild, *The Second Shift*.
11. Allen and Hawkins, "Maternal Gatekeeping"; Marsiglio et al., "Scholarship on Fatherhood"; Fagan and Barnett, "The Relationship between Maternal Gatekeeping."
12. Pehlke et al., "Does Father Still Know Best?" 136.
13. Leavitt, *Make Room for Daddy*.
14. Reed, *Birthing Fathers*, 202.
15. "Nikkole," *16 and Pregnant*, season 2, February 23, 2012.
16. "Jamie," *16 and Pregnant*, season 3, May 3, 2011.
17. "Briana," *16 and Pregnant*, season 4, April 3, 2012.
18. "Chelsea," *16 and Pregnant*, season 2, March 9, 2010.
19. "Briana."
20. "Sabrina," *16 and Pregnant*, season 4, May 15, 2012.
21. "Sarah," *16 and Pregnant*, season 4, May 15, 2012.
22. "Jordan," *16 and Pregnant*, season 4, April 24, 2012.
23. "Nikkole."
24. "Jennifer," *16 and Pregnant*, season 3, April 26, 2011.
25. "Izabella," *16 and Pregnant*, season 3, May 31, 2011.
26. "Cleondra," *16 and Pregnant*, season 3, May 17, 2011.
27. "Kianna," *16 and Pregnant*, season 3, June 7, 2011.
28. Murray, "'I Think We Need a New Name for It,'" 44.
29. "Farrah," *16 and Pregnant*, season 1, June 18, 2009.
30. "Catelynn," *16 and Pregnant*, season 1, July 16, 2009.
31. "Kayla," *16 and Pregnant*, season 3, May 24, 2011.

32. "Sabrina."
33. Thorburn, "Television Melodrama," 538–39.
34. "Jordan."
35. Smith, *The Daddy Shift*, 135.
36. "Cleondra."
37. Belluck, "In Study."
38. "Kayla," *16 and Pregnant*, season 2, December 7, 2010.
39. The daughter says the reason is that Tyler is white and Jordan's family is black.
40. "Jordan."
41. "Jennifer."
42. "Taylor," *16 and Pregnant*, season 3, June 14, 2011.
43. "Jamie."
44. "Nikkole."
45. "Jamie."
46. "Jennifer."
47. "Jordan."
48. "Taylor."
49. "Kianna."
50. "Jordan," *16 and Pregnant*, season 3, April 19, 2011.
51. "Valerie," *16 and Pregnant*, season 2, March 2, 2010.
52. Tichenor et al., "Importance of Fatherhood," 246.
53. "Jenelle," *16 and Pregnant*, season 2, February 16, 2010.
54. "Markai," *16 and Pregnant*, season 2, November 16, 2010.
55. "Sarah."
56. "Alex," *16 and Pregnant*, season 4, April 18, 2012.
57. "Briana."
58. "Hope," *16 and Pregnant*, season 4, May 8, 2012.
59. "Sabrina."
60. "Kayla," *16 and Pregnant*, season 3, May 24, 2011.
61. "Ashley," *16 and Pregnant*, season 2, December 21, 2010.
62. "Valerie."
63. "Devon."
64. Orloff and Monson, "Citizens, Workers or Fathers?" 63.

Part IV

Is This Real Life? Mediating the Whole Story of Teen Pregnancy and Motherhood

Chapter Twelve

"Having an Abortion Is Not Uncommon, but Talking about It Publicly Is"

Exploring the Potential for Positive, Feminist, Pro-Choice Portrayals of Young Women's Experiences with Abortion in Mass Media through MTV's "No Easy Decision"

JoAnne Gordon

This chapter uses the special episode of MTV's documentary-series *16 and Pregnant* entitled "No Easy Decision" as a case study to explore the potential of mass media to disseminate positive, feminist, and pro-choice portrayals of abortion. "No Easy Decision" is an important site of analysis because it specifically focuses on the reality and experiences of young women who have had abortions. Given the current political climate of hostility and regressive federal and state policies against women's reproductive rights and access in the United States,[1] this chapter explores how mass media can be utilized as a tool to fill in the gaps in representations and information pertaining to sexual and reproductive health available to youth. Moreover, this chapter examines how we can look at the show "No Easy Decision" as a counterhegemonic site and a potential feminist success for representations of not only abortion but also teen pregnancy and pregnancy options.

To begin with, I examine the historical and current climate of reproductive and sexual health in the United States. Using the reality of sexual and reproductive health (mis)information and (mis)representation, I then make claims for how mass media can be (re)shaped as an educational tool for sexual and reproductive health information for youth. Next, using "No Easy Decision" as a case study, I look at how mass media constructs representations and discourses of abortion, specifically among young women. Last, using "No Easy Decision," this chapter questions and challenges what the possibility is of mass media being able to convey positive, nonjudgmental, comprehensive, and accurate information about sexual and reproductive health.

HISTORICAL AND CURRENT CLIMATE OF REPRODUCTIVE AND SEXUAL HEALTH IN THE UNITED STATES

The Guttmacher Institute, for advancing sexual and reproductive health worldwide, highlights that in the context of U.S. pregnancies, almost half are unintended and four in ten end in abortion.[2] Furthermore, at current rates, about one-third of American women will have had an abortion by forty-five years of age.[3] Yet even given these realities, abortion remains one of the most regulated elements of health care. To contextualize the frequency of abortion, in 1972, before abortion was legalized in the United States through *Roe v. Wade*, 75 percent of teenage pregnancies resulted in live births, dropping to 50 percent after 1973, when abortion was legalized.[4] Even more important, it must be recognized that the mere legality of abortion does not mean that it is geographically or financially available to all women or that it is always accessible or safe.[5] Additionally, abortion stigma, which is a "negative attribute ascribed to women who seek to terminate a pregnancy that marks them, internally or externally, as inferior to ideals of womanhood," acts as an additional barrier on top of geographical and financial barriers.[6] Abortion stigma is not just harmful as a barrier to abortion access but also works to conceal the reality of abortion as a common experience for women in the United States.

It must be understood that reproductive rights continue to be a controversial issue in the current conservative political climate in the United States.[7] Ongoing attempts to undermine women's access to reproductive health care, contraceptives, and abortion are increasing.[8] According to the Guttmacher Institute, in the first three months of 2011 alone, state legislators across the United States introduced 916 bills related to reproductive health, of which 56 percent were aimed to restrict abortion access (up from 38 percent the year before).[9] As Trina Stout explains, the proposed restrictions included "longer waiting periods, scientifically inaccurate counseling, mandatory ultrasounds, restricted insurance coverage of abortion, and 20-week abortion bans . . . [the proposed banning of] insurance coverage of abortion services in the new health care system, as well as [the elimination of] tax credits and deductions for abortion in private insurance plans."[10] Reproductive health and rights advocates are on the constant defense at both state and federal levels; however, the Democratic victory of the 2012 election suggests that the majority of voting Americans support women's access to sexual and reproductive health, especially abortion.

These restrictions to reproductive and sexual health have not been limited to access of services but have been greatly extended to the sexual and reproductive health information and education that American youth receive. Additionally, young women have been the target of the efforts of the conservative right to limit information related to sexual and reproductive health education and services that are and should be available to them.[11] It is important to acknowledge that the abstinence-only approach currently defines U.S. sex education policy. As Jocelyn Boryczka shockingly states, "Over the past decade, 48 states received nearly $1 billion in federal funding to support abstinence-only programs, and 86% of America's public school districts currently mandate that sex education curricula promote abstinence."[12]

A discussion of the differences between conservative abstinence-only approaches to sexual education and a more liberal comprehensive version of sexual education is important to contextualize how information about sexual and reproductive health is being shaped and promoted to youth. As Tiffany Jones highlights in her article on discursive frameworks for understanding sexuality education, a more conservative orientation to education takes an authoritative approach, with the authority figure "inculcating students with dominant values, beliefs, and practices of the time, and students [are] seen as passive recipients of this knowledge."[13] This approach aims to have students follow the conventions of social, civic, religious, or local community perspectives.[14] Conservative approaches always transmit dominant and privileged sexualities (read: heterosexual, married, and monogamous), and diversity in this model is always "negated, rendered invisible, pathologized, demonized, or declared a fallacy or a mistaken choice."[15] Often, the conservative sexuality education takes on an "abstinence only until marriage" discourse and approach, which calls for students to abstain from sexual activity until marriage and informs that prior sexual activity will result in harm.[16] Additionally, conversations on contraceptive options and abortion are inconsistently and inaccurately covered, shamed, or negated all together.[17]

In contrast to the conservative approach, a more liberal orientation involves the teacher acting as a facilitator in the students' development of knowledge and skills that focus on personal choice and development.[18] Stemming from a liberal approach to sexuality education emerged what is categorized as comprehensive sexual and reproductive health education. As Jones highlights, comprehensive sex education was developed to "get troubling concepts into the open" in the 1960s and was adopted primarily in response to the perceived "epidemic" of teenage pregnancies.[19] Whereas abstinence-only education does not provide information about safer sex practices, pleasure, or abortion services, the comprehensive curriculum's inclusion of spaces to deconstruct complex contexts and structural forces that shape moral decisions has the ability to empower youth by teaching them to critically engage with messages that are being presented to them.[20]

Additionally, drawing on what Jones classifies as the critical approach to sexuality education, linked to feminism, gay liberation, and postcolonialism, progressive comprehensive sex education should adopt a framework that encourages students to think critically and actively about which sexualities and sexual identities society privileges and to undertake actions that lead to a more equitable society.[21] This approach is important because it acknowledges that the "systematic, institutionalized denial of reproductive freedom has uniquely marked Black women's history in America."[22] There exists a powerful link between race and reproductive freedom, or lack thereof, which can be traced back as far as the slave master's economic stake over black women's bodies, to the racist foundations of the birth control movement and the forced sterilization movement in the United States, to the current push for young black women, mothers on welfare, and indigenous women to receive Norplant and Depo-Provera as their "only" options for birth control.[23] Therefore, we need to situate the right to terminate a pregnancy and discussions about reproductive and sexual health within a much broader conversation about the right to bodily autonomy, which includes abortion as well as all other reproductive decision-making choices in the context of marginalized young women's bodies.[24]

Unfortunately, youth are not getting access to comprehensive, accurate, antiracist, decolonial, pro-choice, and feminist information and education related to sexual and reproductive health. Therefore, it is imperative that alternative means of disseminating information are explored to ensure that youth are receiving the information that they need to make empowered and informed decisions that are best suited to their lived realities. The following section examines the possibility of mass media, or popular media, playing the role of educator in the context of sexual and reproductive health.

(RE)SHAPING MASS MEDIA AS AN EDUCATIONAL TOOL

Gavey contends that media representations are an important source of information about societal perceptions because they "provide examples of various discourses in circulation."[25] Dominant groups (e.g., medical, religious, educational, and media institutions) construct, reproduce, and contest domination and social inequality through text and talk or discourse. The extent to which the messaging of these dominant groups is challenged can be understood as determining the degree to which their ideology becomes integrated into the culture, through either law or convention.[26] What becomes known as the dominant discourse, or hegemonic discourse, gets used to set the parameters for what can be discussed.[27] As Anita Shaw reveals, "Regardless of the issue, the mass media usually present the dominant discourse and, by contrasting it to a nonsensical position, convince most media consumers that the dominant discourse simply makes sense."[28] Therefore, we can understand the media as playing a role in reflecting and perpetuating currently existing attitudes and political agendas rooted in stereotypes and oppressive ideologies that implicitly and explicitly marginalize specific voices and experiences.[29] As Yasmin Jiwani states in her work on the ways in which media constructs and reinforces racist and sexist violence, "narrative structure activates previous representations, which then ground and inform the meaning of current representations."[30] Thus, media acts as one dominant avenue for how representations of, for example, young women's sexuality and reproductive health choices are framed, disseminated, naturalized, and legitimized. The reality is that the media has an enormous potential to reach young people in the United States because mass media plays a critical role in shaping culture, reflected by current survey findings that young people watch sixteen to seventeen hours of TV weekly and spend thirty-eight hours each week using media of some kind.[31] This is typically more time than youth spend in school or interacting directly with their parents.[32]

Ward states that there are several theoretical and practical circumstances that can be used to explain why mass media, especially television, has the potential to play a critical role in educating American youth about sexuality.[33] These factors include the fact that sexual content is pervasive in the media; content is highly accessible and widely consumed; the media has the potential to be forthcoming and explicit about sexuality when others are not; and the media is intentionally appealing, compelling, and engaging.[34] In the context of looking at media's impact on young people's understandings of sexual and reproductive health, it is equally important to then question if, how, and in what ways popular media can act as a healthy and comprehensive sex educator. These are important questions because the media is seldom concerned with the lasting outcome of its portrayals of sex and is typically more concerned with attracting audiences and selling products.[35] It is estimated that youth will encounter approximately ten thousand to fifteen thousand sexual references, jokes, and innuendos each year through media.[36] Moreover, in the context of teen pregnancy, the media has profound effects on pregnant and mothering young women by shaping representations of their lives that might not actually be reflective of their lived realities.[37] It is important to highlight that the decisions of pregnant young women are evaluated according to white, middle-class standards that frame these women as being individually responsible for their actions.[38] Part of this framing is the result of white, middle-class, able-bodied, university-educated women represented as dominant voices within the reproductive health and pro-choice movements.[39] Their voices represent what "pro-choice" and adequate reproductive and sexual health are meant to mean for *all* women, regardless of whether they reflect *all* women's realities.[40] Therefore, the question then remains, how can we (re)shape mass media to be a potential educational tool for youth related to sexual and reproductive health? And is there a possibility for the information that media provides to be comprehensive, pro-choice, feminist, and relevant for all young women?

The reality is that popular media often frames issues related to reproductive and sexual health in problematic ways, including framing women who use birth control negatively, providing misinformation about safer contraception (especially condoms), providing little to no resources about access to reproductive health care options, and offering deviant stereotypes of women and reproduction, especially young women.[41] In Amy Hasinoff's work on sexting, she explains that "whether in mass media, legislative hearings, or online safety campaigns, girls are castigated for engaging in media production about their sexualities because this is thought to be inappropriate, to attract online predators, and to damage their reputations."[42] However, the Kaiser Family Foundation reveals that young teens rate the media as their number one source of information about sexuality and sexual health.[43] How then can media examples be (re)shaped and used as teaching tools to help youth deconstruct the ways in which reproductive health and sexuality are framed for their consumption "and the ways in which those framings might reflect or perpetuate certain types of inaccurate information, stereotypes, or prejudices?"[44] Additionally, can we use popular media as a tool to more closely connect sexual health and reproductive health choices as interrelated rather than separate?

Beth Jaworski suggests that "different types of media related to women's reproduction might be used to help young men and women develop skills for critically deconstructing and reframing messages about sex and reproduction put forth by various forms of media."[45] Educational programs placed within mainstream popular television have the potential to teach youth critical media literacy skills as well as information related to sexual and reproductive health. These types of programs are known as "entertainment education," which is "the process of designing and implementing a media message both to intentionally entertain and educate, in order to increase audience members' knowledge about an education issue, and create behavior change."[46] Youth audiences are an important target audience because they can be confronted with many health and social challenges, such as sexually transmitted infections, unwanted pregnancy, and substance (ab)use, and they are also more difficult to reach with traditional marketing and advertising techniques.[47]

According to recent surveys, 78 percent of youth state that they have all the information they need to avoid an unplanned or unwanted pregnancy.[48]

However, approximately half of teens (49 percent) "admit they know 'little or nothing' about condoms and how to use them."[49] As Louisa Allen states in the introduction of her book *Young People and Sexuality Education*, which strives to reimagine sexuality education by incorporating the viewpoints of 1,261 young people between the ages of sixteen and nineteen years, "programmes that fail to acknowledge young people's lived realities are less likely to capture their attention."[50] Without youth input in sexuality education, educators are risking youth disengagement from messaging. Additionally, acknowledging that the media is a dominant source of information for youth means that it is important for sex educators to tap into that resource and find ways to fill in the gaps of sexual and reproductive health information available for youth.

For example, after an episode of the fictional teen series *Friday Night Lights* depicted the decision of a tenth grader to have an abortion in a sensitive and responsible way, Gloria Feldt stated in an article in the *Washington Post* that "this isn't just a television show. Media portrayals, real or fictional, don't merely inform us—they form us. And they miss the profound truth of women's lives when they reduce broad issues such as sexual and childbearing choices to one word—abortion—and reduce abortion to a polarized, black-and-white debate."[51] Therefore, it is important to examine how the shaping of attitudes and perceptions in relation to reproductive information is framed by the mass media and how those framings can affect public opinion and policy.[52] Moreover, Louisa Allen's survey revealed that young women's experience with biased information about abortion in the media served to discourage them from considering it as a viable or safe option.[53] Then, the larger question remains: is it possible for mass media to portray sexual and reproductive health options, specifically abortion, in programming targeted at youth in a comprehensive, accurate, pro-choice, and feminist manner? In the following section, I examine how MTV's "No Easy Decision" has the potential to be a successful step forward in the media as an educational tool that operates as a counterhegemonic site for sexual and reproductive health information available to youth.

MASS MEDIA AND REPRESENTATIONS OF ABORTION

While there have been periodic, not to mention fictional, representations of abortion on youth-focused television shows such as *Friday Night Lights* and *DeGrassi*, there has been little to no representation of abortion on "reality shows" aimed at youth. However, the feminist blogosphere exploded at the end of 2010 with the leaked announcement that MTV would air a special episode of its hit show *16 and Pregnant* that would explicitly deal with abortion. The excitement was also met with serious concern among pro-choice feminists and media critics who feared that "Dr. Drew" Pinsky, who would be hosting the show, would not handle the conversation with the compassion and nuance that it required.

The abortion special, named "No Easy Decision," ran as a thirty-minute spin-off of MTV's smash-success reality series about teen pregnancy *16 and Pregnant*. This episode was particularly important because *16 and Pregnant* and the follow-up series *Teen Mom* and *Teen Mom 2* have shown parenting and adoption as options for young women faced with unexpected pregnancy but have failed to explore or represent the third option for pregnant women, which is abortion. Feminist media critic Jennifer L. Pozner, author of *Reality Bites Back*, states that "while 27 percent of pregnant teens choose abortion . . . in MTV's version of 'reality,' 100 percent of pregnant teens give birth."[54] MTV has come under fire from feminist media critic Jessica Valenti, who rightfully "called out" the show *16 and Pregnant* by questioning,

> Why are some teen pregnancies worth covering while others aren't? There is more than one kind of pregnant teen; even if a teenager decides to have an abortion *she was still pregnant*, her story is still important, and her decision is worth talking about. This absence of teens who choose abortion in *16 and Pregnant* feels like a dismissal of so many young women's experiences.[55]

In December 2010, MTV aired the thirty-minute interview special "No Easy Decision," in which three women sat down with celebrity doctor Dr. Drew to speak about their experiences and decisions, as youth, to have abortions. The segment centered largely on Markai Durham and her partner, James. Markai appeared in season 2 of *16 and Pregnant* and carried her daughter, Zakaria, to term, yet "No Easy Decision" focuses on the young couple's decision-making process that results in her terminating a subsequent pregnancy. The segment also included two other young women, Natalia and Katie, who spoke about their experiences and decisions to choose abortion.

It is important to note that MTV had no intention to promote the show and that the special appeared far past a prime-time hour, at 11:30 pm during the end of December, when most shows usually air reruns due to the holiday season.[56] MTV did, however, partner with postabortion support talkline Exhale, which planned an online campaign called "16 and Loved" to support the young women who were openly talking about their abortions. Nevertheless, "No Easy Decision" has the potential to be read as a feminist success, as the episode accurately revealed "that abortion is safe and common, that abortion has been made difficult to get, and, most importantly, that abortion is a complex decision made by complex human beings."[57] From the very beginning of the episode, Dr. Drew's opening statement set the tone for the framing of how the topic of abortion would be breached throughout the thirty-minute segment:

About 750,000 girls in the U.S. get pregnant every year. And although nearly a third of these teen pregnancies result in abortion, we've never shown this choice on *16 and Pregnant* up until now. It can be a polarizing topic, and there's quite frankly no way to talk about this and please everyone. Although controversial to some, abortion is one of the three viable options, and it's among the safest, most common medical procedures in the U.S., so we thought it was important for us to discuss.[58]

While the 750,000 pregnancies a year may seem alarming, it is important to note that this current figure is down 36 percent since its peak in 1990.[59] These figures indicate vast differences in how teen pregnancy rates are reported, which makes "gauging the prevalence of this phenomenon highly ambiguous, even as seemingly ubiquitous media coverage makes teen pregnancy seem like a growing trend."[60] They also highlight how important discussions of teenage pregnancy and pregnancy options are because they are often not represented comprehensively or accurately.

As mentioned, the episode largely consists of a prerecorded segment in which Markai and her partner James struggle with the reality of their second unplanned pregnancy. Markai reveals that she missed her appointment for her Depo-Provera shot, which she did not realize would cause her to have a much higher chance of becoming pregnant. Markai is not pleased by the option of abortion but does not want to carry the pregnancy to term and place the child for adoption or raise the child under the already tight resources that she and James have available for their family. Dr. Drew contextualizes Markai's reality by stating that "61 percent of women who have abortions already have children."[61] While the show revealed a positive depiction of a multiracial family, inclusive approaches to engagements with spirituality, as well as a positive portrayal of women with families and partners that are loving, supportive, and respectful of a woman's right to choice, the reality is that we often do not hear these stories. I argue that while it is incredibly important to have these experiences depicted, it is crucial to recognize that this is not the reality for a lot of young women, especially racialized and indigenous women in the United States, who often are subject to blatant exclusions from birth control options, including abortion, and for whom discourse fails to acknowledge the historical and ongoing restrictions placed on the reproductive choice to get pregnant—with whom, when and how, and what options are available.[62]

However, I believe that this show can be read as a potential feminist success, as well as a counterhegemonic site for representations and information related to teen pregnancy and pregnancy options, because it includes medically accurate information about abortion procedures; discussion of the challenge of finding the birth control method that works for the individual; the positive presence of supportive family and friends; the compassionate voice of a clinic counselor; the complex emotions of male partners; the cost of abortion ($750 in the case of Natalia, who sold her prom ticket back to the school); the cruelty of parental notification requirements (requiring Natalia to secure a judicial bypass, "begging for permission to make [her] own decision")[63]; the normality of mixed feelings after the procedure; and the characterization of abortion as "a parenting decision."[64] Last, Dr. Drew concludes the segment by stating, "Hopefully this inspires us to be more compassionate when we think about abortions. . . . Having an abortion is not uncommon, but talking about it publicly is."[65] Therefore, the show is optimistic that by capturing the complexities of people's lives, which work to inform their reproductive and sexual health choices, the stigma of abortion and the reality of youth sexuality will start to be challenged in mass media.

DISCUSSION AND CONCLUDING REMARKS

After discussing how abortion gets taken up in "No Easy Decision," I now return to my original question: with "No Easy Decision" as an example, what then is the possibility for mass media being able to convey positive, nonjudgmental, pro-choice, comprehensive, and accurate information about sexual and reproductive health? To begin with, I reiterate that mass media is an important space for youth to learn about sexual and reproductive health. Echoing Deb Levine's research that cautions professionals who are concerned with promoting sexual health for youth to remember that an entire generation of youth has grown up with new channels for gathering and sharing information and that to reach youth, professionals must take advantage of the technology they are using.[66] As Levine explains, "Sexual health education is no longer a linear progression from curiosity to experimentation and consequences, but an interactive learning experience that begins early in young people's lives and, if done correctly, has potential to influence young people toward positive, lifelong sexual and reproductive health."[67] This is particularly why shows such as *16 and Pregnant*, *Teen Mom*, and *Teen Mom 2*, as well as abortion specials such as "No Easy Decision," are important sites of investigation and inquiry about how sexual and reproductive health information is being framed because youth evidently seek knowledge from these spaces.

Therefore, I argue that the segment was successful at demonstrating the complexities and nuances of young women's experiences coping with an unplanned pregnancy through showing three women that chose abortions, why they did it, and how they felt about the choice before and after it. Even more important, Markai's experience with abortion was framed as her personal story, not a caricature of how a woman *should* act. Additionally, the episode was a success because it is supplemented by facts about how abortion is a common procedure and that it is among one of the three viable and safe options available to women when faced with pregnancy. MTV presented the young women with dignity and respect and without perpetuating stereotypes, which it often does in other reality shows.

Additionally, "No Easy Decision" is successful because it works toward adopting Jones's concept of a critical approach to sexuality education that is grounded in the reality that society privileges specific sexualities and experiences over others and works toward deconstructing this norm. Namely, "No Easy Decision" works to promote the idea that young women are able to make sound sexual and reproductive health choices that suit their needs; it promotes all options that are available when one is facing an unplanned pregnancy; and it challenges abortion stigma by grounding personal narratives within the reality of the prevalence of abortion in America. By breaking stigma in mass media, "No Easy Decision" shows young women that abortion is a viable and safe option.

However, for mass media to be a viable site for positive, nonjudgmental, pro-choice, comprehensive, and accurate information about sexual and reproductive health, a degree of critical media literacy skills on the part of youth is also required. Critical media literacy skills are essential for youth to develop to be able to analyze the information and messages they are receiving about sex.[68] Teaching youth the skills needed to become "media literate" ensures that they will think critically about media messaging and challenge what they see instead of passively consuming it.[69] Becoming media literate will allow youth to examine popular sites of media consumption, such as shows on MTV, and in turn offer opportunities where youth can examine and challenge traditional patriarchal, racist, and heterosexist discourses about sexuality and then position themselves differently.[70]

Last, we cannot assume that an individual show related to sexual and reproductive health can be representative of *all* young women or all youth more broadly. However, by being open and honest about, for instance, the diversity of sexualities, relationship styles, gender identities, and cultural approaches to sexual and reproductive health, coupled with comprehensive, accurate, and accessible reproductive and sexual health information, youth will be able to critically engage with the idea that there is not a set definition of "normal." It is therefore important that sexuality education include discussions of both sexual *and* reproductive health, including sexually transmitted infections, barrier methods (e.g., condoms), contraceptive options, positive sexuality, *and* options such as abortion, parenting, and adoption. Sexual health options need to be presented as a range of options for youth to choose from, just as reproductive health options need to be framed as viable choices that youth equally get to make decisions about that suit their needs and realities. These conversations therefore must be integrated, not separated, for youth to understand how their choices are linked so that they may make decisions that *they* decide are best.

MTV's "No Easy Decision" can be understood as an example of how mass media can be used as a vehicle for disseminating comprehensive, accurate, pro-choice, and feminist portrayals of sexual and reproductive health information to youth. However, while this special is a good start, it is imperative that youth have access to more comprehensive, accurate, and accessible conversations about abortion that last longer than thirty minutes and that are in a prime-time time slot. It is also important to see a celebration of particular choices, the inclusion of men's voices, as well as the social constraints of young motherhood represented in these types of shows more fully, as this would help health educators engage young people in the robust discussions of this complex health issue.[71] Nevertheless, I believe that "No Easy Decision" represents the possibility of mass media to be utilized to reach out to youth and fill in the gaps of (mis)information and education related to sexual and reproductive health in a comprehensive, accurate, feminist, and pro-choice manner.

NOTES

1. Guttmacher Institute, *Facts on Induced Abortion.*
2. Guttmacher Institute, *Facts on Induced Abortion.*
3. Guttmacher Institute, *Facts on Induced Abortion.*
4. Luker, *Dubious Conceptions,* 155.
5. Luthra, "Toward a Reconceptualization," 43.
6. Becker et al., "Abortion Stigma," S53.
7. Jaworski, "Reproductive Justice," 106.
8. Jaworski, "Reproductive Justice," 106.
9. Guttmacher Institute, *Laws Affecting Reproductive Health.*
10. Stout, "Framing Abortion Access," 6.
11. Schalet, "Subjectivity, Intimacy," 133.
12. Boryczka, "Whose Responsibility?" 187.
13. Jones, "A Sexuality Education Discourses Framework," 136.
14. Jones, "A Sexuality Education Discourses Framework," 136.
15. Jones, "A Sexuality Education Discourses Framework," 136.
16. Jones, "A Sexuality Education Discourses Framework," 142.
17. Jones, "A Sexuality Education Discourses Framework," 142.
18. Jones, "A Sexuality Education Discourses Framework," 144.
19. Jones, "A Sexuality Education Discourses Framework," 145–46.
20. Boryczka, "Whose Responsibility?" 187.
21. Jones, "A Sexuality Education Discourses Framework," 151.
22. Roberts, *Killing the Black Body,* 4.
23. Roberts, *Killing the Black Body,* 3–7; Smith, *Conquest,* 98–106.
24. See Roberts, *Killing the Black Body*; Smith, *Conquest* and "Beyond Pro-Choice."
25. As cited in Shaw, "Media Representations," 56.
26. Shaw, "Media Representations," 56–57.
27. Shaw, "Media Representations," 56–57.
28. Shaw, "Media Representations," 56.
29. Jaworski, "Reproductive Justice and Media Framing," 111–15.
30. Jiwani, *Discourses of Denial,* 37.
31. Ward, "Understanding the Role of Entertainment Media," 349.
32. Ward, "Understanding the Role of Entertainment Media," 349.

33. Ward, "Understanding the Role of Entertainment Media," 351.

34. Ward, "Understanding the Role of Entertainment Media," 351.

35. Brown and Keller, "Media Interventions," 67.

36. Ward, "Understanding the Role of Entertainment Media," 349.

37. Shaw, "Media Representations," 58.

38. Shaw, "Media Representations," 58.

39. Smith, *Conquest*, 98–106.

40. Smith, *Conquest*, 98–106.

41. Jaworski, "Reproductive Justice and Media Framing," 117.

42. Hasinoff, "Sexting and Media Production," 2.

43. Kaiser Family Foundation and Children Now, as cited in Jaworski, "Reproductive Justice and Media Framing," 116.

44. Jaworski, "Reproductive Justice and Media Framing," 117.

45. Jaworski, "Reproductive Justice and Media Framing," 105.

46. Brewer, "Exploring the Impact," 7–8.

47. Brewer, "Exploring the Impact," 9.

48. Albert, as cited in Brewer, "Exploring the Impact," 16.

49. Brewer, "Exploring the Impact," 16.

50. Allen, *Young People and Sexuality Education*, 5.

51. Feldt, "On *Friday Night Lights*."

52. Jaworski, "Reproductive Justice and Media Framing," 117.

53. Allen, *Young People and Sexuality Education*, 5–6.

54. Harris, "MTV's Shockingly Good Abortion Special."

55. Valenti, "Why No Abortions?"

56. Harris, "MTV's Shockingly Good Abortion Special."

57. Harris, "MTV's Shockingly Good Abortion Special."

58. "No Easy Decision," *16 and Pregnant*, season 2, December 28, 2010.

59. Bute and Russell, "Public Discourses about Teenage Pregnancy," 2.

60. Bute and Russell, "Public Discourses about Teenage Pregnancy," 2.

61. "No Easy Decision."

62. See Roberts, *Killing the Black Body*; Smith, *Conquest* and "Beyond Pro-choice."

63. "No Easy Decision."

64. Harris, "MTV's Shockingly Good Abortion Special."

65. "No Easy Decision."

66. Levine, "Using Technology," 18.

67. Levine, "Using Technology," 18.

68. Ballam and Granello. "Confronting Sex in the Media," 424.

69. Ballam and Granello, "Confronting Sex in the Media," 424.

70. Ashcraft, "Adolescent Ambiguities in *American Pie*," 39.

71. Bute and Russell, "Public Discourses about Teenage Pregnancy," 7–10.

Chapter Thirteen

"I'll See You in Court"

The Collision of Legal Drama Frames and Public Policy

Alison N. Novak and India J. McGhee

As teenagers increasingly draw on media for legal information, understanding the messages and discourses surrounding the topic becomes important. Teenagers are trusting in the media as a means to understand and even research their societal and, thus, legal options.[1] If teens draw their information about legal empowerment from the media, it is important to understand the content and frames that the media uses to depict legal action and policy. In an effort to study the media's content, this chapter looks at the way legal issues are framed in the MTV series *16 and Pregnant*, *Teen Mom*, and *Teen Mom 2*. Drawing from media-framing theories as well as legal studies and policy, we look at the means by which MTV discusses how young mothers interact with the legal system. This is a new and relevant topic in legal and media research because it represents a convergence of the two disciplines and has implications for understanding the way that legal empowerment of young mothers is discussed and showcased in popular media.

Previous research has examined the effects of the shows *16 and Pregnant*, *Teen Mom*, and *Teen Mom 2* on the rates of teen pregnancy and motherhood. Furthermore, other studies have looked at the feminist angles and modes of empowerment in these television shows.[2] However, a gap in the literature exists in considering the legal aspects of teen motherhood and media representations of legal policy. Studying the way that legal action is framed in these shows can help inform conversations on policy specifically related to young American mothers. This will contribute not only to the body of work devoted to studying teen mothers but also to the efforts for young parental legal empowerment, thus providing insight into how young mothers view their own legal potential and informing their access to it.

Family law and policy suggest that the legal system should be supportive of young motherhood through custody rights, child support from the "baby daddies," and federal child care subsidies.[3] This study looks at how these forms of empowerment designed by the legal system are featured in *16 and Pregnant, Teen Mom*, and *Teen Mom 2*. It addresses questions on media representations of legal policy: How are legal actions framed? To what extent are legal actions focused on? Who is helped by the legal system? What are the motivations for the legal intervention? These are important considerations because they focus the analysis of legal drama and address the legal issues portrayed on the three series.

To answer these questions, an inductive framing analysis of 102 episodes of the three series was conducted. "Prevention," "no law is good law," and "revenge" were identified as frames. These frames suggest that, wholly, the legal system is framed within these programs as a hindrance or problem for young mothers, rather than as something that is supportive or helpful. Furthermore, these negative frames are in direct conflict with the purpose depicted by policy studies, described in the next section. This conflict is reflected on in this chapter's discussion and fully explored as a potential for future legal policy analysis.

LITERATURE REVIEW

Legal Policy for Teenage Mothers

Public policy suggests that the law is meant to empower its constituents in an effort to protect them and better their lives. Prue Rains, Linda Davies, and Margaret McKinnon found that this is a popular vein that inspires a variety of social service activities designed for the teen mother's life and family.[4] These authors find that while the effects of social service programs may not fulfill this intention, nearly all social and legal programs begin with the central organizing idea that they should, in fact, empower the mother and assist her.[5] Buss's work supports the concept of empowerment and finds that many legal policies begin with the intention of addressing and rectifying teenage pregnancy problems.[6] This is elaborated by Thomas, who proposes that the efforts of empowerment are often supported by legal and public policy research into the needs of clients and the public.[7]

The federal government devotes considerable time and funding to preventing teenage pregnancy through safe sex campaigns, easier access to contraception, and sex education.[8] Unfortunately, once a teenager actually becomes pregnant and gives birth to a child, funding and federal attention disappear.[9] Teenage parents exist in a legal gray area where their constitutional right to parent is in constant conflict with their limited legal rights as minors.[10] This gray area is seemingly at odds with overall legal policy for teen pregnancy prevention and general family law, where legal policy seeks to actively support and empower young women and adults. Laws may be designed to help; yet, because teenage mothers exist within a gap in the law, there is very little that the courts can actually offer them, in part because legal policy struggles with how to treat teenage mothers. [11]

Indeed, despite the intent of the legislature to promote healthy and stable family units and economically sound support programs, teen moms are often left without clear guidance for expected legal responsibilities and means of financial relief. [12] It is unclear how teenage mothers should be treated by the legal system—are they parents first and minors second? Or the other way around? The first view expects that teen mothers should act as autonomous parties with the right to make legal decisions on behalf of their children without interference. [13] Alternatively, other policies suggest that the teen mothers who are still minors are legal wards of their own parents—the grandparents of the newly born baby. [14] The first model assumes that teenagers are capable of making completely rational, logical, forward-thinking, and self-maximizing decisions absent of outside influences. [15] This adultlike behavior is expected despite numerous studies demonstrating that minors are impulsive, are focused on short-term consequences, and attach positive value to risks. [16] The second model cedes all legal power to the grandparents, ignoring the teen mother's independent right to parent the child. [17] This conflict trickles down into the daily lives of teen mothers, where their fundamental right to raise their children in the manner they see fit is in constant conflict with the legal system.

Due to their age, minors have limited legal rights in practically every arena except child rearing. [18] For instance, a minor may elect, without parental consent, to keep a pregnancy, but she may not elect to *not* keep a pregnancy, via abortion or adoption, depending on the state in which she resides. [19] Minors cannot make a will, borrow money, sign a lease, or get married without parental consent. [20] They have a more difficult time finding jobs that pay above minimum wage, are less successful at finding work, and are often too financially in debt to afford the day care necessary to finish secondary school. [21] Furthermore, although it is clear that teens who finish high school have better economic potential—they can go on to college and reach a higher income—teen moms have no federal right to maternity leave. [22] Instead, they are expected to give birth and immediately return to school, meaning that days missed to recover from labor and bond with their newborn infant are often counted as absences. Furthermore, there is limited academic support while the teen mom is not in class. When she returns, she is typically too far behind the curve to catch up. [23]

The limitations upon their legal rights, combined with their emotional and financial reliance on their parents, put teen mothers in a difficult position. The teen mother is exposed to extreme social and economic pressure both

from her parents and from the state but is often legally and societally prohib-
ited from fulfilling her parental duties.[24] Even when teen mothers are aware
of their minimal legal rights, they may be afraid to assert their parental rights
through the legal system when they are in opposition to the wishes of the
financially supportive and legal guardian grandparents.[25] Society expects
teen mothers to provide the same opportunities and benefits to their children
as adult parents could, but they are legally restricted from doing so.[26]

As reflected in the works by Adam Thomas and Emily Buss, legal policy
begins with the intention of assisting and empowering the young teenage
mother.[27] However, because of the legal gray area, teen mothers are often left
without actualized support. Therefore, a conflict exists in the design of general teen policy and implementation—specifically, the identity of the teen
mother in the eyes of the law.

Framing

Drawing from the work of Dietram Scheufele, this analysis examines the
frames used and projected in the popular MTV shows *16 and Pregnant, Teen
Mom,* and *Teen Mom 2.*[28] As producers select and determine content to
include in the television shows, they employ media frames to construct issues, stories, and plots. Scheufele defines frames as both individually driven
and media created.[29] William Gamson and Andre Modigliani define frames
as "a central organizing idea or story line that provides meaning to an unfolding script of events."[30] By using frames, media producers turn everyday
events into recognizable narratives and storylines that the viewer can relate to
and understand. Todd Gitlin refers to framing as a type of packaging, where
information is edited and selected in an effort to organize ideas for the
audience.[31] Robert Entman furthers this argument, suggesting that selection
and message salience are critical to the function of the media, which attempts
to make some issues more or less recognizably important to the audience.[32]
Because of this, Scheufele concludes that the audience begins to systematically recognize the frames and be affected by the framing process.[33] Thus,
individual frames are partially conceptualized as the result of these media
frames. These frames begin to define the audiences' understanding of reality
as they are combined with individual exposure to and experience with an
issue.

In Scheufele's consideration of media frames as independent variables,
framing research is embedded in media effects. Media effects theories suggest that as viewers are exposed to mass media frames on any topic, they are
likely to develop a mind-set based on the positive or negative framing of that
topic.[34] Zhongdang Pan and Gerald Kosicki propose four types of structural
dimensions of media that influence frames: syntactic, script, thematic, and
rhetorical structures.[35] By considering these four elements of the media text,

researchers are able to exhaustively understand and define the frames that are present. Furthermore, these studies propose that media frames act as the independent variable, causing changes in individual frames, or the dependent variable.[36] Work by K. S. Huang suggests that media frames take precedence over, and shape the audience's understanding of, an issue more prevalently than do individual frames.[37] Thus, media frames become the dominant means by which audiences understand and interpret reality. Works by Gamson and Shanto Iyengar support the conclusions of Huang's study and treat individual frames as outcomes or products of media frames.[38] While this chapter does not consider the individual frames of the audience, it does include an exhaustive search of media frames presented in the shows *16 and Pregnant, Teen Mom,* and *Teen Mom 2.* This chapter's analysis and implication sections propose the possible effects of these media frames and their connection to public policy and legal issues.

METHOD

This work utilizes a qualitative frame analysis in an effort to fully understand the ways in which legal issues are presented in *16 and Pregnant, Teen Mom,* and *Teen Mom 2.* As described by Philip Burnard, we engaged in a process of open coding, or taking notes and creating categories, as we watched the episodes on Netflix, Hulu, and MTV.com.[39] As suggested by the open coding process, we performed a deep reading of all 102 episodes of the three series, creating categories of topics. After the viewing, the categories were grouped and reduced to higher-level headings, or themes, that emerged from the text. The higher-level headings were then analyzed for possible frames employed by producers. Stephen Cavanaugh suggests that in the process of open coding, frames emerge as a means of describing a phenomenon to increase understanding of the narrative.[40] This is alternatively called the process of abstraction.[41] Because there are few studies regarding the framing of the law in reality television shows, we used an inductive framing analysis rather than a deductive one, which would rely on preexisting categories for comparison. For reliability purposes, we have included detailed examples of the frames employed by the various events in the television show. While not an exhaustive listing of all incidents or appearances of frames, these examples do represent an effort to connect the findings to the data set.[42]

The coding process was performed on the universe of data, including *16 and Pregnant,* seasons 1–4; *Teen Mom,* seasons 1–3; and *Teen Mom 2,* seasons 1 and 2. When frames were disagreed on, the coders discussed and argued their subject positions in an effort to come to a single conclusion, a method for code validity supported by the works of U. H. Graneheim and B. Lundman.[43] Overall, three legal frames were located within the television shows: "prevention," "no law is good law," and "revenge." This is an exhaustive listing of the frames, and all legal aspects were displayed by these lenses. The three legal frames are detailed in the following sections.

FRAMES

Prevention

The most common frame regarding the teen mothers' interaction with legal or public policy regards the law's prevention of the young mothers' ability to provide for their families or become successful adults. The law is often depicted as a preventative force on the series, instead of one that empowers the women to care for their young children. Rather than a tool with which the women can engage to help provide for the needs of their children, they instead are featured in conflict with the legal system that was designed to protect and help them.

Consider Catelynn Lowell's episode on *16 and Pregnant*, season 1.[44] As she and boyfriend Tyler contemplated adoption for their daughter, it became clear that their parents disapproved of their plans. At the hospital, Catelynn and Tyler were prevented from giving baby Carly to the adoptive parents until they left hospital grounds because of the unwillingness of Catelynn's mother, April, to sign the proper paperwork. Although they were able to give the baby to the adoptive parents shortly after leaving the hospital, it was the legal system that prevented the process from going as planned and desired. The requirement to wait for the formal exchange of parenting responsibilities for a longer period caused emotional distress to Catelynn and Tyler and further complicated their ability to make a responsible parental choice in their newborn daughter's life.

Catelynn and Tyler's role in the open adoption of their daughter Carly is again complicated by a legal contract that prevents them from knowing her exact location or even her last name. In the second episode of *Teen Mom*, season 1, the parents' frustrations are evoked as they feel helpless against the contract that prevents them from sending gifts or having peace of mind with their decision.[45] Specifically, Catelynn writes an emotional letter to Carly describing the circumstances of her adoption. After reading the letter with Tyler, Catelynn explains that her recent depression is a result of the lack of information. She states, "I have to send it to her, but I don't even know her last name, so I can't send it to her." Tyler responds that he "doesn't understand why" Carly's life is kept hidden from them. Both Tyler and Catelynn are fearful that the secrecy involved in the adoption will result in the adoptive family being able to cut off all ties. The scene ends with Tyler stating, "It's hard not to be angry." Later, in their meeting with the adoption agent, Catelynn emotionally expresses concern that they cannot even know their child's new last name. She comments, "I was just irritated because I thought we had the right to know what her last name is, and I think that as a mother, I deserve to know everything so that I can heal easier." The adoption agent responds by describing the legal contract that gives the adoptive parents the discretion to share Carly's new last name and location. This reinforces that it is the legal contract that prevents Catelynn and Tyler from gaining closure and becoming responsible and emotionally healed adults.

Farrah Abraham's story is also riddled with complications and hindrance by the legal system. *Teen Mom*, season 2, opens with a telephone message of Farrah's call for help when her mother becomes physical during a fight.[46] As a consequence of her mother's arrest, the court forbade her mother from being alone with baby Sophia. Throughout the following season, Farrah must grapple with the consequences of her mother's arrest, which include a court order that prevents her from using her mother as a free babysitter for young Sophia.[47] She also must find an apartment to live in—that is, outside her mother's house—a difficulty for Farrah considering that she is employed in a minimum-wage job.[48] Farrah's story suggests that it is the legal system that requires her to find outside babysitting and housing. The financial burdens accrued because of the legal intervention prevent her from being a good mother to her daughter.

Farrah is shown repeatedly meeting with her lawyer to discuss her mother's court case with state prosecutors. Later, she turns to her lawyer again to seek financial assistance in raising her daughter. Because Sophia's father passed away before acknowledging custody of his daughter, Farrah must get DNA evidence that Sophia is undoubtedly his daughter before she can apply for social security.[49] The DNA test requires that Farrah reach out to Sophia's father's family, from whom she has distanced herself due to family pressures and past relational difficulties. Again, it is the policies regarding social security benefits that prevent Farrah from getting the financial assistance that she needs to provide financially for her daughter.

In the season 1 premiere of *Teen Mom 2*, Jenelle Evans is served with custody papers by her mother regarding the parenting responsibilities of her son Jace.[50] In the episodes that follow, Jenelle agrees to sign the papers because she cannot afford a lawyer or the time for a court hearing.[51] While Jenelle initially agrees that this is best for her son, she soon realizes that her decision places her out of contact with and out of control over Jace: "Signing the papers may have been easy, but dealing with my mom is not."[52] Later in the season, when Jenelle visits the financial aid office of her new college, she is informed that she is not entitled to extra financial aid because she gave up full custody rights to her mother. As she leaves the financial aid office, she states, "I had no idea that signing custody over of Jace could ruin my chances of being able to afford school."[53] Jenelle was relying on the financial aid to help her pay for school so that when she petitioned to regain custody, she would have a degree and be able to support her son. This added financial burden affected her ability to both pay for school and find her own apartment, overall hurting her future efforts to regain custody. Jenelle is prevented from becoming an autonomous adult and acting as a mother because of her decision to give up custody of Jace.

The displays of legal prevention showcase the ambiguous spot in which the legal system places teen mothers. Often depicted as a reaction to this sense of prevention, the teen mothers frequently avoid the legal system as a solution to their needs. This is fully explored and described by the "no law is good law" frame.

No Law Is Good Law

In almost all legal action depicted in the show (such as custody and financial aid issues), there is an effort made by the young families to avoid the legal system altogether. Maci Bookout and Ryan, her son's father, find themselves struggling to set up a custody schedule that works for both parties. In the first season of *Teen Mom*, Maci and Ryan frequently discuss custody after their breakup.[54] However, these conversations are regularly unsupervised, featuring neither party feeling satisfied or fully taken care of. In the beginning of the second season, Maci and Ryan slowly progress toward mediated custody and support discussions but only after five episodes of empty threats to take each other to court and a failed one-on-one meeting to create a parenting schedule.[55] Finally, Maci says that while going to mediation is not ideal, she would rather try that before taking the issue to court. Despite both parties talking to lawyers, Maci's and Ryan's parents suggesting mediated discussions, and Maci's new boyfriend vocally supporting efforts to get them to legally settle the issue, Maci and Ryan are both reluctant, telling viewers that while they are unhappy with their current arrangement, they would rather work things out without entering the legal arena. Importantly, Maci's reluctance to use the courts suggests that the legal system is a force to avoid, rather than one to rely on, in parental conflicts. This frame is reinforced through the stories of Amber and Kailyn on *Teen Mom* and *Teen Mom 2*.

Similarly, Amber Portwood of *Teen Mom* and Kailyn "Kail" Lowry of *Teen Mom 2* work to avoid legal action or reliance on public assistance. Because public assistance is granted by the government through applicant-initiated legal action, the teen mothers are depicted as being reluctant to apply for it. When Amber finds that she cannot afford to live on her own without the financial support from ex-boyfriend Gary, she shuts down the possibility of going on public assistance as suggested by a friend, saying, "I don't want to live off the government."[56] Kailyn similarly protests this as an option until she finds her education and rent to be too expensive for her two-job paycheck. Through a public assistance program, Kailyn finds a new house that she can afford. However, even after she accepts the assistance, she repeatedly states that she does not intend the help to be forever and is already saving to move out of the public housing. She even goes as far as to say that she is not a "bum" or someone who cannot make it on her own but, rather, she needs the assistance because of her unsupportive ex-boyfriend. [57]

The teen mothers' attempts to avoid legal intervention reinforce the perception that the courts and public policy are not designed with them in mind. Rather than relying on legal assistance when their battles over custody and public assistance clearly call for it, the mothers rarely turn to the legal system. However, there are some instances where the mothers request legal assistance—but usually to exact revenge.

Revenge

The legal system is not just depicted as a faulty mechanism for the young mothers to get the money and support they need; it is also used as a vehicle for revenge or getting what they feel they deserve. When Maci is frustrated by Ryan's lack of financial support, she tells her new boyfriend Kyle that "Ryan's custody and court action is unfair because he did nothing during the first year of Bentley's life." [58] Kyle responds by encouraging her to seek legal action, which she initially does before agreeing to try to work things out with Ryan. Maci later says that the court is rewarding Ryan's bad behavior by giving him an extra day of custody, which she challenges under the reasoning that Ryan was unsupportive in the past. She later drops the appeal and agrees to Ryan's custody request for an extra day.

Amber and Gary similarly use the legal system as a means of gaining revenge. In the second season of *Teen Mom*, Amber threatens Gary with court action and a custody fight when he will not tell her who he is moving in with. [59] In three later fights, which turn physical, Amber continues to threaten Gary with court when he does not do what she wants. Gary also calls the police when Amber becomes physically abusive, and he, too, threatens legal action regarding custody when she is verbally aggressive or not doing what he wants. While both parties make threats, neither are shown following up with actual legal action or legal intervention. In their cases, it is the police summoned in the aftermath of a physical fight that initiate legal action. [60]

Kailyn and Jo also use the legal system as a form of revenge. When Kailyn moves out of Jo's family home without taking her belongings, Jo refuses to give them back until she repays him the $500 that she borrowed to pay for college. [61] Kailyn calls the police in an attempt to get her things, but the police officers state that they are unable to help in this private matter. Kailyn later returns to Jo's house with a $500 check, and she collects her belongings. As she leaves the house, she voices her fear that Jo may also take revenge by keeping their son Isaac from her while they have no formal custody agreement.

ANALYSIS OF FRAMES

The presence of the "prevention," "no law is good law," and "revenge" frames suggests that the depiction of legal issues on the popular shows *16 and Pregnant*, *Teen Mom*, and *Teen Mom 2* greatly deviates from the intentions and purpose of family law. However, this conflict is supported by the findings of legal scholarship. While policy is created with the intention of empowering the young women, legal scholarship finds that these efforts are often unfulfilled. While there are opportunities for the law to be conceived of as a positive resource in these young mothers' lives, it is more frequently depicted as a hindrance and obstacle in the three television series. One incident when the law was showcased as a positive resource occurred in *Teen Mom 2*, season 1, when Chelsea's boyfriend Adam failed to pay child support and Social Services acted on her behalf to take Adam to court for the unpaid amount.[62] While all the featured teen mothers in the series accepted or acknowledged that going to court or pursuing legal action to better their family lives would be a good and proactive step, the show continues to focus on the negative aspects of these processes as well as the potential problems associated with them. For example, when Farrah is encouraged to create a will in case her plastic surgery unexpectedly results in a fatality, Farrah argues with her mother that she is being irrational and that creating a will would be too time-consuming. Immediately after this scene, a voice-over by Farrah says, "Maybe my mom is right," suggesting that while she acknowledges that the legal provisions of a will would be beneficial to her young daughter, she does not see the effort required to traverse the legal system to be worth it.[63]

In addition to the mothers viewing the legal system as too unruly, they often refer to legal action with alternative vocabulary. For example, rather than saying that they need to go to court to decide custody rights, Kailyn, Maci, Amber, and Chelsea refer to it as getting custody "in writing." By avoiding the legal terminology or actually saying that they are going to court, the young mothers further avoid the legal system or distance themselves from it.

While all three frames were present in the depiction of interactions with the legal system on the television shows, the majority of legal discussion and action occurred in the seasons of *Teen Mom* and *Teen Mom 2* rather than *16 and Pregnant*. This is potentially a result of the longer time allotted to each mother during the seasons of *Teen Mom* and *Teen Mom 2*, which allows for a more in-depth look at the various aspects of their changed lives. *Teen Mom* chronicles the lives of the young mothers for the first three years, while *16 and Pregnant* can follow them for only three months. Because of the extended time, it is more likely that legal issues will develop further out from the child's birth than in the first few months. The scope of legal issues is reduced when one considers that *Teen Mom* shows only the extended stories of eight young women, greatly limiting the possible variety of issues encountered. Regardless of the reasoning, the lack of legal presence in *16 and Pregnant* is still problematic for the representation of legal issues. The almost total absence of legal issues falsely suggests to the viewer that legal problems are not a prevalent issue for young mothers.

DISCUSSION

The narratives and frames used by the show's producers and included in each mother's plot reflect the conflict within the legal system regarding the policy and protection of teen mothers. As the mothers' stories unfold, the majority of the women work to avoid the law, invoking the legal literature reflecting that the courts are not designed for the betterment of the young parent. The "prevention" frame supports the idea that it is often the courts, not society, peers, or family, that impede adulthood, autonomy, or successful parenting. This is demonstrated by Catelynn, Jenelle, and Farrah, who are shown fighting the legal system and laws that complicate their ability to fulfill various parental responsibilities and needs.

Possibly as a result of the preventative forces of the legal system, the teen mothers begin to avoid the law altogether. The "no law is good law" frame suggests that even when family and friends encourage the pursuit of legal action, the mother is often reluctant to act on her own behalf. Furthermore, this avoidance is incorporated into the vocabulary of the mothers, as they seek alternative words for "going to court" or other legal jargon, as in getting a custody order "in writing." This is supported by Buss, who finds that the mothers have no actual legal legs to stand on because of their minor status.[64] Thus, the experiences of the teen mothers reflect an effort to avoid or ignore the potential assistance that the legal system may be able to provide. Maci, Kailyn, and Amber all work outside the limits of the system in their efforts to establish custody or independent housing.

The "revenge" frame suggests additional conflict between the intentions of legal policy and the representation of the teen mothers. Different than the "prevention" and "no law is good law" frames, the "revenge" frame is often depicted through verbalized threats without follow-up. Amber, Kailyn, and Maci all make threats to their (ex)boyfriends that they will take them to court, but they never actually engage in the legal system because of these problems. Legal intervention occurs as a result of other forces but not specifically out of spite. This again reinforces that the young mothers fail to use the legal system to advocate for themselves and their children.

Schufele's theory of media framing and effects suggests that as media frames are interpreted by the audience, they are integrated into individual members' understanding of issues and events within society.[65] While a study of effects is outside the scope of this chapter, there are many possible avenues for future research within the media's interpretation of the legal system. As these reality shows demonstrate, the legal system complicates the role of the teen mother as an autonomous adult. Various laws and structures prevent the young mothers from pursuing legal action or advocating for their young family within the courts. It is likely that this frame is identified by the audience and possibly integrated into its understanding and perception of the law. Questions remain, such as "How much of an effect do these frames have on the pursuit of young legal action, even by nonteenage mother viewers?" and "What legal actions are perceived as legitimate and potentially successful by the audience?"

Alternatively, this lack of legal action can be read by the audience as a fault of the teen mothers themselves. While it is clear from the legal background that the problems faced by teen mothers are common, there is a potential to misinterpret their legal passivity as laziness, ignorance, or selfishness. Therefore, we must study how the overall view of the teen moms' engagement within the courts structure and affect the audience's understanding of the identity of a teen mom.

Finally, the frames and narratives of the law suggest that it is important for the field of legal studies and public policy to reconsider the role and identity of teen mothers. The frames reflect the confused nature of teen mothers, the courts, and the resulting distance between the two. The young women are shown avoiding the law and reeling from its perceived preventative effects, which go far beyond the shows' main characters. From a legal policy perspective, the law must find a way to consistently balance a minor's right to parent, support, and assert one's independence and adulthood. Without this balance, the confusion and restrictive nature of the law, as shown by the *Teen Mom*, *Teen Mom 2*, and *16 and Pregnant* frames, will prevail and continue to affect multiple groups of people.

CONCLUSION

The legal action available to the teen mothers in *16 and Pregnant*, *Teen Mom*, and *Teen Mom 2* is far from clear. As shown by the frames examined in this chapter, the mothers exist outside the realm of legal action and work to avoid the preventative forces of the unknown system. Thus, the reality shows demonstrate the preventative nature of legal action in the young mothers' quest to become autonomous, responsible adults. Furthermore, the mothers work to evade the legal system by espousing empty threats and changing vocabulary. These frames work together and present the audience with a complicated view of the teen mom's relationship to the law and her ability to traverse the legal system. By knowing how these important and popular shows depict the legal system, we can further understand how teen mothers understand, use, or avoid their legal options. We must continue to study this relationship to better design public policy and the legal system to address the needs of teen mothers.

NOTES

1. Purcell et al., *How Teens Do Research*, 13.
2. Valenti, *The Purity Myth*, 17.
3. Thomas, "Unintended Pregnancy and Public Policy," 514.
4. Rains, Davies, and McKinnon, "Social Services Constructs the Teen Mother," 18.
5. Rains, Davies, and McKinnon, "Social Services Constructs the Teen Mother," 20.
6. Buss, "The Parental Rights of Minors," 788–90.
7. Thomas, "Unintended Pregnancy and Public Policy," 512–13.
8. Thomas, "Unintended Pregnancy and Public Policy," 514.
9. Fershee, "A Parent Is a Parent," 433.
10. Fershee, "A Parent Is a Parent," 431.
11. Fershee, "A Parent Is a Parent," 433.
12. Fershee, "A Parent Is a Parent," 445.
13. Failinger, "Ophelia with Child," 256.
14. Failinger, "Ophelia with Child," 256.
15. Failinger, "Ophelia with Child," 258.
16. Buss, "The Parental Rights of Minors," 799.
17. Failinger, "Ophelia with Child," 258.
18. Buss, "The Parental Rights of Minors," 794–96.
19. Fershee, "A Parent Is a Parent," 436.
20. Failinger, "Ophelia with Child," 260.
21. Fershee, "A Parent Is a Parent," 254.
22. Grome, "The Four-Week Challenge," 543.
23. Grome, "The Four-Week Challenge," 543.
24. Failinger, "Ophelia with Child," 259.
25. Crews, "When Mommy's a Minor," 140.
26. Fershee, "A Parent Is a Parent," 436.
27. Thomas, "Unintended Pregnancy and Public Policy," 514; Buss, "The Parental Rights of Minors," 799.
28. Scheufele, "Framing as a Theory of Media Effects,"
29. Scheufele, "Framing as a Theory of Media Effects,"
30. Gamson and Modigliani, "The Changing Culture of Affirmative Action."
31. Gitlin, *The Whole World Is Watching*, 7.
32. Entman, "Framing U.S. Coverage," 7.
33. Scheufele, "Framing as a Theory of Media Effects," 106.
34. Scheufele, "Framing as a Theory of Media Effects," 112.
35. Pan and Kosicki, "Framing Analysis," 61.
36. Scheufele, "Framing as a Theory of Media Effects," 112.
37. Huang, "A Comparison between Media Frames."
38. Gamson, *Talking Politics*, 115; Iyengar, "Television News," 851.
39. Burnard, "A Method of Analyzing," 463.

40. Cavanaugh, "Content Analysis," 10.
41. Robson, *Real World Research*, 15.
42. Polit and Beck, *Nursing Research,* 50.
43. Graneheim and Lundman, "Qualitative Content Analysis," 108.
44. "Catelynn," *16 and Pregnant*, season 1, July 16, 2009.
45. "How Many Chances?" *Teen Mom*, season 1, December 14, 2009.
46. "Not Again," *Teen Mom*, season 2, July 20, 2010.
47. "Spring Break," *Teen Mom*, season 2, August 10, 2010.
48. "Trial and Error," *Teen Mom*, season 2, August 31, 2010.
49. "Family Bonds," *Teen Mom*, season 2, September 21, 2010.
50. "Nothing Stays the Same," *Teen Mom 2*, season 1, January 11, 2011.
51. "So Much to Lose," *Teen Mom 2*, season 1, January 18, 2011.
52. "Change of Heart," *Teen Mom 2*, season 1, January 25, 2011.
53. "Too Much, Too Fast," *Teen Mom 2*, season 1, February 8, 2011.
54. "Moving On," *Teen Mom*, season 1, December 14, 2009.
55. "Senior Prom," *Teen Mom*, season 2, September 7, 2010.
56. "Lashing Out," *Teen Mom*, season 2, September 28, 2010.
57. "Curveball," *Teen Mom 2*, season 2, December 13, 2011.
58. "See You Later," *Teen Mom*, season 2, October 12, 2010.
59. "Lashing Out."
60. "The Last Straw," *Teen Mom*, season 3, July 19, 2011.
61. "Two Steps Forward," *Teen Mom 2*, season 1, March 15, 2011.
62. "One Step Back," *Teen Mom 2*, season 1, March 22, 2011.
63. "Taking it Slow," *Teen Mom*, season 3, July 5, 2011.
64. Buss, "The Parental Rights of Minors," 794–96.
65. Scheufele, "Framing as a Theory of Media Effects," 105.

Chapter Fourteen

The Young and the Pregnant

Edutainment, Reality Television, and the Question of
Teen Pregnancy Prevention on
16 and Pregnant *and* Teen Mom

Margaret Tally

Recent television episodes about teen pregnancy on such programs as *The Secret Life of the American Teenager* and *Glee* suggest that the taboo subject of teen pregnancy has now become part of mainstream popular media narratives. This has occurred despite the fact that teen pregnancies overall have witnessed an unprecedented decline in American society since the early 1990s.[1] For example, in 2010, the birthrate dropped 9 percent from 2009 for women aged fifteen to nineteen years; in addition, birthrates fell 12 percent for women aged fifteen to seventeen and 9 percent for women aged eighteen to nineteen. The birthrate fell for all races, including African Americans and Hispanics. Some of the reasons cited for the decline include the fact that fewer teens, especially male teens, are having sex than in 1990 (postponing sexual activity until later ages), as well as the fact that there has been a dramatic improvement in the use of contraceptives.[2]

Although teen pregnancies overall have declined, there has, at the same time, been an increasing cultural discussion about pregnancies that occur outside of marriages for women who are of childbearing age, and the rise in media representations of teen pregnancy may be reflective of the increased attention that is now being paid to this phenomenon. In addition, even though overall rates of pregnancy have declined, the United States still leads all other advanced, industrial nations in pregnancy rates for teens. These teens are often at risk, having relationships with older partners, few direct conversations about the use of contraceptives and sex education, and few outlets in the community to engage them in other activities.[3]

More generally, this perception of teen pregnancy as a social problem relates to the fact that single parenthood is correlated with the steep rise in poverty for women and children that has also occurred in the past three decades. In fact, a staggering four of ten children are now raised in poverty. In addition, and related to this, is the so-called feminization of poverty, as women can no longer rely on the income of a husband. This loss of income, combined with the fact that mothers usually make less than the fathers, creates a situation where their low family income can plunge them into poverty. Poverty, though it has many causes, is linked to low incomes and can be cyclical so that the children of these young mothers end up repeating the cycle themselves since they are at higher risk for not having the basics, such as a decent education, housing, food, and crime-free communities.

One strategy that recently has been adopted to combat teen pregnancies is to use media to educate young people about the need to avoid risky behaviors that could result in unplanned pregnancies. Drawing on decades of research by social marketers that has demonstrated that health messages on television can have positive effects, the cable network channel MTV has partnered with the National Campaign to Prevent Teen and Unplanned Pregnancy to produce two reality television programs that deal explicitly with the issue of teen pregnancy: *16 and Pregnant* and *Teen Mom*.[4] As they first follow pregnant sixteen-year-olds through the course of their pregnancy and then through the first years of their children's lives, the young women are held up as a kind of cautionary tale, graphically depicting just how hard it is to raise a baby.

Morgan Freeman, one of the executive producers of the series, believes that these portraits of young women going through this experience provide a powerful public service.[5] The reach of the programs is undeniable, at least in terms of the target demographic, consisting of women under the age of thirty-four, with over two million viewers per episode.[6] And in line with Horace Newcomb's idea that television provides a space or "site" for cultural discussions about difficult social problems,[7] it is clear that these shows have generated a lot of attention in the media because they have been viewed as being able to provide just this kind of space for conversations about teen sexuality and unwanted pregnancies.[8]

One question that then arises is, how do the shows *16 and Pregnant* and *Teen Mom* help shape the larger cultural conversation about pregnancy outside of marriage? In terms of the initial development of the show *16 and Pregnant*, there was an explicit effort (as later shown) to try to reduce teen pregnancies by trying to educate young women with regard to just how difficult it is to raise a baby when one is only a teenager. This form of "health edutainment," as it has sometimes been called, offers one strategy, at the level of explicit messaging, to try to reduce teen pregnancies.

However, while there has been some recent evidence that these shows do indeed help push the conversation into the open, in terms of teens talking to others (including their parents) about the consequences of teen pregnancy, at the same time they do not deal explicitly with the wrenching economic issues that poor single-parent teens have to confront when they have children so young. As Gretchen Sisson notes in her analysis of what is not shown on these programs,

> you know what I haven't seen though? Any of the pregnant high schoolers talking about going to WIC [Women, Infants, and Children] and getting on food stamps. Any of the young mothers dealing with the stigma of receiving public benefits. Any stories of the impossible bureaucracy of Medicaid. Really, I haven't seen any discussion of the huge overlap between economic disadvantage and early parenthood at all.[9]

In fact, as the show progresses from season to season, the young women's economic situation improves because of the heightened profile and stardom of the young women as they become part of the reality television–celebrity tabloid vortex in their own right. In these ways, the shows end up *obscuring* some of the more central reasons why teens get pregnant, which include such factors as their class status and level of poverty. As Sisson concludes,

> it's not that they had a child while they were young, it's that they had a child while they were poor. . . . This is why it's not just another unfortunate misrepresentation; it's not just a glossing over the real issues of class and poverty. *Teen Mom* and *16 and Pregnant* fundamentally misinform while claiming to be legitimate sources of sex education and spaces for activism.[10]

In this chapter, I highlight some of these tensions that exist within the programs in terms of the mixed cultural messages they are conveying to their viewers. On one hand, there is the explicit intent on the part of the shows' creators to offer a narrative that focuses on how an unplanned pregnancy can wreak havoc in these young women's lives. On the other, these shows offer a counternarrative of an increasingly glamorous lifestyle, replete with cosmetic surgery, travel, and new homes, that ends up contradicting the very message of lowered life chances they are trying to highlight as a result of an unplanned pregnancy. Ultimately, in this confusing narrative, the questions of who is getting pregnant and why are lost, and the connections between teen motherhood and poverty are erased; instead, blame is cast on the young women, who are demonized for being sexually loose and having gotten themselves "into trouble" by making poor choices.

HEALTH EDUTAINMENT AND THE CREATION OF REALISTIC NARRATIVES ON TEEN PREGNANCY

"Health edutainment" is a term created by media scholars to describe health messages embedded in entertainment programs. The idea is that these messages can help change behavior so that when health messages are placed in these entertaining formats, they can result in positive health outcomes for the viewing public. Research suggests that including information about a health problem as part of a storyline for a dramatic series can result in positive health behaviors. [11]

This idea of the impact that entertainment can have on our understanding and ability to influence our health care decisions finds its roots in an earlier media theory called "cultivation theory." George Gerbner, describing this phenomenon, noted the ways in which television has saturated our media landscape to such an extent that it plays a large part in cultivating our understanding of, and responses to, our lived experience. [12] Edutainment programs allow the viewer to learn about health issues, while making the message compelling because of its narrative format. To the extent that the stories are realistic, viewers become even more connected to the narratives and therefore more likely to seek support if they find themselves in a similar medical situation.

This notion that television can cultivate a certain orientation or perspective regarding health care information is part of a larger societal phenomenon, namely, that people are getting information now from a variety of sources besides their doctors. Jennifer Gray, for example, wrote about an episode of *Sex and the City* in which a character gets diagnosed with breast cancer and is supported emotionally by her three other friends. Gray found that it was able to offer viewers a vivid example of how this kind of support can help ameliorate the cancer experience. [13] While she felt that this storyline fell short in terms of a prosocial message for its viewers about how to follow up on obtaining health care, she nevertheless noted that programs like this offer the public a way to look for social support if they are diagnosed with a life-threatening disease.

In line with this assumption that social messaging can try to influence behavior, the National Campaign to Prevent Teen and Unplanned Pregnancy has made a concerted effort to work with television producers to help create story lines, as well as offer information on reducing teen pregnancies, without alienating young viewers. In such shows as *Raising Hope*, *The Secret Life of the American Teenager*, *Family Guy*, *How I Met Your Mother*, and even *Gossip Girl*, the campaign has consulted with the shows' producers to help create story lines that touch on the issue of teen pregnancy. What these shows have in common is that they belong to fictional genres, whether dramatic or situation comedy. [14]

The move to highlight the issue of underage pregnancy on reality televi-sion came from Lauren Dolgen, senior vice president of series development at MTV, who wanted to draw on the success of the movie *Juno* and portray "real" young women who were in a similar situation. She explained, "This is an epidemic that is happening to our audience, and it's a preventable epidem-ic. . . . We thought it was so important to shed light on this issue and to show girls how hard teen parenting is." [15]

The National Campaign was consulted throughout the development of the show *16 and Pregnant* and continues to offer advice and work on the web-sites associated with *16 and Pregnant* and *Teen Mom*. In addition, videos of the shows have been distributed to educators in private and public education-al settings to engage in discussions with teens about teen pregnancy. [16] In part, the effort by the National Campaign to be instrumental in shaping the narrative of these shows is a result of the growing awareness that young people are increasingly savvy and jaded about media messages. [17] For this reason, the campaign is trying to find new ways to reach out to young people with the message that teen pregnancies can be prevented. [18]

One immediate question that arises about these programs is whether and how they have been able to effectively communicate their messages about the narrowing of life options for young women that often accompany teen pregnancies. To address this question, the National Campaign commissioned its own research and created an evaluation study to analyze how viewing *16 and Pregnant* influenced young people's perceptions of early pregnancy and parenthood. Working with the Boys and Girls Club of America, it was able to draw on young people from eighteen clubs in one Southern state. The clubs were assigned at random to watch episodes of the shows or not. Out of the 162 teenagers who participated in the study, the average age was 13.5, the majority (62 percent) was female, and three-quarters were African American. [19]

Among its findings, the National Campaign discovered that over one-third of the respondents ended up talking to a parent after watching the show and a third spoke to either a sibling or a boyfriend/girlfriend. The participants also enjoyed watching the show, and nearly 93 percent agreed with the state-ment "I learned that teen parenthood is harder than I imagined from these episodes." The national campaign, acknowledging that some people have claimed that the show "glamorizes" teen pregnancy, found that most teens do not in fact share this view. [20]

In a recent study conducted by the Public Religion Research Institute, over three thousand American adults were polled on their opinions regarding abortion. One of the questions they were asked is whether they have seen or were viewers of shows such as *16 and Pregnant*. The institute found, among other things, that viewers who have watched marathon sessions of the show were more likely to support abortion being legal or legal in most cases. [21]

This position on abortion was linked, in the researchers' minds, to the larger phenomenon of one cohort in particular—the "Millennials, or those who were born between the first half of the 1970s and the second half of the 1990s," who were perceived to view issues such as abortion as depending on the situation. Watching a show like this, which researchers subsequently referred to as "the MTV effect," seems to have influenced this cohort's views over whether abortion should be legal.

Finally, an opinion poll from Social Science Research Solutions, conducted by phone with over one thousand teenagers (twelve to nineteen years old), found that a majority (82 percent) believed that *16 and Pregnant* helped them understand the difficulties that occur for young women when they get pregnant and helped them think about ways to avoid it. [22] In sum, various studies have concluded that these programs do promote the message that teen parenting could have a negative impact on the futures of young women.

CAN A TV SHOW PREVENT TEEN PREGNANCY?

Although the research has found that the social message about the difficulties accompanying teen pregnancy have been "heard" by its intended audience, the question remains whether these shows have been able to affect the behavior of young people and ultimately prevent teen pregnancies. There has, after all, been a continual drop in the rate of teen pregnancies both before and after the show *16 and Pregnant* was introduced in 2009.

Some individuals, for example, believe that the recent drop in teen pregnancy is a result of changes in the economy; others cite the factor of the television shows *16 and Pregnant* and *Teen Mom* as playing an important role in reduced pregnancy rates among teens. Sarah Brown, chief executive of the National Campaign to Prevent Teen and Unplanned Pregnancy, was quoted as saying that "there is no question that these shows are affecting the conversation about teen pregnancy and teen motherhood." [23]

Other advocates in the field, however, while acknowledging the benefits of this kind of edutainment, believe that the show does not go far enough in presenting its viewers with more information about sex in general, as well as the issues that go along with preventing teen pregnancy, including discussions around dating and sexuality. Overall, however, most sex educators are in agreement that for their message about sex education to get out, there needs to be some outreach within popular culture. [24] For example, Deb Levine, who is the executive director of a sex health education program, recently sponsored a conference on technology and sex education. At the conference, the participants included Morgan Freeman and Dia Sokol Savage, who are the executive producers of *16 and Pregnant* and *Teen Mom*. Noting that these producers were asked a number of pointed questions about the series,

Levine commented, "All day long, that's all everyone was talking about [*Teen Mom* and *16 and Pregnant*] . . . how sex education has to intersect with popular culture."[25]

Even if *16 and Pregnant* and *Teen Mom*, then, could be shown to have influenced the conversation on teen pregnancy in the United States and to have been effective in conveying the message that unplanned pregnancies can have unintended and negative effects, the question of whether this can lead to behavioral changes on the part of the viewers remains unanswered. For example, much of the recent literature on poverty and social class has pointed to the fact that poverty itself is a key determinant in pregnancy rates among teenagers. This finding relates to a small but growing consensus among some researchers that young women get pregnant and have babies because they are *already* poor and do not see many viable economic alternatives to their situation.[26] Furthermore, there are a host of other demographic factors that are more influential in determining whether a teen will become pregnant and carry an unplanned pregnancy to term, including how much education the mothers of the girls have, whether the girls live in a low-income community, and more generally, how much economic inequality the girls experience. In this sense, the frequency of teen motherhood is more a function of poverty than it is a cause.

Perhaps as a corollary, there has been little evidence that reforming social policies to be more liberal or conservative seems to measurably affect the teen birthrate among poor young women. Additionally, sex education, social messages from television, or, indeed, abortion restrictions do not seem to make a large impact on this group of young women. Matthew Iglesias observes,

> Instead, family life seems to follow real economic opportunities. Where poor people can't see that hard work and "playing by the rules" will reward them, they're more likely to abandon mainstream norms. Those who do so by becoming single teen moms end up fairing poorly in life, but those bad outcomes seem to be a result of bleak underlying circumstances rather than poor choices.[27]

If poor women are the most likely to get pregnant and carry their pregnancies to term, it would seem helpful to have that group of women portrayed on these shows—or at least explicitly discuss how poverty affects life decisions such as teen pregnancy. On *16 and Pregnant* and *Teen Mom*, however, the conversation about poverty and teen pregnancy is dealt with on an individual basis and is not always consistent. As Gretchen Sisson concludes,

> There's occasionally a nod to getting financial aid for school, or a brief exclamation of "diapers are expensive!" But there's certainly no real, meaningful

exploration of the fact that poverty is the single largest indicator of whether or not a young woman will become a teen mom. [28]

Teen motherhood, in short, exacerbates what these young women already struggle with in their daily lives, including poor educational outcomes, scant job prospects, housing insecurity, and access to basic public supports. Their pregnancy did not cause these problems, yet *Teen Mom* leaves this social fact unexplored.

Part of the impact of this silence is that viewers are often left confused as to what life options there are for these women. For example, when the young women are shown driving late-model cars as a result of having earned money from appearing on the shows, there is no acknowledgment that they have been paid to do the show, and it is not clear whether they were more middle class than it first appeared on earlier episodes. Another way that the show obscures the links between poverty and high teen pregnancy rates is to portray most of the young women who get pregnant as white, rather than Latina or African American. The lack of diversity on *Teen Mom* as well as *16 and Pregnant* (which has had only a few African American and Latina women) makes it seem as if race and social class are not linked to higher pregnancy rates. The geographical distribution of the young women, finally, also obscures the fact that poverty is oftentimes higher in cities, yet the young women are mostly from small towns, in either the Midwest or the South.

Some viewers have noted that the lower social class of a few of the young women on the show was more prominent in the first season of *Teen Mom*. They point out, for example, that the young woman Amber had to go to an SRO (single-room occupancy) because she had nowhere to live and could not even afford a motel room. In addition, Catelynn, who was the only young woman to place her baby for adoption, offered the reason that she did not have the financial resources available to raise the child. Overall, however, and as the series progressed from one season to the next, the young women became progressively wealthier, and their life situations seemed to have improved, although it was never made explicit to the audience how this occurred.

REALITY TELEVISION AS EDUTAINMENT

Writing about the ways in which contemporary reality television programs attempt to educate their viewers, Laurie Ouellette and James Hay have described the links between this form of instruction and a changing societal understanding of the individual as responsible for one's own fate. [29] The individual went from someone who was embedded in a larger community and social welfare system to one who is self-governed and in need of being taught how to make the best consumer and lifestyle choices to sustain oneself. The individual, with the help of such cultural forces as reality television, learns how to "empower" herself to make the right choices and help herself. The authors write, "These are not abstract ideologies imposed from above, but highly dispersed and practical techniques for reflecting on, managing, and improving the multiple dimensions of our personal lives with the resources available to us. Reality TV has become one of these resources."[30]

In this construction, reality television shows such as *16 and Pregnant* and *Teen Mom* can be understood as attempting to educate young women through warning them about the difficulties they will encounter if they get pregnant and carry the pregnancy to term. By combining this message within an entertaining reality soap opera format, the program effectively offers a form of edutainment that reinforces the private nature of the experience of the young women who get pregnant while exhorting them to take personal responsibility for their choices. Even though the National Campaign to Prevent Teen and Unplanned Pregnancy is not a governmental agency per se, it is instructive that it is partnering with a cable channel to provide a platform for its message about personal responsibility.

Speaking more generally of television as a kind of "cultural technology," Ouellette and Hay prompt us to think more explicitly about the ways in which *16 and Pregnant* and *Teen Mom* help to "nurture citizenship" and serve as an instrument for "educating, improving, and shaping subjects" by exhorting its young viewers to avoid unplanned pregnancies.[31] For our purposes, it is important to note that in this understanding, these programs are meant to try to influence the individual viewer to make "good choices" regarding her sexual behavior. In reality, however, these series obscure the fact that she has no reason to expect that her future will be any better whether she chooses to carry the pregnancy to term or not.

DISCUSSION: REFRAMING THE PICTURE OF TEEN PREGNANCY ON REALITY TELEVISION?

With a singular focus on the individual, the question of the economic situation of the young mother and its influence on her decision to carry her baby to term is left unanswered on *16 and Pregnant* as well as *Teen Mom.* One way that these shows can begin to offer a more realistic portrait, then, of the economic context that informs these choices is to raise this topic more explicitly. For that to occur, however, several issues need to be addressed.

The first question is whether it is reasonable or indeed desirable to assume that a television show can serve as the primary vehicle for educating young people about their sexuality and the consequences of unprotected sex? It is perhaps a clichéd point but nevertheless true that the business of television is business, and in an environment where public television has been radically defunded, to expect that a for-profit channel should carry the societal responsibility for sex education is disingenuous at best.

A second problem is that even if you do try to make a responsible television show that highlights the consequences of teen pregnancy, the media environment of MTV and, indeed, cable television in general ends up offering wildly mixed messages. If *Jersey Shore* and *Real World* are celebrating the same sexualized behaviors that got the young women on *16 and Pregnant* and *Teen Mom* into their predicaments, how can one assume that the viewers for these programs will not be confused with the "takeaway" messages, as they identify with and at the same time attempt to take responsibility for their sexual behavior?

A third problem relates to the remaining cultural taboo that surrounds the portrayal of abortion on television. With the exception of a few storylines and one episode that carried a storyline about a teen who was making this "difficult choice" about whether to have an abortion, there is scant discussion of abortion as a strategy to resolve the dilemma of an unintended pregnancy. Whatever one's belief about whether abortion should be legal or not, the fact that it is a choice is never explicitly dealt with on these programs.

In conclusion, both *16 and Pregnant* and *Teen Mom* can be read as cultural morality plays about the need to place restrictions on women's sexuality more generally, whether those restrictions are internally imposed or not. In this way, these programs fit within a different kind of larger political discussion now taking place, one that seeks to regulate a whole host of medical and legal rights for women, including access to contraception, abortion, and their right to make their own difficult choices in the event of an unintended pregnancy. This is precisely the opposite message of "empowerment" that young women were supposed to be learning in the new millennium—that is, the power to make better choices based on that information, without the interference of outside agencies, including the state. As such, the battle over reproductive rights that is now taking place in the larger society—from which these kinds of television programs are perhaps one example—has ended up silencing the question of why young women get pregnant in the first place, as well as what options they might have if they get pregnant, including termination of the pregnancy. Perhaps the real public service message, then, that these programs can promote would be to offer young women a frank discussion of what options they have if they find themselves pregnant, including the option to have an abortion.

More generally, these series can broaden the discussion by being clear about the demographic that is mostly affected by teen pregnancy—that is, young women in poverty. The public conversation that might take place would focus first on the real circumstances that low-income young women find themselves in and then highlight their life stories and the ways in which they have to struggle to survive on a daily basis. Ideally, this will have the effect of seriously engaging the larger public in a morality play of its own, where the question can be raised more explicitly about the need to address the sources of poverty and growing inequality that have occurred over the past three decades. If that were to happen, it would be a real "Rock the Vote" public service that MTV could initiate and, hopefully, one that would result in some meaningful social changes for the most disadvantaged young women in our society.

NOTES

1. Centers for Disease Control and Prevention, http://www.pearsonhighered.com/educator/product/Dimensions-of-Social-Welfare-Policy-Plus-MySearchLab-with-eText/9780205223510.page#downlaoddiv.
2. National Campaign to Prevent Teen and Unwanted Pregnancy, "Teen Pregnancy Birth."
3. Christenson and Ivancin, "The 'Reality' of Health."
4. Seltzer, "MTV's *16 and Pregnant.*"
5. Thompson, "16, Pregnant . . . and Famous."
6. Hoffman, "Fighting Teenage Pregnancy."
7. Newcomb and Hirsch, "Television as a Cultural Forum."
8. Brewer, "Exploring the Impact of MTV's *16 and Pregnant.*"
9. Sisson, "The 99%."
10. Sisson, "The 99%."
11. Signorielli, "Health Images on Television."
12. Gerbner et al., "Living with Television."
13. Gray, "Interpersonal Communication."
14. Bazilian, "Social Messages Seek Out."
15. Bazilian, "Social Messages Seek Out."
16. Albert, "Is Media Glamorizing Teen Pregnancy?"
17. Bazilian, "Social Messages Seek Out."
18. Bazilian, "Social Messages Seek Out."
19. National Campaign to Prevent Teen and Unwanted Pregnancy, "Teen Pregnancy Birth."
20. National Campaign to Prevent Teen and Unwanted Pregnancy, "Teen Pregnancy Birth."
21. Public Religion Research Institute, "Committed to Availability."
22. Albert, "Is Media Glamorizing Teen Pregnancy?"
23. Hoffman, "Fighting Teenage Pregnancy."
24. Hoffman, "Fighting Teenage Pregnancy."
25. Hoffman, "Fighting Teenage Pregnancy."
26. Yglesias, "Why Are Teen Moms Poor?"
27. Yglesias, "Why Are Teen Moms Poor?"
28. Yglesias, "Why Are Teen Moms Poor?"
29. Ouellette and Hay, *Better Living through Reality TV.*
30. Ouellette and Hay, *Better Living through Reality TV,* 2.
31. Ouellette and Hay, *Better Living through Reality TV,* 14.

Chapter Fifteen

Isolated and Struggling

A Real-Life "Sixteen and Pregnant" Narrative

Allison Bass

The popular MTV show *16 and Pregnant* aired first in the summer of 2009 with quite controversial responses. Initially, MTV audiences, followed by much of American popular culture, became captivated with the stories of Maci, Farrah, Amber, Ebony, and Catelynn and their journeys through their pregnancies.[1] Catelynn, Farrah, Maci, and Amber continued to raise their children in the public gaze while filming *Teen Mom*. While the show *16 and Pregnant* certainly aims to provide "a unique look into the wide variety of challenges pregnant teens face: marriage, adoption, religion, gossip, finances, rumors among the community, graduating high school, getting (or losing) a job,"[2] it also demonstrates a vastly positive community created by the mere appearance of the show itself. While many of the girls lack supportive community within their own lives (take, for instance, Amber and Catelynn from season 1 of *16 and Pregnant*), they tend to receive support from the show, in terms of the cast and crew and the American public. MTV notes, "There is an optimism among them; they have the dedication to make their lives work and to do as they see fit to provide the best for their babies."[3] With over 5.5 million "likes" on Facebook, the popularity around this show is hard to deny, particularly when one compares this number to the 2.4 million "likes" that the ultrapopular American actress, director, and humanitarian Angelina Jolie has received.

Certainly, many opposed to the content of *16 and Pregnant* accuse the show of "glamorizing teenage pregnancy, and conferring girls-gone-wild celebrity [status] on their stars."[4] In contrast, those who are proponents of the show often note the positive lessons that young girls can learn. Megan Clark, a high school teacher in Kansas, uses the show in her classroom to open up

219

discussion of the "hard" topics, such as teenage sex and pregnancy. She notes that her students are "sucked into the drama of it . . . but they see that they don't ever want to be in that situation. I talk about abstinence first and foremost, but I listen to them, so I know they're not abstinent. So the show offers a good opportunity to teach them about condoms and birth control. "[5] Although the show does not particularly address these concerns, it certainly can be, and often is, used to "prompt discussion about sex education, family and romantic relationships and shattered dreams."[6] Even teenage pregnancy prevention organizations are finding the show useful for promoting awareness about the issues surrounding teen pregnancy. The National Campaign to Prevent Teen and Unplanned Pregnancy's chief program officer, Bill Albert, notes, "I think any effort that puts this issue in front of millions of teenagers week in and week out is a net win. . . . I might go so far as to say this is the best public service announcement I have seen for preventing teen pregnancy in decades."[7] Regardless of the public sentiment, much of popular culture's national attention is focused on these types of reality TV shows (particularly for those in the preteen, teen, and young adult age groups). A 2011 *New York Times* article notes, "Despite the tabloid derision and paparazzi attention that are almost a necessary byproduct of reality TV shows, the impact extends far beyond their ratings triumphs. (The season finale of *Teen Mom 2* on March 29 drew 4.7 million viewers, and was the top-rated show that day in the 12 to 34 demographic.)"[8] That more than the simple teenage, dominantly female, audience is viewing *16 and Pregnant* is evident by the many male users, ranging in age groups, who are commenting on the Facebook page on a regular basis. The shows' impact can be seen and heard across a variety of social media sources and around the proverbial "water cooler," from the high school locker room to the "grown-up" world of men, and particularly women, in the workforce.

Many scholars interested in popular culture studies[9] have shown that perceptions of life are often shaped by media, including these so-called reality television shows.[10] Yet, these shows can often create a skewed version of reality. This is frequently the case with media, as a token person serves to stand for the entirety of those who claim that identity. Nancy Hartsock notes this danger in her essay "The Feminist Standpoint: Toward a Specifically Feminist Historical Materialism," when she says that "knowledge produced from the dominant group's perspective distorts reality."[11] In *16 and Pregnant*, this misconception of teenage pregnancy can be seen in the money paid to the girls per episode (know any other teenage moms being paid simply to tell their story?), in the overwhelming ambition or outrageous spectacle of the moms' journeys (I am sure that much has been, or will be, written about the *types* of girls who seek this spotlight), and in the sheer production of the narratives (with extensive editing for dramatic effect). But perhaps one of the most notable delusions created by the show is the community of support the girls gained simply by appearing on the show: a community that is perhaps largely virtual. As I noted, the girls of *16 and Pregnant* and *Teen Mom* do live in a world where they certainly receive slanderous remarks from the general public, but it seems that the majority of viewers support the girls in their journey and encourage them toward success. This can prominently be seen in social media responses to the shows. In addition to the 5.5 million "likes" on Facebook, the moms have a huge fan base in the "Twittersphere," where the public awaits pictures and comments from the girls themselves. The stars of the shows seem to adhere to the public's desire to constantly want to know more about them. They load comments, pictures, and gossip about themselves and others on a constant basis. Maci Bookout, from the first season of *16 and Pregnant*, notes, "Before [the show], I just had my friends and family in Chattanooga, and that was really the only thing I knew. . . . Now, it's like everyone in the world knows me or knows something about me and is watching me."[12] The girls on *16 and Pregnant* and *Teen Mom* have no shortage of popularity or community, a characteristic that is highly valued among all teen girls—pregnant or not.

To gain a sense of the multifaceted implications and explanations of the public's fascination and obsession with shows such as *16 and Pregnant* and *Teen Mom*, one must look beyond the hype of the show itself and search for the more common, less glamorized narratives of being a teen mom. Finding the sources for these anecdotes is not a difficult task to tackle. *Being* a teen mom is not as unusual as one might think. Indeed, "the United States has the highest teenage birth rate among the fully industrialized countries, although that number has slowly declined over the last 20 years. Even so, in 2009, 410,000 teenagers, ages 15 to 19, gave birth—or 1,100 a day."[13] The reasons for such high rates of teenage pregnancy are fiercely debated, particularly in the most recent presidential election year, but the implications are clear. This country has many teen moms looking for what all teens—and, often, what many first-time moms (regardless of age)—are looking for: a support system. The variations of this search are probably as wide as the list of baby names is long. But for me, a real-life "sixteen and pregnant" mom, lack of community was one of the most crippling issues that I dealt with. New moms, regardless of their age, need supportive community to help them make the adjustments that come with being a mother. Often teenagers confuse popularity with community or support. Feeling popular makes teens feel as though they have the support they need. Since teen moms are simultaneously moms and teens, they seek both popularity and community and often confuse the two. For me, popularity, although quite prominent on the show, was not a part of my reality. Instead, isolation and shame became a part of my daily life. Although it is true that the teen moms of *16 and Pregnant* cannot completely escape this ubiquitous side effect of teen pregnancy, the cast continues to have access to many other avenues of support, such as the virtual communities noted earlier. I, much like some of the moms on the MTV show, had a strong determination to do right by myself and my daughter, but unlike the moms on the show, I experienced a loneliness so palpable that I was often left reeling from it. Although I longed for some sort of community in which I could feel a sense of belonging, it was years before I learned how to develop it for myself. Developing this makeshift family was imperative for my success and my daughter's, and yet, it was no easy task.

Growing up in a fundamental Christian household in the southern United States, I often heard the premise "There is no such thing as 'safe sex' just as there is no safe sin! When a person chooses to live in direct contradiction to the laws of God, there is no place to hide."[14] Now as a mother of a young teen, I understand the purpose of urging abstinence. Our society and our teenagers would benefit from having children when they are older, wiser, more educated, and financially stable; however, my household and community chose to ignore the very real sexual pressures and desires that young men and women face. Instead of helping me to be aware of the responsibilities, consequences, and decision making that come with being sexually active, I was simply told, "Don't have sex because God says not to." As early as age twelve, I attended many "True Love Waits" rallies, where teens are made "aware" of their sexual responsibility of chastity to God. During this ceremony, teens are encouraged to sign a commitment pledge before God and their church community promising to be "pure" until marriage. The ceremony focuses on the "love and sacrifice" that Jesus gave while being crucified. Prompted by the emotional rhetoric and peer pressure, I signed the pledge, indicating that I would "make a commitment to God, myself, my family, my friends, my future mate, and my future children to a lifetime of purity including sexual abstinence from this day until the day I enter a biblical marriage relationship."[15] I proudly wore my "True Love Waits" ring on my wedding finger and, for a short time, felt involved and accepted. I was also told that when I did enter a partnership, it was God's will for me to be submissive to my male partner.[16] I was told that sex was natural and healthy but only *after* marriage. Sexual desires of a teenager were rarely, if at all, discussed. I tried to adhere to these strict guidelines for my sexuality.

When I was fourteen, my parents divorced, and my mother was much more permissive with me than I was accustomed to. I began having sex occasionally at the age of fifteen. Soon after, I met a boy whom I became enamored with quite quickly. He was older, exciting, and different from what I had been exposed to before. He was one of the first boys whom I had met outside of church, school, or youth group. His parents did not belong to any specific church, and as he was twenty years old, he was not subject to any stringent rules, although he still lived with his parents. In December 1998, I turned sixteen; feeling confused and lonely, I began having sex with my boyfriend, not seriously thinking of any specific consequences. When I did preemptively question the thought of unsafe sex, I was told by my boyfriend that he could prevent any disease or pregnancy by controlling the timing of his ejaculation. Naïve and uneducated, I submitted to his coercion and began engaging in sexual activity regularly.

Three short months later, I began to feel sick often. I was always tired, exhausted, and moody. All the tell-tale signs of pregnancy were there, and I knew something peculiar was going on with my body, but I was not sure exactly what. I certainly did not want to entertain the thought that I might be pregnant. The two largest sins that a female can commit against God, according to my church, were premarital sex and abortion. If my boyfriend was wrong and I was actually pregnant, I virtually had no viable options. After I missed my first period in February, I took a pregnancy test; it came back negative. I was overjoyed. I hid the test in the trash, thanked my boyfriend for being so "concerned" with preventing a pregnancy, and continued on with my life.

I still felt terrible—sick, tired, depressed, and tender—but I just attributed these feelings to my changing body. After all, I was a teenager. In late March, I missed another period and asked my mom to take me to the doctor. I had many tests, including urinary tract, pregnancy, and kidney stone tests, run with no concrete results. I was at a loss as to what was wrong with me. My mother knew that I was sexually active, and she verbally disapproved but often turned her head rather than enforce any rules. Two weeks later, on April 1, 1999, still feeling sick and prompted by an older coworker, I took another pregnancy test. This time it came back positive.

Sitting in the bathroom, I could hear my boyfriend in the other room watching TV. It is odd to describe the thoughts that ran through my head that afternoon, but I wasn't feeling as desperate as one might think a sixteen-year-old pregnant girl would feel at that moment. Instead, my head was full of naïvely positive thoughts. Probably in an attempt to deny the gravity of the situation, I felt that my boyfriend would be tolerant of the news, perhaps even happy. Instead of thinking of the obstacles that surely awaited me, I thought of the fact that perhaps we could get married, rent a house, and live on our own. After all, he was four years older than me; surely, he would know what to do. I approached him within minutes of the test coming back positive, with a big smile on my face. "I'm pregnant," I announced. His head jerked in my direction, and his mouth dropped open. His reaction was not at all what I thought it would be. His face, grief stricken and filled with anger, went pale, and he demanded, "What are you going to do?" Minutes later, my mom arrived home, and I broke the news to her. Her response, perhaps naturally, was one of anger. She exclaimed, "This is just great, Allison. Do you know what your father is going to do to me?" I interpreted her statement as one implying responsibility. I knew this meant that my father, the male, would be angry with my mother, just as my boyfriend, the male, was holding

me responsible for the pregnancy. Though I was young, naïve, and uneducated, I would shoulder the responsibility and guilt that would be associated
with this pregnancy. Though I knew nothing of gender norms at the time, I
took the statement to mean that I was solely responsible for this child—that
because I was female, regardless of age or previous experience, I would be
the one to raise and care for my future baby. Suddenly, the realization of how
alone I really was hit me.

Four days later, my boyfriend went to jail for ninety days. Over the next
few months, my life became more and more isolated. I went through the
motions of school and work at a local fast-food joint. I walked (which in rural
North Carolina is not easy) from school to work to home to the grocery store.
I continued to live with my mother, who was rarely home. Often, I would go
days without speaking to someone supportive. I spent hours sleeping or lying
around in my home, listless, lonely, and scared. When I did go out, I received
disgusted looks from strangers and felt ashamed and belittled. A few times,
while at work, elderly ladies asked to pray over my stomach. When they did,
they prayed for God to forgive me and not punish my child as a result of my
own sin. My friends' parents would not allow my friends to visit with me any
longer; my church community had long ago written off my mother (and me,
as long as I lived with her) during the divorce; and I focused only on working
and writing letters to my jailed boyfriend. Very few stopped to ask how I
was, and if they did, the framing of their questions made me feel ashamed or
ostracized. Life was lonely and sad. I felt overwhelmed and helpless, yet in
characteristic teenage naivety, I refused to be hopeless. I could not see the
full implications of my pregnancy and resulting lack of supportive community.

I began to visit other churches, as this was the only means of community I
had been raised to know. Some churches would employ outright disdain, and
I often felt as though I was treated like I had some type of disease. Others
would be kind to my face yet do their best to avoid me otherwise. Many were
politely distant. After searching for a month or two, I did find one church
through my boyfriend's mother that was kind to me. Though I was often
treated as a charity case, it made me feel loved and valued. It provided me
with a confidence that I might be able to move through this pregnancy in
some sort of graceful manner. It even went as far as throwing a baby shower
for me.

It was at this church where the idea of marriage to my baby's father grew
in abundance. Somehow, I already had a motherly instinct, and I thought that
I knew from a lifetime of listening to Dr. James Dobson's radio broadcast
Focus on the Family that the family most pleasing to God's eyes was one
with a mother *and* a father. Because of the political rhetoric I had been
exposed to, I feared that the traditional family faced "imminent demise from
politicians, radical feminists, homosexual activists, and liberal journalists."[17]

I felt as though my unborn daughter faced a huge disadvantage in life. She was being born to a single mom at the tender age of only sixteen. I wanted to give her the best chance possible; I wanted to make her life "right" before God. Though my boyfriend was verbally abusive and controlling in his collect phone calls from jail, I thought if we could just get married, he would straighten out, thus creating a family for my daughter and me. I heavily pressured him to marry me. We decided to get married on July 17, five days after he got out of jail and six months into my pregnancy.

We went through with the marriage and, with the money that I saved while he was in jail, moved into a small trailer in a nearby town. Over the last few months of my pregnancy, I worked at a grocery store and tried to focus on getting the house ready for the baby, working, and trying to not fight with my twenty-year-old husband. Once we were married, the church, though still very kind to me, abandoned the daily talks of pseudo-encouragement. I had done the "right thing"; now, I had to just go on with my life. I once again felt that I had lost any type of makeshift support system I had found. I did not have many others to turn to. My father and brother lived relatively close by and tried to help out. But because my dad was a single father with a prepubescent boy, he didn't have much time to give. I attended an enormous mega church, one that I had gone to with my father as a child, but in the thousands of faces, I often felt alone and unimportant. On the show *16 and Pregnant*, the girls often have their fans to turn to when they are feeling this way. In addition, the show doesn't portray the daily monotonous tasks any mom must perform. They are often overwhelming and endless. For a sixteen-year-old, it is even more so. For me, I had only myself to perform these everyday jobs, decide if I was making the right decisions, and interpret the world around me.

As I moved through my "normal" daily tasks, I would contemplate my life, wondering how I might make this pregnancy "okay." I turned to the local library; it was my place of refuge. I spent hours in the stacks, reading about childbirth and child rearing, hoping that this would not only pass my time but enable me to be the best mom that I could be. Education, though it was self-attained at this point, became the place where I learned self-advocacy. Though I had no one else to turn to, I learned to turn to learning as a place where I could grow and evolve. In a way, books became my support system: my way of learning and growing.

The birth of my daughter came, and I figuratively traveled through the first year of her life. Though the first year of her life seemed to pass rapidly, many events occurred that helped me to gain experience and knowledge. I endured abuse and poverty. Often, my husband would jump from job to job, and he struggled with drug addiction. We would fight over his lack of responsibility, but eventually, I would stop probing him to look for another job, out of fear. Without an education and with the $500-per-month bill of child care, it was extremely difficult for me to find a job. I took low-paying jobs where I could take my daughter with me, such as my church's day care. It didn't pay much, but at least I didn't have to pay for care for the baby; I would simply bring her along. My husband threatened my life on numerous occasions. At night, I was literally afraid to sleep for fear of being killed. I was despondent and terrified, but I didn't know where to turn. I felt if I let someone know what was happening, I would be breaking up the morally "right" family my daughter so deserved. I was filled with shame and guilt and had no one to turn to. I continued through her first year with my head held down, focusing only on my love for my daughter.

I decided to go to school, planning to get a degree and a job so that in five years I would be able to leave my abusive husband. I felt that until I had a degree, I had no power and would cause only detriment to my daughter's well-being by prematurely leaving. Education (although it was via my own direction and, therefore, a lonely act in and of itself) had helped me through my loneliness and had guided me in the course of my first year of mothering. Surely, I surmised, it would carry me somewhere else, particularly if that meant learning with peers around me and under the instruction of a mentor.

I have realized in my life that one's perspective often determines the hardships that one encounters as viable or impractical. It seemed to me that because of my daughter, I had no choice but to survive. For me, everything I hoped to do to achieve my education would be extremely difficult. I had no car, no license, no access to public transportation. I had no money, no child care, no parents able to babysit. But I felt that this was my only means of survival for my daughter and me. Since I had worked independently to finish my high school diploma while pregnant, I applied and was admitted to my local community college for the spring semester of 2001. This was a feat in and of itself, as I had to learn how to apply for the college, find a way to obtain my license, and apply for financial aid. Since, while applying, I was technically still under 18, these steps required extra provisions, having to prove that I lived separately from my parents, that I was married, that I was responsible for my own taxes and living expenses. I spent countless hours in various social service and college offices stating and restating my situation. I received a variety of reactions throughout this process: skepticism, weariness, reverence, cynicism, and disdain. Through it all, I thought only of my daughter and my obligation to be a "good" mother to her. Once all the legalities were out of the way for applying for college, I had to move on to finding ways to get a car and a place for my child to go while I attended school. At the time, the going rate for a week's worth of child care was about $200. There was no way that I could afford that at the time, so I applied for financial assistance. I received a portion of the monies needed for child care from the state, but I knew that it would require more for me to be able to attend college full-time. I spent weeks researching and applying for other scholarships in the school that pertained to child care. Once I secured the money needed to get her into day care, I spent much of the month of December interviewing multiple child cares. Finally having found the funds for child care, school, books, and a day care for her to attend, I moved on to finding a work-study job that I could do. As the semester start approached, I was filled with anxieties. I was afraid that no one would respect me or view me as important. It seemed that I had been dismissed so often. But I had an overwhelming desire to make my daughter proud. She was my community.

Only a few weeks after I began my first semester of college, my husband told me that he was going to his cousin's for dinner. He never came back. This was over twelve years ago, and I have seen him only twice since then, both times within the first year of him being gone. Looking back, I see his abrupt abandonment as an immense blessing that many battered women are never offered. At the time, however, I was devastated. I had been trained to believe that a family must include a mother *and* a father. My heart was broken that my daughter was destined to live a life with only a mom. Hindsight is twenty-twenty, and with my thirty-year-old eyes, it seems incredulous that I feared for our well-being. My husband had hardly worked; he was abusive to me; and he paid little to no attention to his daughter, even when she was in the same room. Yet I was very distressed. I continued moving through the motions, not quite sure what else to do.

It didn't take me very long to figure out that, although being a single mom was difficult, it was better than being a married single mom who was enduring abuse. I learned how to navigate the waters of education, single motherhood, jobs, financial assistance, and the world of toddlers. Every lesson I learned at my community college, I found a way to apply to my job as a parent. When I learned how to write persuasive essays, I wrote a letter to James Dobson, asking him to "focus" on my "family." I wrote a letter to my daughter's favorite television show, *Veggie Tales*, asking the producers to portray types of families other than the nuclear family typically shown by this Christian children's show. I used my newly honed math skills to make a plan for saving money from tax returns, and I used my critical thinking skills to determine good advice from bad advice. It was an extremely productive point in my life. Yet, I could not escape the pervasive feeling of loneliness. My classmates would try to speak with me, but I was always rushing away to get homework done before I had to pick my daughter up. Time was a precious commodity to me. I spent long hours studying, getting to bed by two or three in the morning, and back up to start my day around six or seven. I did have a few friends who came and went from my life, one or two who are still around today (the youngest of whom is twelve years older than me), but for the most part, I journeyed through the first nine years of my daughter's life quite alone. Because I had a child, I could not relate to my own peers and therefore found that older women were better able to identify with my daily life issues.

My age significantly hindered my ability to find a supportive community. As a single woman, I could make community within the singles group at my church, but most of the people who attended were either ten to fifteen years older than me or had no children (and were still at least five years older). Though my church had often isolated me after my pregnancy and I had endured many traumatic events throughout my upbringing within its doors, it was the only way of life I knew. I found myself constantly hoping for some type of community there. I feared that removing myself from that situation would serve only to further isolate me. In a region where churches were much more prevalent than fast-food restaurants, it didn't seem possible to escape that. As with anything in life, particularly within the more unhealthy aspects of someone's journey, the church community and structure were quite complex. Though the church served to damage my self-esteem and cause me to question my worth and self-efficacy, it was a place where I felt that I had some purpose: to serve God. Leaving that meant that I was not only isolated but would lead a purposeless life. It meant that I would fail my daughter again. Not only would she have to face the world as the child of a teenage mom, but she would also likely be destined to hell. I knew that the people within the church, ones I was working very hard to gain redemption from, would write me and, more important, my daughter, off as completely lost. Having been raised this way since birth, I saw no other way to live life. So, I continued to live my solitary life, struggling to make my presence and my daughter's vindicated.

Additionally, finding friends at college wasn't really an option, as no one there had children, and most were much more concerned with the local party than changing diapers or buying the newest *Veggie Tales* VHS. I learned to navigate through life, depending on only myself. I learned how to always ask questions for my daughter's future. I learned how to apply myself in all aspects of life. I learned how to look to officials within my geographic community to advocate for financial assistance. I learned how to clean my house, cook my meals, and care for my daughter, turning to self-help and how-to books to learn how to create a better me. Still, I was left with the persistent loneliness that often accompanies being a single mom. I often turned to radio call-in shows such as *Delilah* or sitcoms that portrayed close communities, such as *Friends*, to make a pseudo-community for myself. Sure, I met a few young moms along the way, but the number of young moms who would qualify as a healthy, supportive community was scarce. For the cast of *16 and Pregnant*, this community—sometimes virtual, sometimes not—exists inherently through the show. For me, I had to learn how to exist within my own world of self-approval and self-discipline.

It was after many life circumstances—some happy, many devastatingly sad—that I ended up in a state some eight hundred miles away from my home. Making the decision to move to Connecticut was tough, but I felt that it was a chance for me to start over, to build a new life in a new place. In 2007, I arrived in New Haven, just my daughter and myself, only knowing two people in the whole state. Only after age was no longer an issue (age differences do not seem as important once you reach twenty-five) did I begin to feel that I could create my own community, my own family, to serve the purposes that my daughter and I needed so desperately. Because one could no longer see youth as prominently in my face, I began to develop confidence in being able to reach out to others without instantaneous judgment. I learned through age, experience, and grief that community is imperative for survival. Humans are, at the core, communal creatures, and we require some sense of belonging to thrive. I did eventually learn how to create that for myself but only after many years of being alone and ostracized. I had to learn to change the way that I saw community, the way that I searched for it. For the women on the show *16 and Pregnant*, they receive money and stardom as a result of being pregnant. For me and many other teen moms like me, being sixteen and pregnant did not mean fame and fortune but, rather, poverty and isolation.

It is true that in today's social media climate, many moms, regardless of age, have a different sort of experience than I had at the turn of the millennium. At that time, social media was not nearly as popular as it is now. There was the occasional "MySpacer," but the Internet was not as readily accessible, and I certainly did not have the time or the money to access it. Though there are many Americans without access to Internet sources today, there are a variety of other ways to utilize social media (3G phone service being a prominent example). In this modern American cultural climate, social media can provide a place for "powerful competition," a version of mothering that Susan Douglas and Meredith Michaels term "the ultimate female Olympics."[18] Yet, it also has provided a place for mothers to ask questions, find answers, and, more important, seek out a sense of community. No longer does a new mom have to make the frantic 2:00 am call to her own mother (if she is lucky enough to have a mom who would listen). She can simply find her answer online, post her cry for help in her status, or read the comments at the end of an article. She never has to feel alone.

For the average teenage mom in this decade, access to a virtual community may no longer be a problem. Even young moms who are facing poverty often can access this community. Today, as cell phones are seen by many as a necessity of daily living, many socioeconomically disadvantaged moms can apply for a cell phone and service through their local Department of Social Services. The same place where women seek assistance with food, housing, and utilities can now provide access to a cell phone plan and carrier.[19] Though the plan is limited, the moms often still have the ability to access Facebook through 3G connections. In addition, libraries are often utilized for social media purposes. A girl can find people who are willing to engage at any moment via Facebook, Twitter, e-mail, and texting—so much so that she will face new obstacles, such as setting boundaries for herself on how *much* social media will be healthy for herself and her child. This is true for the average teenage pregnancy as well as the stars of the MTV show, as suggested by its website article "A Little Laughing Gas Won't Stand in the Way of Chelsea Houska's Texting."[20] Moms (and their babies' fathers) can post their daily triumphs as well as their contrition for their shortcomings. In this way, a community can be both supportive and invasive, even for the average girl.

Yet, learning to navigate the world by finding the healthiest community for one's life is all part of growing up, particularly for today's teens. It is imperative that any mom feel as though she has a strong community with which she can share her daily mommy fears, triumphs, insecurities, and joys. Those on the show *16 and Pregnant* have an automatic built-in community. They are sharing this experience with other girls who are in the exact same situation as they. Though they may be miles apart, they have the resources to connect with one another.

In addition, and more pointedly, it seems that they have an entire country rooting for them. Though it may be true that they receive some negativity and harsh words based on their lifestyles throughout their stint on *16 and Pregnant* and *Teen Mom*, the majority of viewers seem to be fans (if we use Facebook, Twitter, and online comments on MTV's website as indicators). If Amber, Maci, Catelynn, and Farrah feel at a loss with their confidence or desire someone to share in their joy, they might simply jump online or open up the latest copy of *Ok!* or *People* magazine. The girls on *16 and Pregnant* experience this daily via the feedback they receive from the viewers. Maci— mother of Bentley, from the first season of the popular MTV show—notes that she "is positive she has her own happy ending within her sights."[21] She can feel good about having another child, marrying another man, knowing that she has the fan base to encourage her. The mere thought of having another child close to my daughter's birth was, perhaps logically, often met with disdain and disgust. I recall a time when I took my then four-year-old daughter to the doctor for a wellness check-up. She had been going to the same pediatrician for years at this point and always received clean health reports. While waiting for the doctor to come in, I fiddled with a pregnancy due-date indicator that was lying on the counter. The doctor walked in, raised his eyebrows, and snidely said, "You aren't pregnant *again* are you?" Shame and embarrassment flooded my face, as it turned red and flushed at the obvious reaction that a second pregnancy would have received.

Even Amber—the mother of Leah and the notorious "bad girl" from the first season of *16 and Pregnant*—has her own fan base. Though she is currently in jail for violating probation, she has a large community rooting for her success, as noted by her exclusive interview with Dr. Drew.[22] Many mothers in jail today face not only separation from their children but also estrangement from any community they might seek. The women and children from shows such as *16 and Pregnant* have, over the years, experienced the benefits that come with being a celebrity: money, fame, and access to services they might normally not have. Despite their numerous struggles, they have typically been assured of being loved, looked after, and cheered on. They still have to work at balancing their careers, schooling, parenting, and outside relationships, but they all are receiving a hefty paycheck simply by sharing their story with others.

While I certainly am not championing the idea that teen moms join shows such as *16 and Pregnant* or *Teen Mom* to solve their struggles with isolation and fear, I do think that it is important to point out that as we watch these moms on TV, we should view them and other nonfamous teen moms through a multifaceted lens that helps us to see the situation as one that is complex and layered. An average teenage mom cannot expect the same lifestyle merely by carrying on with her motherly duties. She must learn to balance finances, school, work, home, cleaning, grocery shopping, meetings, driving, and self-care, not to mention the very astute task of caring for the cognitive, physical, and emotional well-being of her child. She certainly does not receive a paycheck for sharing her narrative. Often, these moms figuratively pay the price of unhealthy relationships, simply to have the benefit of someone who will even remotely *listen* to their story. In addition, we must ask questions about the sustainability of this type of lifestyle for the moms and their children on *16 and Pregnant* and *Teen Mom*. Eventually, the show will end—and what will become of the cast then? The mothers must go on with their daily lives, adjust to being forgotten publicly, and learn to create new lives for themselves. The mothers will have to learn self-advocacy and self-worth, without MTV around to show them how.

Indeed, it certainly can be debated whether an abundance of fame is healthy for individuals, particularly those who are still cognitively and emotionally developing while caring for a new, fragile, and impressionable child. Yet one cannot deny that the girls of *16 and Pregnant* have access to their own, usually positive, community from which to receive advice, encouragement, and even adoration. And yet, there are dangers that come with one being constantly affirmed and spotlighted. One might argue for the lifetime of benefits that accompany the struggling that it takes to create a positive community for oneself, a notion that has proven true in my own life. There is always a danger in not learning how to advocate for oneself. Often, the best growth comes from struggle. Indeed, if it weren't for the loneliness and feelings of insecurity that arose from my trials of ostracism, I might not have learned the triumph of education and self-advocacy, something I strive to pass on to my daughter and students today. Yet, no one can deny a girl the short-term satisfaction of feeling as though she is not alone in her journey toward adulthood and successful child rearing or the possibility of learning these lessons in an environment that serves to engage mothers through self-confidence and support.

The type of instant community and support created by virtual communities and fame is quite powerful for mothers at any age but particularly for a young mom, who is caught somewhere between the stage of typical teenage drama and mothering an infant. This mom desperately needs some type of supportive community, even if it is only virtual. Most teen moms are fortunate today to find these advantages at their fingertips any time they need them. In 2010, I started an electronic newsletter[23] primarily for this purpose: to create a sense of community among single moms who are going to school, are typically young, and are in need of a fast-forming, supportive community. I hope that young mothers can read the newsletter and feel inspired to create their own physical supportive community. It is my intention that this publication will serve the same purpose. I hope that by sharing my narrative, two responses might come about. One is that from the people who surround or come in contact with the young teen mom. I hope that they will better understand her, her hopes and her fears, and what she is battling personally in her day-to-day life. The second is the response from the teen mom herself. My hope is that she will read this and know that she can advocate for herself. I hope that she will be able to grow and change and not fear the world but rather realize that much of her life and dreams are hers for the taking, if she chooses to participate in self-advocacy.

For me, it took years of isolation and suffering before I was able to form a community of "family" that I can trust to help guide me in the right direction, listen to my struggles, and cheer me on as I accomplish my goals. I continue to balance all the typical responsibilities that any mom, but particularly a single mom, struggles to maintain. Every moment that I announce to a co-worker, my classroom, a new acquaintance, or another mom that I have a thirteen-year-old, I am met with the same response: "My! You look so young to have a teenager!" A comment that at one time filled my heart with dread and shame now brings a sense of pride and a heartfelt smile. What once was a shameful secret of mine I now carry as a part of my identity. Sure, I still don't "fit" exactly in any one place. The parents of my daughter's peers are often my own parents' age. My peers are just starting to have children. My colleagues often don't have children at all. And yet, it is nothing that I hide from anymore. Having a child at sixteen is part of who I am, how I belong, by *not* belonging.

NOTES

1. Thompson, "16, Pregnant . . . and Famous."
2. "About MTV's *16 and Pregnant*."

3. "About MTV's *16 and Pregnant.*"

4. Hoffman, "Fighting Teenage Pregnancy."

5. Hoffman, "Fighting Teenage Pregnancy."

6. Hoffman, "Fighting Teenage Pregnancy."

7. Albert quoted in Thompson, "16, Pregnant . . . and Famous."

8. Hoffman, "Fighting Teenage Pregnancy."

9. See Douglas and Michaels, *The Mommy Myth*; hooks, "Paulo Freire"; Mackoff, "Consider Her Conditioning"; or Orenstein, *Cinderella Ate My Daughter*.

10. Perhaps the word *reality* lends itself to this phenomenon happening in a more intense manner. By labeling the shows as "reality TV," people often intuitively suppose that the shows are a true and realistic depiction of the characters being portrayed.

11. Hartsock, "The Feminist Standpoint," 304.

12. Bookout quoted in Thompson, "16, Pregnant . . . and Famous."

13. Hoffman, "Fighting Teenage Pregnancy."

14. Dobson, "My Family Talk: Virtue."

15. "True Love Waits Pledge."

16. Ephesians 5:22 (King James version).

17. Dobson, "My Family Talk: Traditional?"

18. Douglas and Michaels, *The Mommy Myth*, 2–45.

19. "Who Qualifies for a Free Cell Phone?"

20. Donnelly, "A Little Laughing Gas."

21. "*Teen Mom* Drama."

22. Donnelly, "Imprisoned Amber Portwood."

23. *Single Is Enough: Embracing, Loving and Thriving as a Single Mother*, available at http://www.southernct.edu/womenscenter/singleisenough.

Episode Bibliography

16 AND PREGNANT

Season 1

"Amber." June 25, 2009.
"Catelynn." July 16, 2009.
"Ebony." July 2, 2009.
"Farrah." June 18, 2009.
"Life after Labor." July 24, 2009.
"Maci." June 11, 2009.
"Whitney." July 9, 2009.

Season 2

"Ashley." December 21, 2010.
"Chelsea." March 9, 2010.
"Christinna." November 30, 2010.
"Felicia." November 2, 2010.
"Jenelle." February 16, 2010.
"Kailyn." April 20, 2010.
"Kayla." December 7, 2010.
"Leah." April 6, 2010.
"Life after Labor." April 20, 2010.
"Life after Labor." December 28, 2010.
"Lizzie." April 13, 2010.
"Lori." March 16, 2010.
"Markai." November 16, 2010.
"Nikkole." February 23, 2010.

"No Easy Decision." December 28, 2010.
"Samantha." March 23, 2010.
"Unseen Moments (Season 2)." December 14, 2010.
"Valerie." March 2, 2010.

Season 3

"Cleondra." May 17, 2011.
"Izabella." May 31, 2011.
"Jamie." May 3, 2011.
"Jennifer." April 26, 2011.
"Jordan." April 19, 2011.
"Kayla." May 24, 2011.
"Kianna." June 7, 2011.
"Taylor." June 14, 2011.

Season 4

"Alex." April 18, 2012.
"Briana." April 3, 2012.
"Devon." May 22, 2012.
"Hope." May 8, 2012.
"Jordan." April 24, 2012.
"Kristina." May 29, 2012.
"Mackenzie." March 27, 2012.
"Sabrina." May 15, 2012.
"Sarah." May 15, 2012.

TEEN MOM

Season 1

"Finale Special: Check-Up with Dr. Drew." February 1, 2010.
"How Many Chances?" December 14, 2009.
"A Little Help." December 29, 2009.
"Looking for Love." December 8, 2009.
"Moving On." December 14, 2009.

Season 2

"Family Bonds." September 21, 2010.
"Finale Special: Check-Up with Dr. Drew." October 19, 2010.
"Lashing Out." September 28, 2010.

"Not Again." July 20, 2010.
"Secrets and Lies." August 16, 2010.
"See You Later." October 12, 2010.
"Senior Prom." September 7, 2010.
"Spring Break." August 10, 2010.
"Trial and Error." August 31, 2010.
"Valentine's Day." August 3, 2010.

Season 3

"Finale Special: Check-Up with Dr. Drew—Part 1." September 27, 2011.
"Finale Special: Check-Up with Dr. Drew—Part 2." October 4, 2011.
"The Last Straw." July 19, 2011.
"Pros and Cons." September 20, 2011.
"Stay with Me." September 6, 2011.
"Taking It Slow." July 5, 2011.
"Teen Dads Special." September 18, 2011.
"Without You." August 16, 2011.

Season 4

"Letting Go." June 12, 2012.
"The Next Step." August 1, 2012.
"Places You'll Go." June 19, 2012.
"Separation Anxiety." June 12, 2012.
"Wake Up." August 29, 2012.

TEEN MOM 2

Season 1

"Change of Heart." January 25, 2011.
"Nothing Stays the Same." January 11, 2011.
"One Step Back." March 22, 2011.
"So Much to Lose." January 18, 2011.
"Too Much, Too Fast." February 8, 2011.
"Two Steps Forward." March 15, 2011.

Season 2

"Curveball." December 13, 2011.

Bibliography

"*16 and Pregnant*: Is Devion the Worst New Dad in the History of the Show?" Huffington Post. September 24, 2010. http://www.huffingtonpost.com/20120/04/04/16-and-pregnant-is-devon-worst-dad-ever-video_n_1402148.html.

Aapola, Sinikka, Marnina Gonick, and Anita Harris. *Young Femininity: Girlhood, Power and Social Change.* New York: Palgrave Macmillan, 2005.

"About MTV's *16 and Pregnant*." MTV.com. http://www.mtv.com/shows/16_and_pregnant/season_4/series.jhtml.

"About *Teen Mom* (Season 3)." MTV.com. 2012. http://www.mtv.com/shows/teen_mom/season_3/series.jhtml.

"About Teen Pregnancy: Teen Pregnancy in the United States." Centers for Disease Control and Prevention. 2012. http://www.cdc.gov/teenpregnancy/AboutTeenPreg.htm.

Abramovitz, Mimi. *Regulating the Lives of Women: Social Welfare Policy from Colonial Times to the Present.* Revised ed. Cambridge, MA: South End Press, 1996.

Acs, Gregory, and Heather L. Koball. "TANF and the Status of Teen Mothers under Age 18." Urban Institute. June 2, 2003. http://www.urban.org/publications/310796.html.

Agger, Ben. *Cultural Studies as Critical Theory.* Washington, DC: Falmer Press, 1992.

Ahola-Sidaway, Janice, and Sandra Fonseca. "When Schooling Is Not Enough: Support, Empowerment and Social Regulation of the Teen Mother in Contemporary Canada." *Journal of the Association for Research on Mothering* 9, no. 1 (2007): 53–61.

Albert, Bill. "Is Media Glamorizing Teen Pregnancy? New Research of Teens Suggests the Answer Is No." National Campaign to Prevent Teen and Unplanned Pregnancy. October 10, 2010. http://www.thenationalcampaign.org/media/press-release.aspx?releaseID-200.

Allen, Louisa. *Young People and Sexuality Education: Rethinking Key Debates.* New York: Palgrave Macmillan, 2011.

Allen, Sarah M., and Alan J. Hawkins. "Maternal Gatekeeping: Mothers' Beliefs and Behaviors That Inhibit Greater Father Involvement in Family Work." *Journal of Marriage and the Family* 61 (1999): 199–212.

Allen, William D., and William J. Doherty. "The Responsibilities of Fatherhood as Perceived by African American Teenage Fathers." *Families in Society* 77, no. 3 (1996): 142–55.

"Amber Portwood Chooses Prison over Her Child." Hollywood Gossip. June 11, 2012. http://www.thehollywoodgossip.com/2012/06/amber-portwood-chooses-prison-over-her-child/.

Arai, Lisa. *Teenage Pregnancy: The Making and Unmaking of a Problem.* Bristol, England: Policy Press, 2009.

Armstrong, Jennifer. "*16 and Pregnant* Delivers Big." *Entertainment Weekly*, March 19, 2010, 84.

Arrington, Michael Irvin, and Bethany Crandell Goodier. "Prostration before the Law: Representations of Illness, Interaction, and Intimacy in the NYPD Blue Prostate Cancer Narrative." *Popular Communication* 2, no. 2 (2004): 67–84.

Arthur, Shirley M. *Surviving Teen Pregnancy: Your Choices, Dreams and Decisions.* Buena Park, CA: Morning Glory Press, 1996.

Ashcraft, Catherine. "Adolescent Ambiguities in *American Pie*: Popular Culture as a Resource for Sex Education." *Youth and Society* 35, no. 1 (2003): 37–70.

———. "Ready or Not . . . ? Teen Sexuality and the Troubling Discourse of Readiness." *Anthropology and Education Quarterly* 37, no. 4 (2006): 328–46.

Bailey, Nicole, Geraldine Brown, Gayle Letherby, and Corinne Wilson. "'The Baby Brigade': Teenage Mothers and Sexuality." *Journal of the Association for Research on Mothering* 4, no. 1 (2002): 88–100.

Ballam, Stacey M., and Paul F. Granello. "Confronting Sex in the Media: Implications and Counseling Recommendations." *Family Journal: Counseling and Therapy for Couples and Families* 19, no. 4 (2011): 421–26.

Baretto, Melissa, and Janice Gatti. "MTV Press: About *16 and Pregnant.*" MTV Press. http://mtvpress.com/shows/16_and_pregnant.

———. "Network Greenlights *16 and Pregnant* Spinoff Series *Teen Mom.*" MTV Press. September 9, 2009. http://mtvpress.com/press/release/labor_day_marathon/.

Baxter, Judith. "Feminist Post-structuralist Discourse Analysis: A New Theoretical and Methodological Approach?" In *Gender and Language Research Methodologies*, edited by Kate Harrington, Lia Litosseliti, Helen Sauntson, and Jane Sunderland, 243–55. New York: Palgrave, 2008.

Bazilian, Emma. "Social Messages Seek Out New Tactics for Teens." Adweek.com. June 13, 2012. http://www.adweek.com/news/advertising-branding/social-messages-seek-out-new-tactics-teens-141026.

Becker, Davida, Danielle Bessett, Megan L. Kavanaugh, Alison Norris, Julia R. Steinberg, and Silvia De Zordo. "Abortion Stigma: A Reconceptualization of Constituents, Causes, and Consequences." *Women's Health Issues* 21, no. 3 (2011): S49–S54.

Belluck, Pam. "In Study, Fatherhood Leads to Drop in Testosterone." *New York Times*, September 12, 2011.

Berlant, Lauren. *The Female Complaint: The Unfinished Business of Sentimentality in American Culture.* Durham, NC: Duke University Press, 2008.

———. *The Queen of America Goes to Washington City: Essays on Sex and Citizenship.* Durham, NC: Duke University Press, 1997.

Berman, Rachel C., Susan Silver, and Sue Wilson. "'Don't Look Down on Me Because I Have One': Young Mothers Empowered in a Context of Support." *Journal of the Association for Research on Mothering* 9, no. 1 (2007): 42–52.

Boryczka, Jocelyn. "Whose Responsibility? The Politics of Sex Education Policy in the United States." *Politics and Gender* 5 (2009): 185–210.

Bowlby, John. *Child Care and the Growth of Love.* Baltimore: Pelican Books, 1953.

Brewer, Tiffany. "Exploring the Impact of MTV's *16 and Pregnant* on Parents and Teenage Girls." Master's thesis, American University. April 21, 2011. http://www.american.edu/soc/communication/upload/Tiffany-Brewer.pdf.

Briggs, Laura. *Somebody's Children: The Politics of Transracial and Transnational Adoption.* Durham, NC: Duke University Press, 2012.

Brooks, Ann. *Postfeminisms: Feminism, Cultural Theory and Cultural Forms.* London: Routledge, 1997.

Brown, Jane D., and Sarah N. Keller. "Media Interventions to Promote Responsible Sexual Behavior." *Journal of Sex Research* 39, no. 1 (2002): 67–72.

Brown, Richard Harvey. *Society as Text: Essays on Rhetoric, Reason and Reality.* Chicago: University of Chicago Press, 1987.

Brown, William, and Arvind Singhal. "Ethical Dilemmas of Prosocial Television." *Communication Quarterly* 38, no. 3 (1990): 268–80.

Bunting, Lisa, and Colette McAuley. "Research Review: Teenage Pregnancy and Parenthood. The Role of Fathers." *Child and Family Social Work* 9, no. 3 (2004): 295–303.

Burnard, Philip. "A Method of Analyzing Interview Transcripts in Qualitative Research." *Nurse Education Today* 11 (1991): 461–66.

Buss, Emily. "The Parental Rights of Minors." *Buffalo Law Review* 48 (2000): 785–833.

Bute, Jennifer L., and Laura D. Russell. "Public Discourses about Teenage Pregnancy: Disruption, Restoration, Ideology." *Health Communication* 27, no. 7 (October 2012): 712–22.

Butler, Judith. *Gender Trouble: Feminism and the Subversion of Identity.* New York: Routledge, 1990.

———. "Is Kinship Always Already Heterosexual?" *Differences: A Journal of Feminist Cultural Studies* 13, no. 1 (2002) : 14–44.

Cantor, Muriel G. "Prime-Time Fathers: A Study in Continuity and Change." *Critical Studies in Mass Communication* 7 (1990): 275–86.

Carmon, Irin. "MTV Airing Teen Abortion Special." Jezebel. December 22, 2010. http://jezebel.com/5716000/mtv-airing-teen-abortion-special.

Catlett, Beth Skilken, and Patrick C. McKenry. "Class-Based Masculinities: Divorce, Fatherhood, and the Hegemonic Ideal." *Fathering* 2, no. 2 (2004): 165–90.

Cavanaugh, Stephen. "Content Analysis: Concepts, Methods and Applications." *Nurse Researcher* 4 (1997): 5–16.

Chang, Juju, and Taylor Behrendt. "*Teen Mom* Star Portwood Hospitalized in Apparent Suicide Attempt." ABC News. 2011. http://abcnews.go.com/Entertainment/teen-mom-star-amber-portwood-hospitalized-apparent-suicide/story?id=13843481#.Tybu6HOrXSw.

Cherrington, Jane, and Mary Breheny. "Politicizing Dominant Discursive Constructions about Teenage Pregnancy: Re-locating the Subject as Social." *Health* (London) 9, no. 1 (2005): 89–111.

Chow, Rey. *The Protestant Ethnic and the Spirit of Capitalism.* New York: Columbia University Press, 2002.

Christenson, Peter, and Maria Ivancin. "The 'Reality' of Health: Reality Television and the Public Health." Henry Kaiser Family Foundation. October 10, 2006. http://www.kff.org/entmedia/7567.cfm.

Chudnofsky, Lisa. "Fond Farewell to MTV's Original Teen Moms." MTV Remote Control. August 28, 2012. http://remotecontrol.mtv.com/2012/08/28/teen-mom-goodbye-series-finale/.

Connell, Robert W. *Masculinities.* 2nd ed. Berkeley: University of California Press, 1995.

———. "Teaching the Boys: New Research on Masculinity, and Gender Strategies for Schools." In *Women, Culture and Society: A Reader*, edited by Barbara Balliet and Patricia McDaniel, 151–73. Dubuque, IA : Kendall/Hunt, 1998.

Cope-Farrar, Kristie M., and Dale Kunkel. "Sexual Messages in Teens' Favorite Prime-Time Television Programs." In *Sexual Teens, Sexual Media: Investigating Media's Influence on Adolescent Sexuality*, edited by Jane D. Brown, Jeanne R. Steele, and Kim Walsh-Childers, 59–78. Mahwah, NJ: Erlbaum, 2002.

Corcorran, Farrell. "Television as Ideological Apparatus: The Power and the Pleasure." *Critical Studies in Mass Communication* 1 (1984): 131–45.

Crews, Jami L. "When Mommy's a Minor: Balancing the Rights of Grandparents Raising Grandchildren against Minors' Parental Rights." *Law and Psychology Review* 28 (2004): 133–48.

Dallas, Constance M., and Shu-Pi C. Chen. "Experiences of African American Adolescent Fathers." *Western Journal of Nursing Research* 20, no. 2 (April 1998): 210–22.

Danielle625. "Teens Want Fame through Pregnancy at Being Pregnant." Babble: For a New Generation of Parents. December 10, 2010. http://blogs.babble.com/being-pregnant/2010/12/10/teens-want-fame-through-pregnancy/.

Danziger, Sandra K. "The Decline of Cash Welfare and Implications for Social Policy and Poverty." *Annual Review of Sociology* 36 (2010): 523–45.

Darisi, Tanya. "'It Doesn't Matter If You're 15 or 45, Having a Child Is a Difficult Experience': Reflexivity and Resistance in Young Mothers' Constructions of Identity." *Journal of the Association for Research on Mothering* 9, no. 1 (2007): 29–41.

Davies, Bronwyn, Suzy Dormer, Sue Gannon, Cath Laws, Sharn Rocco, Hillevi Lenz Taguchi, and Helen McCann. "Becoming Schoolgirls: The Ambivalent Project of Subjectification." *Gender and Education* 13, no. 2 (2001): 167–81.

Davis, Allison. "Baby Mama." *Teen Vogue*, June/July 2010.

Davis, Deborah, ed. *You Look Too Young to Be a Mom: Teen Mothers Speak Out on Love, Learning and Success*. New York: Perigee, 2004.

Dill, Karen E. *How Fantasy Becomes Reality: Seeing through Media Influence*. New York: Oxford University Press, 2009.

Doan, Alesha, and Jean Calterone Williams. *The Politics of Virginity: Abstinence in Sex Education*. Westport, CT: Praeger, 2008.

Dobson, James. "My Family Talk: Traditional Family Still Viable?" Dr. James Dobson's Family Talk. 2012. http://drjamesdobson.org/Solid-Answers/Answers?a=b40de61b-b4ca-43b8–bad8–b8f4803f5a01.

———. "My Family Talk: Virtue Is a Necessity." Dr. James Dobson's Family Talk. 1995. http://www.drjamesdobson.org/real-love/virtue-is-a-necessity.

Donnelly, Matthew Scott. "Imprisoned Amber Portwood on Life without Her Daughter: 'I Don't Even Matter' (Sneak Peak)." MTV Remote Control. October 8, 2012. http://remotecontrol.mtv.com/category/shows/teen_mom/.

———. "A Little Laughing Gas Won't Stand in the Way of Chelsea Houska's Texting." MTV Remote Control. October 3, 2012. http://remotecontrol.mtv.com/2012/10/03/teen-mom-2-chelsea-houska-text-dentist-photo/.

Douglas, Susan J. *Enlightened Sexism: The Seductive Message That Feminism's Work Is Done*. New York: Times Books, 2010.

———. *The Rise of Enlightened Sexism: How Pop Culture Took Us from Girl Power to Girls Gone Wild*. New York: St. Martin's Griffin, 2010.

Douglas, Susan J., and Meredith W. Michaels. *The Mommy Myth: The Idealization of Motherhood and How It Has Undermined All Women*. New York: Free Press, 2004.

Dowd, John. "'Telling It Like It Is': Subject Positions on Reality Television." *Kaleidoscope: A Graduate Journal of Qualitative Communication Research* 5 (fall 2006): 17–33.

Dubrofsky, Rachel E. "Fallen Women in Reality TV: A Pornography of Emotion." *Feminist Media Studies* 9, no. 3 (2009): 353–68.

Duffy, Janellen, and Jodie Levin-Epstein. "Add It Up: Teen Parents and Welfare . . . Undercounted, Oversanctioned, and Underserved." Center for Law and Social Policy. April 2002. http://www.clasp.org/admin/site/publications/files/0090.pdf.

Duggan, Lisa. *The Twilight of Equality: Neoliberalism, Cultural Politics and the Attack on Democracy*. Boston: Beacon, 2003.

Duke, Alan. "*Teen Mom* Amber Portwood Ordered to Prison." CNN. June 5, 2012. http://www.cnn.com/2012/06/05/showbiz/teen-mom-prison/index.html.

Durham, Jessica. "'My Teenage Dream Ended': Farrah Abraham Lands on *New York Times* Bestseller List; Reveals Drug Abuse and One-Night Stands." Books and Review. August 23, 2012. http://www.booksnreview.com/articles/791/20120823/my-teenage-dream-ended-farrah-abraham-lands-on-new-york-times-bestseller-list-reveals-drug-abuse-and-one-night-stands.htm.

Edelman, Lee. *No Future: Queer Theory and the Death Drive*. Durham, NC: Duke University Press, 2004.

"Employment and Unemployment among Youth Summary." Bureau of Labor Statistics. August 21, 2012. http://www.bls.gov/news.release/youth.nr0.htm.

Englander, Anrenee. *Dear Diary, I'm Pregnant: Teenagers Talk about Their Pregnancy*. Toronto, ON: Annick Press, 1997.

Entman, Robert M. "Framing US Coverage of International News." *Journal of Communication* 41, no. 4 (1991): 6–27.

"Episode 1 Maci Discussion Guide." Stayteen.org. http://www.stayteen.org/sites/default/files/discussion_guides/16-and-Pregnant-1-01-Maci.pdf.

"Episode 2 Farrah Discussion Guide." Stayteen.org. http://www.stayteen.org/sites/default/files/discussion_guides/16-and-Pregnant-1-02-Farrah.pdf.

"Episode 3 Amber Discussion Guide." Stayteen.org. http://www.stayteen.org/sites/default/files/discussion_guides/16-and-Pregnant-1-03-Amber.pdf.

"Episode 4 Ebony Discussion Guide." Stayteen.org. http://www.stayteen.org/sites/default/files/discussion_guides/16-and-Pregnant-1-04-Ebony.pdf.

"Episode 5 Whitney Discussion Guide." Stayteen.org. http://www.stayteen.org/sites/default/files/discussion_guides/16-and-Pregnant-1-05-Whitney.pdf.

"Episode 6 Catelynn Discussion Guide." Stayteen.org. http://www.stayteen.org/sites/default/files/discussion_guides/16-and-Pregnant-1-06-Catelynn.pdf.

Everett, Christina. *"Teen Mom* Star Begins Five-Year Prison Sentence." *New York Daily News.* June 15, 2012. http://articles.nydailynews.com/2012-06-15/news/32258957_1_gary-shirley-amber-portwood-teen-mom.

"Exclusive: *Teen Mom*'s Farrah Opens Up about Death of Sophia's Dad." USMagazine.com. August 18, 2010. http://www.usmagazine.com/celebrity-moms/news/teen-moms-farrah-opens-up-about-death-of-sophias-dad-2010188.

Fagan, Jay, and Marina Barnett. "The Relationship between Maternal Gatekeeping, Paternal Competence, Mothers' Attitudes about the Father Role, and Father Involvement." *Journal of Family Issues*, no. 24 (2003): 1020–43.

Failinger, Marie A. "Ophelia with Child: A Restorative Approach to Legal Decision-Making by Teen Mothers." *Law and Inequality: A Journal of Theory and Practice* 28 (2010): 255–88.

"Farrah Abraham 'On My Own' Music Video: Even Worse Than Her First Song?!" Hollywood Gossip. August 17, 2012. http://www.thehollywoodgossip.com/2012/08/farrah-abraham-on-my-own-music-video-even-worse-than-her-first-s/.

Feldstein, Ruth. *Motherhood in Black and White: Race and Sex in American Liberalism, 1930–1965.* Ithaca, NY: Cornell University Press, 2000.

Feldt, Gloria. "On *Friday Night Lights*, a Brave and Honest Abortion Story." *Washington Post.* July 25, 2010. http://www.washingtonpost.com/wpdyn/content/article/2010/07/23/AR2010072302432.html.

Fershee, Kendra Huard. "A Parent Is a Parent, No Matter How Small." *William and Mary Journal of Women and the Law* 18 (2012): 425–73.

Fessler, Ann. *The Girls Who Went Away: The Hidden Story of Women Who Surrendered Children for Adoption in the Decades Before Roe v. Wade.* New York: Penguin, 2006.

Fields, Jessica. "'Children Having Children': Race, Innocence, and Sexuality Education." *Social Problems* 52, no. 4 (2005): 549–71.

Fields, Jessica, and Deborah Tolman. "Risky Business: Sexuality Education and Research in U.S. Schools." *Sexuality Research and Social Policy: Journal of NSRC* 3, no. 4 (2006): 63–76.

Finn, Natalie, and Katie Rhames. "Kim Kardashian vs. Teen Mom: Amber Portwood and Jenelle Evans Fire Back." E! Online. January 19, 2011. http://uk.eonline.com/news/221508/kim-kardashian-vs-teen-mom-amber-portwood-and-jenelle-evans-fire-back.

Fogel, Jennifer M. "Reality Parenting 101: Celebrity Dads, Reality Sitcoms, and New 'Old School' Family Values." Paper presented at the Conference of the International Communication Association, Chicago, 2009.

Foucault, Michel. *Discipline and Punish: The Birth of the Prison.* New York: Random House, 1975.

———. *The History of Sexuality: An Introduction.* Vol. 1. New York: Vintage, 1978; reprinted 1990.

———. *"Society Must Be Defended": Lectures at the College de France, 1975–1976.* New York: Picador, 2003.

Frankel, Daniel. "MTV Plans 16 New Reality Shows." *Variety*, December 19, 2008.

"Funders." National Campaign to Prevent Teen and Unplanned Pregnancy. http://www.thenationalcampaign.org/about-us/funders.aspx.

Furrow, James L. "The Ideal Father: Religious Narratives and the Role of Fatherhood." *Journal of Men's Studies* 7, no. 1 (1998): 17–32.

Furstenberg, Frank F. "Good Dads–Bad Dads: Two Faces of Fatherhood." In *Changing American Family and Public Policy*, edited by Andrew J. Cherlin, 193–218. Washington, DC: Urban Institute, 1988.

Gamson, William A. *Talking Politics.* New York: Cambridge University Press, 1992.

Gamson, William A., and Andre Modigliani. "The Changing Culture of Affirmative Action." In *Research in Political Sociology*, edited by Robert Braungart and Michael Braungart, 137–77. Greenwich, CT: JAI Press, 1987.

Georgia State Board of Education. "Comprehensive Health and Physical Education Program Plan." July 21, 2011. http://www.doe.k12.ga.us/External-Affairs-and-Policy/State-Board-of-Education/SBOE Rules/160-4-2-.12.pdf.

Gerbner, George, Larry Gross, Michael Morgan, and Nancy Signorielli. "Living with Television: The Dynamics of the Cultivation Process." In *Perspectives on Media Effects*, edited by Jennings Bryant and Dolf Zillman, 17–40. Hillsdale, NJ: Erlbaum, 1984.

Giddens, Anthony. *Modernity and Self Identity: Self and Society in the Late Modern Age.* Stanford, CA: Stanford University Press, 1991.

Gill, Rosalind. "Culture and Subjectivity in Neoliberal and Postfeminist Times." *Subjectivity* 25 (2008): 432–45.

———. "Postfeminist Media Culture: Elements of a Sensibility." *European Journal of Cultural Studies* 10 (2007): 147–66.

Gitlin, Todd. *The Whole World Is Watching.* Berkeley: University of California Press, 1980.

Gomez, Laura. *Misconceiving Mothers: Legislators, Prosecutors, and the Politics of Prenatal Drug Exposure.* Philadelphia: Temple University Press, 1997.

Gonick, Marnina. *Between Femininities: Ambivalence, Identity, and the Education of Girls.* New York: State University of New York Press, 2012.

———. "Between 'Girl Power' and 'Reviving Ophelia': Constituting the Neoliberal Girl Subject." *NWSA Journal* 18, no. 2 (2006): 1–23.

Gore, Ariel. *Breeder: Real-Life Stories from the New Generation of Mothers.* Seattle: Seal Press, 2001.

Gorman, Bill. "Tuesday Cable Ratings: *Teen Mom* > *Sons of Anarchy*, Plus *Stargate Universe*, *Bad Girls Club* and Much More." TV by the Numbers. September 29, 2010. http://tvbythenumbers.zap2it.com/2010/09/29/tuesday-cable-ratings-teen-mom-sons-of-anarchy-plus-stargate-universe-bad-girls-club-much-more/65850/.

Graneheim, U. H., and B. Lundman. "Qualitative Content Analysis in Nursing Research: Concepts, Procedures, and Measures to Achieve Trustworthiness." *Nurse Education Today* 24, no. 1 (2004): 105–12.

Gravelle, Karen. *Teenage Fathers.* Blomington, IN: iUniverse, 2000.

Gray, Jennifer B. "Interpersonal Communication and the Illness Experience in the *Sex and the City* Breast Cancer Narrative." *Communication Quarterly* 55, no. 4 (2007): 397–414.

Grigsby Bates, Karen. "MTV's *Teen Mom* Makes for Teaching Moments." National Public Radio, August 10, 2007.

Grome, Brittany L. "The Four-Week Challenge: Student Mothers, Maternity Leaves, and Pregnancy-Based Sex Discrimination." *Albany Government Law Review* 4 (2011): 538–61.

Grose, Jessica. "Does MTV's *16 and Pregnant* Keep Girls from Getting Pregnant? Or Does It Just Exploit the Teen Moms on the Show?" Slate. February 22, 2010. http://www.slate.com/articles/double_x/doublex/2010/02/does_mtvs_16_and_pregnant_keep_girls_from_getting_pregnant.html.

———. "Lauren Dolgen, Creator of *16 and Pregnant* and *Teen Mom*, Makes Advocacy TV That Works." Slate. July 26, 2011. http://www.slate.com/articles/technology/top_right/2011/07/lauren_dolgen_creator_of_16_and_pregnant_and_teen_mom.html.

———. "Lauren Dolgen, Creator of *16 and Pregnant* and *Teen Mom* Talks about Her Inspiration for the Series." Slate. July 25, 2011. http://www.slate.com/articles/technology/top_right/2011/07/questions_for_lauren_dolgen.html.

———. "Study: Watching *16 and Pregnant* Makes Americans More Likely to Support Abortion." Slate. June 9, 2011. http://www.slate.com/blogs/xx_factor/2011/06/09/the_mtv_effect_and_abortion_watching_16_and_pregnant_makes_americans_more_likely_to_be_prochoice.html.

Grossbart, Sarah, and Rachel Paula Abrahamson. *"Teen Mom*: Inside Their Brave Struggle." *Us Weekly*, August 30, 2010, 38–45.

Guttmacher Institute. *Facts on Induced Abortion in the United States*. New York: Guttmacher Institute, 2011.

———. *Laws Affecting Reproductive Health and Rights: Trends in the First Quarter of 2011*. New York: Guttmacher Institute, 2011.

Hancock, Ange-Marie. *The Politics of Disgust: The Public Identity of the Welfare Queen*. New York: NYU Press, 2004.

Hao, Lingxin, and Andrew J. Cherlin. "Welfare Reform and Teenage Pregnancy, Childbirth, and School Dropout." *Journal of Marriage and Family* 66, no. 1 (2004): 179–94.

Harris, Anita. *Future Girl: Young Women in the Twenty-First Century*. New York: Routledge, 2004.

Harris, Lynn. "MTV's Shockingly Good Abortion Special." Salon. December 29, 2010. http://www.salon.com/2010/12/29/mtv_abortion_show_no_easy_choice/.

Hartsock, Nancy C. M. "The Feminist Standpoint: Toward a Specifically Feminist Historical Materialism." In *Feminist Theory Reader: Local and Global Perspectives*, edited by Carole R. McCann and Seung-Kyung Kim, 316–31. New York: Routledge, 2009.

Hasinoff, Amy. "Sexting as Media Production: Re-thinking Social Media." Unpublished manuscript. March 2012. http://mcgill.academia.edu/AmyHasinoff/Papers/1514754/Sexting_as_media_production_Re-thinking_social_media.

Havemann, Judith, and Helen Dewar. "Dole Courts Consensus on Welfare: Reform Plan Carries Tough Work Mandates." *Washington Post*, August 8, 1995.

Hays, Sharon. *The Cultural Contradictions of Motherhood*. New Haven, CT: Yale University Press, 1998.

Heath, D. T. "The Impact of Delayed Fatherhood on the Father-Child Relationship." *Journal of Genetic Psychology: Research and Theory on Human Development* 155, no. 4 (1994): 511–30.

Hennessy, Rosemary. *Profit and Pleasure: Sexual Identities in Late Capitalism*. New York: Routledge, 2000.

Henry J. Kaiser Family Foundation. *Issue Brief: Entertainment and Health Education in the United States*. Spring 2004. http://www.kff.org/entmedia/upload/entertainment-education-and-health-in-the-united-states-issue-brief.pdf.

Hernández, Rudy. *Fatherwork in the Crossfire: Chicano Teen Fathers Struggling to "Take Care of Business."* East Lansing, MI: Julian Samora Research Institute, 2002.

Hill, Annette. *Reality TV: Audiences and Popular Factual Television*. New York: Routledge, 2005.

———. *Restyling Factual TV: Audience and News, Documentary and Reality Genres*. London: Routledge, 2007.

Hochschild, Arlie. *The Second Shift*. New York: Penguin, 2003.

Hoffman, Jan. "Fighting Teenage Pregnancy with MTV Stars as Exhibit A." *New York Times*. April 8, 2011. http://www.nytimes.com/2011/04/10/fashion/10TEEN.html.

hooks, bell. "Paulo Freire." In *Teaching to Transgress*, 45–58. New York: Routledge.

Huang, K. S. "A Comparison between Media Frames and Audience Frames: The Case of the Hill-Thomas Controversy." Paper presented at the annual conference of the International Communication Association, Chicago, May 1996.

Hudley, Cynthia A. "Issues of Race and Gender in the Educational Achievement of African American Children." In *Gender, Equity, and Schooling: Policy and Practice*, edited by Barbara J. Bank and Peter M. Hall, 113–34. New York: Routledge, 1997.

If These Walls Could Talk. Directed by Cher and Nancy Savoca. New York: HBO NYC Productions, 1996.

Ingraham, Chrys. *White Weddings: Romancing Heterosexuality in Popular Culture*. New York: Routledge, 1999.

Iyengar, Shanto. "Television News and Citizens Explanations of National Affairs." *American Political Science Review* 81, no. 1 (1987): 815–31.

Jacobs, Janet. "Gender, Race, Class, and the Trend toward Early Motherhood: A Feminist Analysis of Teen Mothers in Contemporary Society." *Journal of Contemporary Ethnography* 22, no. 4 (1994): 442–62.

Jaworski, Beth K. "Reproductive Justice and Media Framing: A Case-Study Analysis of Problematic Frames in Popular Media." *Sex Education* 9, no. 1 (2009): 105–21.

Jay, Samuel. "De-racializing 'Deadbeat Dads': Paternal Involvement in MTV's *Teen Mom*." Flow. September 24, 2010. http://flowtv.org/2010/09/de-racializing-deadbeat-dads/.

Jilani, Zaid. "Three Leading GOP Presidential Nominees Pledge to Be Tough on Porn." Think Progress. January 10, 2012. http://thinkprogress.org/politics/2012/01/10/401517/three-leading-gop-nominees-porn/.

Jiwani, Yasmin. *Discourse of Denial: Meditations of Race, Gender, and Violence*. Vancouver, BC: UBC Press, 2006.

Jones, Tiffany. "A Sexuality Education Discourses Framework: Conservative, Liberal, Critical, and Postmodern." *American Journal of Sexuality Education* 6 (2011): 133–75.

Jonsson, Patrick. "A Force Behind the Lower Teen Birth Rate: MTV's *16 and Pregnant*." *Christian Science Monitor*. December 21, 2010. http://www.csmonitor.com/USA/Society/2010 /1221/A-force-behind-the-lower-teen-birthrate-MTV-s-16-and-Pregnant.

Kardashian, Kim. "To All Young Girls Out There . . ." Blog. Kim Kardashian: Official website. January 19, 2011. http://kimkardashian.celebuzz.com/2011/01/19/kim-kardashian-teen-mom-teenage-pregnancy-young-girls/.

Katz, Michael B. "The Urban 'Underclass' as a Metaphor of Social Transformation." In *The "Underclass" Debate: Views from History*, edited by Michael B. Katz, 3–23. Princeton, NJ: Princeton University Press, 1993.

Kavka, Misha. *Reality TV*. Edinburgh, Scotland: Edinburgh University Press, 2012.

Kearney, Melissa Schettini, and Phillip B. Levine. "Why Is the Teen Birth Rate in the United States So High and Why Does It Matter?" National Bureau of Economic Research. Working Paper 17965. March 2012. http://www.nber.org/papers/w17965.pdf.

Kelly, Deidre M. *Pregnant with Meaning: Teen Mothers and the Politics of Inclusive Schooling*. New York: Peter Lang, 2000.

———. "Stigma Stories: Four Discourses about Teen Mothers, Welfare, and Poverty." *Youth and Society* 27, no. 4 (2006): 421–49.

———. "Young Mothers, Agency and Collective Action: Issues and Challenges." *Journal of the Association for Research on Mothering* 9, no. 1 (2007): 9–19.

Kelly, Maura. "Virginity Loss Narratives in 'Teen Drama' Television Programs." *Journal of Sex Research* 47, no. 5 (2010): 479–89.

Kerber, Linda. *No Constitutional Right to Be Ladies: Women and the Obligations of Citizenship*. New York: Hill and Wang, 1998.

Kidger, Julie. "Stories of Redemption? Teenage Mothers as the New Sex Educators." *Sexualities* 8, no. 4 (2005): 481–96.

Kimmel, Michael. *Guyland: The Perilous World Where Boys Become Men*. New York: HarperCollins, 2008.

Kinser, Amber. "Mothering as Relational Consciousness." In *Feminist Mothering*, edited by Andrea O'Reilly, 123–42. Albany: State University of New York Press, 2008.

Kiselica, Mark S. *When Boys Become Parents: Adolescent Fatherhood in America*. New Brunswick, NJ: Rutgers University Press, 2011.

Klein, Jonathan D. "Adolescent Pregnancy: Current Trends and Issues." *Pediatrics* 116, no. 1 (2005): 281–86.

Kunzel, Regina G. "White Neurosis, Black Pathology: Constructing Out-of-Wedlock Pregnancy in the Wartime and Postwar United States." In *Not June Cleaver: Women and Gender in Postwar America, 1945–1960*, edited by Joanne Meyerowitz, 304–31. Philadelphia: Temple University Press, 1994.

Ladd-Taylor, Molly, and Lauri Umansky. *"Bad" Mothers: The Politics of Blame in Twentieth Century America*. New York: NYU Press, 1998.

Lamb, Michael. "The History of Research on Father Involvement: An Overview." *Marriage and Family Review* 29, nos. 2–3 (2000): 23–42.

LaRossa, Ralph. "Fatherhood and Social Change." In *Men's Lives*, edited by Michael S. Kimmel and Michael A. Messner, 448–60. Needham Heights, MA: Pearson, 1995.

Leavitt, Judith Walzer. *Make Room for Daddy: The Journey from Waiting Room to Birthing Room*. Chapel Hill: University of North Carolina Press, 2009.

Lemay, Celeste A., Suzanne B. Cashman, Dianne S. Elfenbein, and Marianne E. Felice. "A Qualitative Study of the Meaning of Fatherhood among Young Urban Fathers." *Public Health Nursing* 27, no. 3 (2010): 221–31.

Lerman, Evelyn. *Teen Moms: The Pain and the Promise*. Buena Park, CA: Morning Glory Press, 1997.

Levine, Deb. "Using Technology, New Media, and Mobile for Sexual and Reproductive Health." *Sexuality Research and Social Policy* 8 (2011): 18–26.

Lewis, Oscar. *La Vida: A Puerto Rican Family in the Culture of Poverty—San Juan and New York*. New York: Random House, 1966.

Lieberman, Lisa, and Haiyan Su. "Impact of the Choosing the Best Program in Communities Committed to Abstinence Education." Sage Open. March 22, 2012. http://sgo.sagepub.com/content/2/1/2158244012442938.

"Life of a Teen Father." YouTube. February 13, 2012. http://www.youtube.com/watch?v=e8awJO-S_4k.

Loke, Jaime, and Dustin Harp. "Evolving Themes of Masculinity in *Seventeen Magazine*: An Analysis of 1945–1955 and 1995–2005." *Journal of Magazine and New Media Research* 12, no. 1 (2010): 1–21.

Lord, Alexandra. *Condom Nation: The U.S. Government's Sex Education Campaign from World War I to the Internet*. Baltimore: Johns Hopkins University Press, 2010.

Lotz, Amanda. *Redesigning Women: Television after the Network Era*. Urbana: University of Illinois Press, 2006.

Luker, Kristin. *Dubious Conceptions: The Politics of Teen Pregnancy*. Cambridge, MA: Harvard University Press, 1996.

Luthra, R. "Toward a Reconceptualization of 'Choice': Challenges by Women at the Margins." *Feminist Issues* 13, no. 1 (1993): 41–54.

Luttrell, Wendy. *Pregnant Bodies, Fertile Minds: Gender, Race, and the Schooling of Pregnant Teens*. New York: Routledge, 2003.

Mackoff, Barbara. "Consider Her Conditioning." In *Growing a Girl: Seven Strategies for Raising a Strong, Spirited Daughter*, 81–88. New York: Random House.

Macleod, Catriona. *"Adolescence," Pregnancy and Abortion: Constructing a Threat of Degeneration*. New York: Routledge, 2011.

Marks, Loven, and Rob Palkovitz. "American Fatherhood Types: The Good, the Bad, and the Uninterested." *Fathering: A Journal of Theory, Research, and Practice about Men and Fathers* 2, no. 2 (2004): 113–29.

Marshall, P. David. *Celebrity and Power: Fame in Contemporary Culture*. Minneapolis: University of Minnesota Press, 1997.

Marsiglio, William, ed. *Fatherhood: Contemporary Theory, Research, and Social Policy*. Thousand Oaks, CA: Sage, 1995.

———. *Procreative Man*. New York: NYU Press, 1998.

Marsiglio, William, Paul Amato, Randal D. Day, and Michael E. Lamb. "Scholarship on Fatherhood in the 1990s and Beyond." *Journal of Marriage and Family* 62, no. 4 (2000): 1173–91.

Martin, Joyce A., Brady E. Hamilton, Stephanie J. Ventura, Michelle J. K. Osterman, Sharon Kirmeyer, T. J. Mathews, and Elizabeth Wilson. *Births: Final Data for 2009*. Washington, DC: U.S. Department of Health and Human Services, 2011.

Maushart, Susan. *The Mask of Motherhood: How Becoming a Mother Changes Our Lives and Why We Never Talk about it*. New York: Penguin, 2000.

McCarthy, Anna. "Stanley Milgram, Allen Funt, and Me: Postwar Social Science and the 'First Wave' of Reality TV." In *Reality TV: Remaking Television Culture*, edited by Susan Murray and Laurie Ouellette, 19–39. New York: NYU Press, 2004.

McClelland, Sarah I., and Michelle Fine. "Rescuing a Theory of Adolescent Excess: Young Women and Wanting." In *Next Wave Cultures: Feminism, Subcultures, Activism*, edited by Anita Harris, 83–102. New York: Routledge, 2008.

———. "Writing on Cellophane: Studying Teen Women's Sexual Desires, Inventing Methodological Release Points." In *The Methodological Dilemma: Creative, Critical and Collaborative Approaches to Qualitative Research*, edited by Kathleen Gallagher, 232–60. New York: Routledge, 2008.

McDermott, Elizabeth, and Hilary Graham. "Resilient Young Mothering: Social Inequalities, Late Modernity and the 'Problem' of Teenage Motherhood." *Journal of Youth Studies* 8, no. 1 (2005): 59–79.

Michel, Sonya. *Children's Interests/Mothers' Rights: The Shaping of America's Child Care Policy.* New Haven, CT: Yale University Press, 1999.

Middleton, Amy. "Mothering under Duress: Examining the Inclusiveness of Feminist Mothering Theory. *Journal of the Association for Research on Mothering* 8, nos. 1–2 (2006): 72–82.

Miller, Diana. "Masculinity in Popular Sitcoms, 1955–1960 and 2000–2005." *Culture, Society and Masculinities* 3, no. 2 (2011): 141–59.

Mitchell, Wendy A., Paul Crawshaw, Robin Bunton, and Eileen E. Green. "Situating Young People's Experiences of Risk and Identity." *Health, Risk, and Society* 3, no. 2 (2001): 217–33.

Morman, Mark T., and Kory Floyd. "Good Fathering: Father and Son Perceptions of What It Means to Be a Good Father." *Fathering: A Journal of Theory, Research, and Practice about Men as Fathers* 4, no. 2 (2006): 113–36.

Moynihan, Daniel P. *The Negro Family: The Case for National Action.* Washington, DC: Office of Policy Planning and Research, 1965.

"MTV's *16 and Pregnant* Is Casting Now." MTV.com. April 7, 2011. http://www.mtv.com/news/articles/1661526/mtvs-16-pregnant-casting-now.jhtml.

"MTV's *16 and Pregnant* > Season 1 > Ep. 01." http://www.mtv.com/shows/16_and_pregnant/season_1/episode.jhtml?episodeID=153833#moreinfo.

Murphy, Caryn. "Teen Momism on MTV: Postfeminist Subjectivities in *16 and Pregnant*." *Networking Knowledge: Journal of the MeCCSA-PGN* 5, no. 1 (2012): 84–99.

Murray, Susan. "'I Think We Need a New Name for It': The Meeting of Documentary and Reality TV." In *Reality TV: Remaking Television Culture*, edited by Susan Murray and Laurie Ouellette, 65–81. New York: NYU Press, 2004.

Murray, Susan, and Laurie Ouellette, eds. *Reality TV: Remaking Television Culture.* New York: NYU Press, 2004.

Muskal, Michael. "U.S. Teen Births Fall to Record Lows." *Los Angeles Times*, April 11, 2012, 6.

National Campaign to Prevent Teen and Unplanned Pregnancy. "*16 and Pregnant*: Important Things to Know about Teen Pregnancy." 2010. http://www.thenationalcampaign.org/resources/pdf/16-and-preg-fact-sheet.pdf.

———. "*16 and Pregnant* Season 1 Discussion Guide." http://www.thenationalcampaign.org/resources/pdf/16-and-preg-discussion-guide.pdf.

———. "About Us." http://www.thenationalcampaign.org/about-us/PDF/AboutUs.pdf.

———. "Accomplishments." http://www.thenationalcampaign.org/about-us/accomplishments.aspx.

———. "Evaluating the Impact of MTV's *16 and Pregnant* on Teen Viewers' Attitudes about Teen Pregnancy." 2010. http://www.thenationalcampaign.org/resources/pdf/SS/SS45_16andPregnant.pdf.

———. "Fast Facts: Teen Pregnancy in the United States." July 2012. http://www.thenationalcampaign.org/resources/pdf/FastFacts_TeenPregnancyinUS.pdf.

———. "Risky Business: A 2000 Poll: Teens Tell Us What They Really Think of Contraception and Sex." March 8, 2000. http://www.thenationalcampaign.org/national-data/pdf/poll2000.pdf.

———. "Teen Pregnancy Birth and Sexual Activity Data." http://www.thenationalcampaign.org/national-data/teen-pregnancy-birth-rates.aspx.

Negra, Diane. "Quality Postfeminism? Sex and the Single Girl on HBO." *Genders.* 2004. http://www.genders.org/g39/g39_negra.html.

Neubeck, Kenneth J., and Noel A. Cazenave. *Welfare Racism: Playing the Race Card against America's Poor.* London: Routledge, 2001.

Newcomb, Horace M., and Paul M. Hirsch. "Television as a Cultural Forum: Implications for Research." *Quarterly Review of Film Studies* 8, no. 3 (1983): 45–55.

O'Connor, Alice. *Poverty Knowledge: Social Science, Social Policy, and the Poor in Twentieth-Century U.S. History.* Princeton, NJ: Princeton University Press, 2001.

Oliver, Kelly. "Motherhood, Sexuality, and Pregnant Embodiment: Twenty-Five Years of Gestation." *Hypathia* 25, no. 4 (2010): 761–77.

O'Reilly, Andrea, ed. *21st Century Motherhood: Experience, Identity, Policy, Agency.* New York: Columbia University Press, 2010.

———. *Mother Outlaws: Theories and Practices of Empowered Mothering.* Toronto, ON: Women's Press, 2004.

———. "Outlaw(ing) Motherhood: A Theory and Politic of Maternal Empowerment for the Twenty First Century." *Hecate* 36, nos. 1–2 (2010): 17–29.

Orenstein, Peggy. *Cinderella Ate My Daughter.* New York: HarperCollins.

Orloff, Ann Shola, and Renee A. Monson. "Citizens, Workers or Fathers? Men in the History of US Social Policy." In *Making Men into Fathers: Men, Masculinities and the Social Politics of Fatherhood,* edited by Barbara Hobson, 61–91. Cambridge, England: Cambridge University Press, 2002.

Ouellette, Laurie. "'Take Responsibility for Yourself': Judge Judy and the Neoliberal Citizen." In *Reality TV: Remaking Television Culture,* edited by Susan Murray and Laurie Ouellette, 231–50. New York: NYU Press, 2004.

Ouellette, Laurie, and James Hay. *Better Living through Reality TV: Television and Postwelfare Citizenship.* Malden, MA: Blackwell, 2008.

Pan, Zhongdang, and Gerald M. Kosicki. "Framing Analysis: A New Approach to News Discourse." *Political Communication* 10, no. 1 (1993): 55–75.

Parra-Cardona, José Rubén, Richard S. Wampler, and Elizabeth A. Sharp. "'Wanting to Be a Good Father': Experiences of Adolescent Fathers of Mexican Descent in a Teen Fathers Program." *Journal of Marital and Family Therapy* 32, no. 2 (2006): 215–31.

Paschal, Angelia M. *Voices of African-American Teen Fathers: "I'm Doing What I Got to Do."* Binghamton, NY: Haworth Press, 2006.

Pehlke, Timothy Allen, Charles B. Hennon, M. Elise Radina, and Katherine A. Kuvalanka. "Does Father Still Know Best? An Inductive Thematic Analysis of Popular TV Sitcoms." *Fathering: A Journal of Theory, Research, and Practice about Men as Fathers* 7, no. 2 (2009): 114–39.

Peters, Sara, and Jennifer Aubrey. "MTV's Docu-series Delivers Platform for Teen Parenthood: A Content Analysis of *16 and Pregnant.*" Unpublished essay, 2012.

Piazza, Joe. "What Are the Most Dangerous Shows Your Kids Are Watching without You?" FoxNews.com. December 5, 2011. http://www.foxnews.com/entertainment/2011/12/05/what-are-most-dangerous-shows-your-kids-are-watching-without/.

Pillow, Wanda. *Unfit Subjects: Educational Policy and the Teen Mother.* New York: Routledge, 2004.

Polit, Denise F., and Cheryl T. Beck. *Nursing Research: Principles and Methods.* Philadelphia: Lippincott Williams and Wilkins, 2004.

Pozner, Jennifer L. *Reality Bites Back: The Troubling Truth about Guilty Pleasure TV.* Berkeley, CA: Seal Press, 2010.

PR NewsWire. "MTV Chronicles the Challenges of Teen Pregnancy in *16 and Pregnant.*" May 18, 2009.

Projansky, Sarah. "Mass Magazine Cover Girls: Some Reflections on Postfeminist Girls and Postfeminism's Daughters." In *Interrogating Postfeminism: Gender and the Politics of Popular Culture,* edited by Yvonne Tasker and Diane Negra, 40–72. Durham, NC: Duke University Press, 2007.

———. *Watching Rape: Film and Television in Postfeminist Culture.* New York: NYU Press, 2001.

Prusank, Diane T. "Masculinities in Teen Magazines: The Good, the Bad, and the Ugly." *Journal of Men's Studies* 15, no. 2 (2007): 160–77.

Public Religion Research Institute. "Committed to Availability, Conflicted about Morality: What the Millennial Generation Tells Us about the Future of the Abortion Debate." June 9, 2011. http://publicreligion.org/research/2011/06/committed-to-availability-conflicted-about-morality-what-the-millennial-generation-tells-us-about-the-future-of-the-abortion-debate-and-the-culture-wars/.

Purcell, Kristen, Lee Rainie, Alan Heaps, Judy Buchanen, Linda Friedrich, Amanda Jacklin, Clara Chen, and Katheryn Zickuhr. *How Teens Do Research in the Digital World.* Washington, DC: Pew Research Center, 2012.

Rains, Prue, Linda Davies, and Margaret McKinnon. "Social Services Constructs the Teen Mother." *Families in Society* 85, no. 1 (2004): 17–27.

Reed, Richard K. *Birthing Fathers: The Transformation of Men in American Rites of Birth.* New Brunswick, NJ: Rutgers University Press, 2005.

"Relationship Details: Farrah Abraham and Derek Underwood." Famous Hookups. http://www.famoushookups.com/site/relation-ship_detail.php?name=FarrahAbrahamandreId=21446andcelebid=24161.

Renold, Emma, and Jessica Ringrose. "Schizoid Subjectivities? Re-theorizing Teen Girls' Sexual Cultures in an Era of 'Sexualization.'" *Journal of Sociology* 47, no. 4 (2011): 389–409.

Ringrose, Jessica. "Are You Sexy, Flirty, or a Slut? Exploring 'Sexualization' and How Teen Girls Perform/Negotiate Digital Sexual Identity on Social Networking Sites." In *New Femininities: Postfeminism, Neoliberalism, and Subjectivity*, edited by Rosalind Gill and Christina Scharff, 99–116. New York: Palgrave, 2011.

Roberts, Dorothy. *Killing the Black Body: Race, Reproduction and the Meaning of Liberty.* New York: Vintage, 1999.

Robson, Colin. *Real World Research: A Resource for Social Scientists and Practitioner-Researchers.* Oxford, England: Blackwell, 1993.

Rochman, Bonnie. "*16 and Pregnant*: Tuned-In Teens Are Turned Off by Teen Pregnancy." Time.com. October 22, 2010. http://healthland.time.com/2010/10/22/16-and-pregnant-tuned-in-teens-are-turned-off-by-teen-pregnancy/.

Rock, Lindsey. "The 'Good Mother' vs. the 'Other' Mother: The Girl-Mom." *Journal of the Association for Research on Mothering* 9, no. 1 (2007): 20–28.

Romney, Mitt. "The Best of America." Mitt Romney for President. July 4, 2012. http://www.mittromney.com/forms/best-america.

Rose, Lacey. "MTV's David Janollari Opens Up about *Jersey Shore*'s Uncertain Future, *Teen Mom* Controversy and What's Next." Hollywood Reporter. http://www.hollywoodreporter.com/news/david-janollari-jersey-shore-mtv-260289.

Roy, Kevin M. "You Can't Eat Love: Constructing Provider Role Expectations for Low-Income and Working-Class Fathers." *Fathering* 2, no. 3 (2004): 253–76.

Roy, Kevin, and Omari Dyson. "Making Daddies into Fathers: Community-Based Fatherhood Programs and the Construction of Masculinities for Low-Income African American Men." *American Journal of Community Psychology* 45, no. 1 (2010): 139–54.

Rubin, Gayle. "Thinking Sex: Notes for a Radical Theory of the Politics of Sexuality." In *Pleasure and Danger: Exploring Female Sexuality*, edited by Carole S. Vance, 267–319. Boston: Routledge, 1984.

Salomone, Gina. "Debra Danielson, Mother of MTV *Teen Mom* Farrah Abraham, Arrested after Hitting Daughter." *New York Daily News.* January 19, 2010. http://articles.nydailynews.com/2010-01-19/gossip/17945303_1_teen-mom-young-mothers-mtv.

Schalet, Amy. "Subjectivity, Intimacy, and the Empowerment Paradigm of Adolescent Sexuality: The Unexplored Room." *Feminist Studies*, 35, no. 1 (2009): 133–60.

Scheufele, Dietram A. "Framing as a Theory of Media Effects." *Journal of Communication* 49, no. 1 (1999): 103–22.

Schreffler, Laura. "Twits-War! Pregnant Kourtney Kardashian Slams *Teen Mom* Star Farrah Abraham after Online Attack." *Daily Mail.* December 3, 2011. http://www.dailymail.co.uk/tvshowbiz/article-2069410/Pregnant-Kourtney-Kardashian-slams-Teen-Mom-star-Farrah-Abraham-online-attack.html.

Seltzer, Sarah. "MTV's *16 and Pregnant*, Exploits Teen Moms but Addresses Abortion with Dignity." *Washington Post.* December 30, 2010. http://www.washingtonpost.com/wpdyn/content/article/2010/12/30/AR2010123001953.html?referrer=emailarticle.

Shaw, Anita. "Media Representations of Adolescent Pregnancy: The Problem with Choice." *Atlantis* 34, no. 2 (2010): 55–65.

Shoveller, Jean, Cathy Chabot, Joy L. Johnson, and Ken Prkachin. "'Aging Out': When Policy and Social Orders Intrude on the 'Disordered' Realities of Young Mothers." *Youth and Society* 43, no. 4 (2011): 1355–80.

Signorielli, Nancy. "Health Images on Television." In *Health Communication Research: A Guide to Developments and Directions,* edited by Bernard K. Duffy and Lorraine D. Jackson, 163–79. Westport, CT: Greenwood Press, 1998.

Sisson, Gretchen. "The 99%: The Hidden Class Politics of *Teen Mom 2.*" BitchMagazine.com. December 7, 2011. http://bitchmagazine.org/post/the-99-class-politics-of-teen-mom-2-feminism-MTV.

Skolfield, Melissa. "Draft Talking Points." Fol. 3, box 24, News Clips, Domestic Policy Council, Bruce Reed, Welfare Reform (1993–2001) Subject File. Systematic Processed Collections, William J. Clinton Presidential Library, Little Rock, AK.

Slocum, Charles. "The Real History of Reality TV: Or, How Alan Funt Won the Cold War." Writers Guild of America, West. 2008. http://www.wga.org/organizesub.aspx?id=1099.

Smith, Andrea. "Beyond Pro-choice versus Pro-life: Women of Color and Reproductive Justice." *Feminist Formations,* 17, no. 1 (2005): 119–40.

———. *Conquest: Sexual Violence and American Indian Genocide.* Cambridge, England: South End Press, 2006.

Smith, Debra C. "Critiquing Reality-Based Televisual Black Fatherhood: A Critical Analysis of Run's House and Snoop Dogg's Father Hood." *Critical Studies in Media Communication* 25, no. 4 (2008): 393–412.

Smith, Jeremy Adam. *The Daddy Shift: How Stay-at-Home Dads, Breadwinning Moms, and Shared Parenting Are Transforming the American Family.* Boston: Beacon, 2009.

Smith, Sarah H. "Scripting Sexual Desire: Cultural Scenarios of Teen Girls' Sexual Desire in Popular Films, 2000–2009." *Sexuality and Culture* 16, no. 3 (2012): 321–41.

"So True? So False? Does *Teen Mom*'s Amber Portwood Really Earn Six Figures?!" E! Online. December 30, 2010. http://uk.eonline.com/news/218334/so-true-so-false-does-teen-mom-s-amber-portwood-really-earn-six-figures.

Soliger, Rickie. *Beggars and Choosers: How the Politics of Choice Shapes Adoption, Abortion and Welfare in the United States.* New York: Hill and Wang, 2001.

———. *Wake Up Little Susie: Single Pregnancy and Race before* Roe v. Wade. London: Routledge, 2000.

Sparks, Holloway. "Queens, Teens, and Model Mothers: Race, Gender, and the Discourse of Welfare Reform." In *Race and the Politics of Welfare Reform,* edited by Sanford F. Schram, Joe Soss, and Richard C. Fording, 171–95. Ann Arbor: University of Michigan Press, 2003.

Stout, Trina. "Framing Abortion Access for the Abortion Grays: Moving the Middle toward Wider Support for Abortion Rights in the United States." Master's thesis, American University, 2011.

Sun, FeiFei. "Baby Mamas: Teen Moms Are Reality TV's New Stars. Is This a Good Thing?" Time.com. July 16, 2011. http://www.time.com/time/magazine/article/0,9171,2081928,00.html.

Sylvester, Kathleen. *Second-Chance Homes, Breaking the Cycle of Teen Pregnancy.* Washington, DC: Progressive Policy Institute, 1995.

Tasker, Yvonne, and Diane Negra. "Introduction: Feminist Politics and Postfeminist Culture." In *Interrogating Postfeminism: Gender and the Politics of Popular Culture,* edited by Yvonne Tasker and Diane Negra, 1–25. Durham, NC: Duke University Press, 2007.

"*Teen Mom* Drama." *OK! Cover Story,* August 13, 2012, 30–33.

"*Teen Mom* Stars Earn More Than $60,000 a Season!" *Life and Style.* October 28, 2010. http://www.lifeandstylemag.com/2010/10/teen-mom-1.html.

Thomas, Adam. "Unintended Pregnancy and Public Policy." *Notre Dame Journal of Law, Ethics & Public Policy* 26 (2012): 501–31.

Thompson, Arienne. "16, Pregnant . . . and Famous: Teen Moms are TVs New Stars." *USA Today*, November 23, 2010.

Thompson, Stacy, and Andrea Walker. "Satisfaction with Parenting: A Comparison between Adolescent Mothers and Fathers." *Sex Roles* 50, no. 9 (2004): 677–87.

Thorburn, David. "Television Melodrama." In *Television: The Critical View*, edited by Horace Newcomb, 537–50. New York: Oxford University Press, 1994.

Thornberry, Terence P., Carolyn A. Smith, and Gregory J. Howard. "Risk Factors for Teenage Fatherhood." *Journal of Marriage and Family* 59, no. 3 (1997): 505–22.

Thorne, Barrie. *Gender Play: Girls and Boys in School*. New Brunswick, NJ: Rutgers University Press, 1993.

Thurer, Shari. *The Myths of Motherhood: How Culture Reinvents the Good Mother*. New York: Penguin, 1994.

Tichenor, Veronica, Julia McQuillan, Arthur L. Greil, Raleigh Contreras, and Karina M. Shreffler. "The Importance of Fatherhood to U.S. Married and Cohabiting Men." *Fathering* 9, no. 3 (2011): 232–51.

Tolman, Deborah. "Found(ing) Discourses of Desire: Unfettering Female Adolescent Sexuality." *Feminism and Psychology* 15, no. 1 (2005): 5–9.

Tolman, Deborah L., Celeste Hirschman, Emily A. Impett. "There Is More to the Story: The Place of Qualitative Research on Female Adolescent Sexuality in Policy Making." *Sexuality Research and Social Policy: Journal of NSRC* 2, no. 4 (2005): 4–17.

Tolman, Deborah L., and Sara I. McClelland. "Normative Sexuality Development in Adolescence: A Decade in Review 2000–2009." *Journal of Research on Adolescence* 21, no. 1 (2011): 242–55.

Townsend, Nicholas. *Package Deal: Marriage, Work and Fatherhood In Men's Lives*. Philadelphia: Temple University Press, 2002.

Trice-Black, Shannon. "Perceptions of Women's Sexuality in the Context of Motherhood." *Family Journal: Counseling and Therapy for Couples and Families* 18, no. 2 (2010): 154–62.

"True Love Waits Pledge." LifeWay Ministries. http://www.lifeway.com/Article/true-love-waits.

Twisty. "Blaming XPress: Blurb + Open Thread." I Blame the Patriarchy. http://blog.iblamethepatriarchy.com.

Tyler, Imogen. "Pramface Girls: The Class Politics of 'Maternal TV.'" In *Reality Television and Class*, edited by Helen Wood and Beverley Skeggs, 210–24. London: Palgrave Macmillan, 2011.

U.S. Congress, House of Representatives, Committee on Government Reform and Oversight, Subcommittee on Human Resources and Intergovernmental Relations. "Preventing Teen Pregnancy: Coordinating Community Efforts." 104th Cong., 2nd sess., April 30, 1996.

U.S. Congress, House of Representatives, Committee on Small Business, Subcommittee on Empowerment. "Social and Economic Costs of Teen Pregnancy." 105th Cong., 2nd sess., July 16, 1998.

U.S. Congress, House of Representatives, Committee on Ways and Means, Subcommittee on Human Resources. "Teen Pregnancy Prevention." 107th Cong., 1st sess., November 15, 2001.

"U.S. Teen Birth Rate Fell to Record Low in 2009: Still, More Than 400,000 Teen Girls Give Birth Each Year in United States." CDC Newsroom. http://www.cdc.gov/media/releases/2011/p0405_vitalsigns.html.

Valenti, Jessica. "MTV's Abortion Special Treats Issue with Compassion, Facts." Jessica Valenti. December 29, 2010. http://jessicavalenti.com/2010/12/29/mtvs-abortion-special-treats-issue-with-compassion-facts/.

———. *The Purity Myth: How America's Obsession with Virginity Is Hurting Young Women*. Berkeley, CA: Seal Press, 2010.

———. "Why No Abortions on MTV's 16 and Pregnant?" Jessica Valenti. February 2, 2010. http://jessicavalenti.com/2010/02/10/why-no-abortions-on-mtvs-16-and-pregnant/.

Van Damme, Elke. "Gender and Sexual Scripts in Popular U.S. Teen Series: A Study on the Gendered Discourses in *One Tree Hill* and *Gossip Girl.*" *Catalan Journal of Communication and Cultural Studies* 2, no. 1 (2010): 77–92.

Vavrus, Mary Douglas. "Putting Ally on Trial: Contesting Postfeminism in Popular Culture." *Women's Studies in Communication* 23, no. 3 (2000): 413–28.

Walzer, Susan. *Thinking about the Baby: Gender and Transitions into Parenthood.* Philadelphia: Temple University Press, 1998.

Ward, L. Monique. "Understanding the Role of Entertainment Media in the Sexual Socialization of American Youth: A Review of Empirical Research." *Developmental Review* 23 (2003): 347–88.

Warren Lindsay, Jeanne. *Teen Dads: Rights, Responsibilities and Joys.* Buena Park, CA: Morning Glory Press, 2008.

Warren Lindsay, Jeanne, and Jean Brunelli. *Your Pregnancy and Newborn Journey: A Guide for Pregnant Teens.* Buena Park, CA: Morning Glory Press, 2004.

Weber, Brenda. *Makeover TV: Selfhood, Citizenship, and Celebrity.* Durham, NC: Duke University Press, 2009.

Weber, Jennifer Beggs. "Becoming Teen Fathers: Stories of Teen Pregnancy, Responsibility, and Masculinity." *Gender and Society* (published online before print, October 10, 2012).

Welter, Barbara. "The Cult of True Womanhood: 1820–1860." *American Quarterly* 18 (1966): 151–74.

Wetzstein, Cheryl. "Congress Hopes to Cut Illegitimacy at Any Age: Clinton Targets Teen Pregnancies." *Washington Times*, January 14, 1997.

White, Naomi Rosh. "About Fathers: Masculinity and the Social Construction of Fatherhood." *Journal of Sociology* 30, no. 2 (1994): 119–131.

"Who Qualifies for a Free Cell Phone?" Free Government Cell Phones. 2011. http://www.freegovernmentcellphones.net/basics/qualify.

Wilson, Helen, and Annette Huntington. "Deviant (M)Others: The Construction of Teenage Motherhood in Contemporary Discourse." *Journal of Social Policy* 35, no. 1 (2006): 59–76.

Yardley, Elizabeth. "Teenage Mothers' Experience of Stigma." *Journal of Youth Studies* 11, no. 6 (2008): 671–84.

Yglesias, Matthew. "Why Are Teen Moms Poor?" Slate. May 14, 2012. http://www.slate.com/articles/business/moneybox/2012/05/teen_moms_how_poverty_and_inequality_cause_teens_to_have_babies_not_the_other_way_around_.html.

Index

About the Editor and Contributors

Letizia Guglielmo is associate professor of English at Kennesaw State University who also teaches in the gender and women's studies program and serves as the assistant director of composition for the English department. She teaches writing courses in the undergraduate writing minor and the master of arts in professional writing, in face-to-face and fully online formats. Her research and writing focus on feminist rhetoric and pedagogy, multiliteracies, digital media in the writing classroom, and the intersections of feminist action and digital communication. Her work has appeared in *Computers and Composition Online* and in collections, including *Race and Identity in Barack Obama's "Dreams from My Father": A Collection of Critical Essays*, *Teachers as Avatars: English Studies in a Digital Age*, *Who Speaks for Writing: Stewardship in Writing Studies in the 21st Century*, and *Performing Feminism and Administration in Rhetoric and Composition Studies*.

* * *

Allison Bass recently graduated with her master of arts in English and a graduate certificate in women's studies from Southern Connecticut State University. Having a baby at the age of sixteen, she has learned to advocate for herself and her baby throughout their entire lives. She has obtained associate, bachelor, and master's degrees all while having a child in tow. She is a firm believer in learning how to be responsible for one's health and wellness. At age twenty-nine, she is the loving mother of a quirky twelve-year-old, an adjunct English professor, and a grant assistant for the Connecticut Campus Coalition to End Violence against Women. She enjoys healthy eating and engaging with her daughter.

Clare Daniel is a doctoral candidate in American studies at the University of New Mexico. She is interested in the intersections of citizenship studies, race theory, and histories of the welfare state. She is currently working on a dissertation examining the contemporary discourses of teenage pregnancy and parenthood in public policy, popular culture, and nonprofit advocacy, as well as the biopolitical implications of these discourses.

Jennifer A. Fallas is a visiting lecturer at Bridgewater State University, where she teaches rhetoric and composition and literature courses around the themes of feminisms, LGBTQ (lesbian, gay, bisexual, transgender, queer) activisms, and Latina studies.

May Friedman blends social work, teaching, research, writing, and parenting, often in the same five-minute period. May's passions include social justice and reality TV, and she is firmly in favor of living with contradiction. She has published on the topic of motherhood and transnationalism and has presented on mothers who are sex workers and on representations of teen mothers. May's most recent research was on *mommyblogs*, a mode of writing that has transformed her life and many of her relationships. May lives in downtown Toronto with her partner and three young children and works as an assistant professor of social work at Ryerson University.

JoAnne Gordon is a first-year master-of-arts student in the Institute of Women's Studies at the University of Ottawa, Ontario, Canada. Her research focuses on intersectional feminist theory; representations and theorizing of young motherhood; the use of art-based methodologies, specifically *zines*, as a means of integrating marginalized voices into the research process; and critical examinations of social policies in Canada. She has worked in, and coordinated, women-and-gender resource centers for the past five years and is an antiviolence and reproductive justice activist both on and off campus. Her activism and advocacy have greatly shaped her research interests and pushed her to strive to ensure that all of her research is grounded in critical praxis.

Andrea M. McClanahan is an associate professor and chairperson of the Department of Communication Studies and an affiliated faculty member with the Department of Women's Studies at East Stroudsburg University of Pennsylvania. She teaches courses in communication theory, feminist theory, mass media, and rhetorical theory. Her research focuses on media representations of masculinity and femininity and alternative life choices, such as the choice to remain single or to become a single parent. She has a chapter in *Critical Thinking about Sex, Love, and Romance in the Mass Media: Media Literacy Applications* and a coauthored chapter in *Constructing Our Health: The Implications of Narrative for Enacting Illness and Wellness*.

India J. McGhee is a second-year student at Drexel University's Earle Mack School of Law. She has previously worked for the Domestic Violence Unit at family court in Philadelphia, where she frequently helped young mothers navigate legal issues, such as custody orders and the requirements for legal protection from abuse.

Caryn Murphy is an assistant professor of communication at the University of Wisconsin–Oshkosh. She holds a doctorate in media and cultural studies from the University of Wisconsin–Madison. Her research on the uses of film and television in the construction of social roles and individual identity has appeared in the anthologies *The Business of Entertainment* (2008) and *Dear Angela: Remembering My So-Called Life* (2007) and will appear in the forthcoming *Beyond Saturday Night: "Saturday Night Live" and American Television Culture* (2012).

Alison N. Novak is a doctoral student in the Department of Culture and Communication at Drexel University. Her primary research studies the media's depiction of and contribution to generational identity. She has been published on new forms of political engagement in the millennial generation.

Enid Schatz is an assistant professor in the Department of Occupational Therapy and the Department of Women's and Gender Studies at the University of Missouri. Her research focuses on the social and structural impacts of HIV/AIDS on gender, aging, and families in rural South Africa. She teaches research courses and a class titled "*16 and Pregnant*: Teen Pregnancy and Parenthood in a Global Perspective."

Melanie Anne Stewart is a master's candidate in women's studies at the University of Oxford, St. Catherine's College. She completed her bachelor's degree in theatre studies and English literature at Lancaster University, United Kingdom. Her interests bring together queer theory, gender studies, cultural studies, and popular culture.

Margaret Tally is chair of policy studies and professor of social policy in the School for Graduate Studies at the State University of New York, Empire State College. Her current research interests include critical media theory, media and public policy, gender and society, and family policy. She has written and presented on the marketing of *tweens* in Hollywood, on the representation of middle-aged women's sexuality in popular culture, and on changing gender roles as portrayed in television series from the 1990s.

Martina Thomas is a doctoral student at the University of Alabama. She graduated with a master of arts in anthropology at the University of Alabama in 2010. She is currently pursuing her doctorate in medical anthropology and is pursuing a certificate in gender and race studies. Her thesis project explored body image perceptions among low socioeconomic status African American mothers and daughters in Mobile, Alabama. Her dissertation project examines HIV knowledge among African American adolescent girls in Tuscaloosa, Alabama. Her other research interests include visual anthropology, digital storytelling, human sexuality, and media representations of race and gender.

Anastasia Todd is a doctoral student in women and gender studies at Arizona State University. Her research interests include girls' sexuality and representations of subversive girlhoods in popular culture.

Laura Tropp received her doctorate at New York University. She is currently an associate professor and chair of the communication arts department at Marymount Manhattan College. Her work includes "Faking a Sonogram: Representations of Motherhood on *Sex and the City*," which was published in the *Journal of Popular Culture*, and a chapter in *Mental Illness in Popular Media* entitled "Off Their Rockers: Representations of Postpartum Depression in Popular Culture." She also has a forthcoming book, *A Womb with a View: America's Growing Public Interest in Pregnancy*.

Kimberly Wallace Stewart recently completed a bachelor of science in psychology and is currently preparing for and applying to graduate schools in counseling psychology. Throughout her undergraduate career, she contributed to several research projects concerning religious freedom, personality testing, and dominant narratives of teen sexuality. She plans to continue developing knowledge in similar research areas through graduate school.

Jennifer Beggs Weber is a doctoral candidate in the Department of Sociology at the University of Missouri. Her teaching and research interests include gender, youth, family, culture, and identity. Her dissertation focuses on teen fatherhood.

52178180R00166

Made in the USA
Lexington, KY
20 May 2016